NEW CENTURY BIBLE COMMENTARY

General Editors

RONALD E. CLEMENTS
(Old Testament)

MATTHEW BLACK
(New Testament)

COLOSSIANS
and
PHILEMON

THE NEW CENTURY BIBLE COMMENTARIES

EXODUS (J. P. Hyatt)
LEVITICUS AND NUMBERS (N. H. Snaith)*
DEUTERONOMY (A. D. H. Mayes)
JOSHUA, JUDGES, AND RUTH (John Gray)*
EZRA, NEHEMIAH, AND ESTHER (L. H. Brockington)*
JOB (H. H. Rowley)
PSALMS Volumes 1 and 2 (A. A. Anderson)
ISAIAH 1-39 (R. E. Clements)
ISAIAH 40-66 (R. N. Whybray)
EZEKIEL (John W. Wevers)*
THE GOSPEL OF MATTHEW (David Hill)
THE GOSPEL OF MARK (Hugh Anderson)
THE GOSPEL OF LUKE (E. Earle Ellis)
THE GOSPEL OF JOHN (Barnabas Lindars)
THE ACTS OF THE APOSTLES (William Neil)
ROMANS (Matthew Black)
1 and 2 CORINTHIANS (F. F. Bruce)
GALATIANS (Donald Guthrie)
EPHESIANS (C. Leslie Mitton)
PHILIPPIANS (Ralph P. Martin)
COLOSSIANS AND PHILEMON (Ralph P. Martin)
1 PETER (Ernest Best)*
THE BOOK OF REVELATION (G. R. Beasley-Murray)

*Not yet available in paperback
 Other titles are in preparation

NEW CENTURY BIBLE COMMENTARY

Based on the Revised Standard Version

COLOSSIANS
and
PHILEMON

RALPH P. MARTIN

WM. B. EERDMANS PUBL. CO., GRAND RAPIDS

MARSHALL, MORGAN & SCOTT PUBL. LTD., LONDON

Copyright © Marshall, Morgan & Scott 1973
First published 1973 by Marshall, Morgan & Scott, England
Softback edition published 1981

Reprinted, April 1992

All rights reserved
Printed in the United States of America
for
Wm. B. Eerdmans Publishing Company
255 Jefferson Ave. S.E., Grand Rapids, Mich. 49503
and
Marshall, Morgan & Scott
1 Bath Street, London ECIV 9LB
ISBN 0 551 009 10 1

Library of Congress Cataloging in Publication Data

Martin, Ralph P.
Colossians and Philemon.

(New century Bible commentary)
Reprint. Originally published: London: Oliphants,
1978. (New century Bible)
Bibliography: p. xv
Includes indexes.
1. Bible. N.T. Colossians — Commentaries. 2. Bible.
N.T. Philemon — Commentaries. I. Title. II. Series.
III. Series: New century Bible.
BS2715.3.M36 1981 227'.707 81-5574
ISBN 0-8028-1908-7 (pbk.) AACR2

UXORI   CARISSIMAE

EDITOR'S FOREWORD

The original instructions issued to the editors of the individual biblical books in the New Century Bible series were that they should follow, in general, the pattern of the old series, both with regard to format and size of the volume.

In course of the preparation of the new series, two departures from this plan and policy were found to be desirable and have already been made. It was felt to be unnecessary to print the Revised Standard Version biblical text above the commentary, and this text is now omitted. The instructions about length of manuscript were considered, in some cases, to impose much too severe limitations on the range and scope of the commentary.

The old Century Bible devoted one volume to Ephesians, Philippians, Colossians and Philemon, and this model was followed in the new series in the volume edited by Dr. George Johnston of Montreal. This was again thought to be unduly restrictive, especially in view of the new and important work which has been appearing on the Colossian epistle. When Dr. R. P. Martin offered a manuscript on Colossians to the publishers, it was decided—provided Dr. Johnston agreed—to include it as a separate supplementary volume in the series. The proposal has Dr. Johnston's full approval, and we now include this additional volume in the series.

MATTHEW BLACK

CONTENTS

PREFACE

Elsewhere in the introductory pages of this commentary Principal Matthew Black has explained the relationship of the following work to an earlier edition of the New Century Bible commentary on the 'prison epistles' prepared by Principal George Johnston. It remains for me to express appreciation for the opportunity to offer another work on the letters to the Colossians and to Philemon which attempts to interrogate and explain the text at a somewhat deeper level than was possible on that earlier occasion.

I have gladly made ample use of the resources available in the English translation of Professor (now Bishop) Eduard Lohse's commentary in the Meyer series, which appeared in the series Hermeneia (Fortress Press, Philadelphia, 1971). It would have been negligent to have despised this mine of information and erudition; and the same goes for the use which has been freely made of Kittel's *Theological Dictionary of the New Testament* (Eerdmans, Grand Rapids, 1964–) of which nine volumes are accessible in English, thanks to the translation work of my colleague Geoffrey W. Bromiley. Both sources, however, require a fair knowledge of Greek, and it is my hope that this commentary may fulfil a role in mediating the fruits of these larger books to a wider public than has access to Lohse and Kittel.

These two Pauline letters exercise an undiminished fascination in spite of the time-span which separates us in the modern world from the era of Paul's day with its strange views on cosmology, demonology and ascetic religious practice on the one hand, and the oppressing institution of slavery and authoritarianism on the other hand. Much of what the apostle wrote was culturally conditioned and inevitably expressed in the thought-forms and idiom of his time. But when due allowance of this fact has been made and regard is had to the need for him to address himself to a set of pastoral problems in the churches of the Lycus valley in Asia Minor, it still may be claimed that these two brief epistles not only give us insight into Paul's agile mind and illustrate his pastoral sensitivity, but have something important to say to our culture and our problems.

My thanks are due for the efficient help of Mrs. Jane Beattie, who typed the manuscript and improved the text of the commentary by her questions and comments as a student.

R. P. M.

ABBREVIATIONS

BIBLICAL

OLD TESTAMENT (*OT*)

Gen.	Jg.	1 Chr.	Ps.	Lam.	Ob.	Hag.
Exod.	Ru.	2 Chr.	Prov.	Ezek.	Jon.	Zech.
Lev.	1 Sam.	Ezr.	Ec.	Dan.	Mic.	Mal.
Num.	2 Sam.	Neh.	Ca.	Hos.	Nah.	
Dt.	1 Kg.	Est.	Isa.	Jl	Hab.	
Jos.	2 Kg.	Job	Jer.	Am.	Zeph.	

APOCRYPHA (*Apoc.*)

1 Esd.	Tob.	Ad. Est.	Sir.	S. 3 Ch.	Bel.	1 Mac.
2 Esd.	Jdt.	Wis.	Bar.	Sus.	Man.	2 Mac.
			Ep. Jer.			

NEW TESTAMENT (*NT*)

Mt.	Ac.	Gal.	1 Th.	Tit.	1 Pet.	3 Jn
Mk	Rom.	Eph.	2 Th.	Phm.	2 Pet.	Jude
Lk.	1 C.	Phil.	1 Tim.	Heb.	1 Jn	Rev.
Jn	2 C.	Col.	2 Tim.	Jas	2 Jn	

DEAD SEA SCROLLS

1QpHab	Habakkuk Commentary
1QS	The Rule of the Community
1QH	Hymns of Thanksgiving
1QM	War of the Sons of Light against the Sons of Darkness
4QpPs	Commentary on Psalms

GENERAL

'Ābôth	*Sayings of the Jewish Fathers*
Adv. Haer.	*Against all Heresies* (Irenaeus)
AJT	*Americal Journal of Theology* (Chicago)
Ann.	*Annals* (Tacitus)
Ant.	*Antiquities of the Jews* (Josephus)
Arndt-Gingrich	W. Bauer, *A Greek–English Lexicon of the New Testament and Other Early Christian Literature.*

	Translated by W. F. Arndt and F. W. Gingrich (Cambridge, 1957)
ATR	*Anglican Theological Review* (Evanston)
Att.	*Letters to Atticus* (Cicero)
AV	Authorized Version/King James Version
Barn.	*Epistle of Barnabas*
BJRL	*Bulletin of the John Rylands Library* (Manchester)
Blass-Debrunner-Funk	*A Greek Grammar of the New Testament.* Translated and edited by R. W. Funk (Cambridge, 1961)
CBQ	*Catholic Biblical Quarterly* (Washington, DC)
De Praescr. Haer.	*Objections to Heretics* (Tertullian)
Ep.	Epistle
Eph.	*Letter to the Ephesians* (Ignatius)
EQ	*Evangelical Quarterly* (Exeter)
ET	English Translation
ExpT	*Expository Times* (Edinburgh)
Geogr.	*Geographica* (Strabo)
Gr.	Greek
HE	*Church History* (Eusebius)
Heb.	Hebrew
Hist. Nat.	*Natural History* (Pliny)
HTR	*Harvard Theological Review* (Cambridge, Mass.)
JBL	*Journal of Biblical Literature* (Philadelphia)
JR	*Journal of Religion* (Chicago)
JTS	*Journal of Theological Studies* (Cambridge)
LXX	Septuagint
NEB	New English Bible
NovT	*Novum Testamentum* (Leiden)
ns	New Series
NTS	*New Testament Studies* (Cambridge)
os	Old Series
Philo	
Agric.	*On Husbandry*
Conf. Ling.	*On the Confusion of Tongues*
Fug.	*On Flight and Finding*
Leg. All.	*Allegorical Interpretation*
Som.	*On Dreams*
Polyc.	Polycarp
Prep. Ev.	*The Preparation of the Gospel* (Eusebius)
RSV	Revised Standard Version

RV	Revised Version
SB	H. Strack and P. Billerbeck, *Kommentar zum Neuen Testament aus Talmud und Midrasch* (Munich, 1922–56)
SJT	*Scottish Journal of Theology* (Edinburgh)
ST	*Studia Theologica* (Lund)
Strom.	*Miscellanies* (Clement of Alexandria)
sv	under the word (entry)
Test. Zeb.	*Testament of Zebulun* in *The Testament of the Twelve Patriarchs*
TDNT	*Theological Dictionary of the New Testament* (Grand Rapids, 1964–)
ThLZ	*Theologische Literaturzeitung* (Leipzig)
ThZ	*Theologische Zeitschrift* (Basel)
TSK	*Theologische Studien und Kritiken* (Hamburg/Gotha)
Vermes	G. Vermes, *The Dead Sea Scrolls in English* (Harmondsworth, 1962)
VT	*Vetus Testamentum* (Leiden)
ZKTh	*Zeitschrift für katholische Theologie* (Innsbruck)
ZNTW	*Zeitschrift für die neutestamentliche Wissenschaft* (Giessen/Berlin)

BIBLIOGRAPHY

COMMENTARIES ON COLOSSIANS AND PHILEMON

Benoit, P. *Les épîtres de saint Paul aux Philippiens, a Philémon, aux Colossiens,* etc. La Sainte Bible. Paris, 1949.

Conzelmann, H. *Die kleineren Briefe des Apostels Paulus.* Neue Testament Deutsch 8. Göttingen, 1965.

Dibelius, M. and Greeven, H.. *An die Kolosser, Epheser, an Philemon.* Handbuch zum Neuen Testament 12. Tübingen, 1953.

Houlden, J. L. *Paul's Letters from Prison.* Pelican New Testament Commentaries. Harmondsworth, 1970.

Lightfoot, J. B. *St Paul's Epistles to the Colossians and Philemon.* London, 1879.

Lohmeyer, E. *Die Briefe an die Philipper, an die Kolosser und an Philemon.* Meyer Kommentar 9 (additional notes by W. Schmauch, 1964). Göttingen, 1953.

Lohse, E. *Colossians and Philemon.* Hermeneia. Philadelphia, 1971.

Moule, C. F. D. *The Epistles of Paul the Apostle to the Colossians and to Philemon.* The Cambridge Greek New Testament Commentary. Cambridge, 1957.

Thompson, G. H. P. *The Letters of Paul to the Ephesians, to the Colossians, and to Philemon.* Cambridge Bible Commentary. Cambridge, 1967.

COMMENTARIES ON COLOSSIANS

Barclay, W. *The Letter to the Colossians,* Daily Study Bible, Edinburgh, 1957.

Beare, F. W. *The Epistle to the Colossians.* Interpreter's Bible 11. New York/Nashville, 1955.

Bruce, F. F. *Commentary on the Epistles to the Ephesians and Colossians* (with E. K. Simpson). New London/International Commentary. London/Grand Rapids, 1957.

Masson, Ch. *L'épître de saint Paul aux Colossiens.* Commentaire du Nouveau Testament 10. Neuchâtel/Paris, 1950.

Mussner, F. *Der Brief an die Kolosser.* Geistliche Schriftlesung. Düsseldorf, 1965.

Synge, F. C. *Philippians and Colossians.* Torch Bible Commentary. London, 1951.

PERTINENT ESSAYS APPEARING IN VOLUMES OF COLLECTED STUDIES (*including Festschriften*)

Benoit, P. 'Rapports litteraires entre les épîtres aux Colossiens et aux Ephésiens' in *Neutestamentliche Aufsätze. Festschrift für Prof. Josef*

Schmid zum 70. Geburtstag. Ed. J. Blinzler, *et al.* Regensburg, 1963, pp. 11–22.

Bornkamm, G. 'Die Häresie des Kolosserbriefes', *Das Ende des Gesetzes. Paulusstudien.* Gesammelte Aufsätze Band 1. Munich, 1952, pp. 139–56.

—— 'Das Bekenntnis im Hebräerbrief', *Studien zu Antike und Urchristentum.* Gesammelte Aufsätze Band ii. Munich, 1959, pp. 188–203.

—— 'Die Hoffnung im Kolosserbrief–zugleich ein Beitrag zur Frage der Echtheit des Briefes' in *Studien zum Neuen Testament und zur Patristik. Festschrift für Erich Klostermann.* Berlin, 1961, pp. 56–64.

Foerster, W. 'Die Irrelehrer des Kolosserbriefes' in *Studia Biblica et Semitica. Theodoro Christiano Vriezen . . . dedicata.* Wageningen, 1966, pp. 71–80.

Lohse, E. 'Christologie und Ethik im Kolosserbrief' in *Apophoreta, Festschrift für Ernst Haenchen.* Ed. W. Eltester. Berlin, 1964, pp. 156–68.

—— 'Die Mitarbeiter des Apostels Paulus im Kolosserbrief' in *Verborum Veritas. Festschrift für Gustav Stählin zum 70. Geburtstag.* Ed. O. Böcher and K. Haacker. Wuppertal, 1970, pp. 189–94.

Reicke, B. 'Caesarea, Rome, and the Captivity Epistles' in *Apostolic History and the Gospel. Biblical and Historical Essays presented to F. F. Bruce.* Ed. W. W. Gasque and R. P. Martin. Exeter, 1970, pp. 277–86.

Schweizer, E. 'Die "Elemente der Welt" Gal. 4. 3, 9; Kol. 2. 8, 20' in *Verborum Veritas. Festschrift für Gustav Stählin zum 70. Geburtstag.* Ed. O. Böcher and K. Haacker. Wuppertal, 1970, pp. 245–59.

—— 'Die Kirche als Leib Christi in den paulinischen Antilegomena'; and 'The Church as the Missionary Body of Christ' in *Neotestamentica: Deutsche und Englische Aufsätze.* Zürich, 1963, pp. 293–316, 317–29.

SUPPLEMENTARY BIBLIOGRAPHY (1974–81)

Since a new printing of this commentary is called for, it has been possible to include these few pages of additional material in which note is taken of some recent studies of the two epistles. It has not been feasible to introduce these items of bibliography into the body of the commentary, but their place here seems appropriate. Conventional headings to divide the literature have been used, and the authors' names stand in alphabetical order.

COMMENTARIES

Caird, G. B. *Paul's Letters from Prison.* New Clarendon Bible, Oxford, 1976.

Ernst, J. *Die Briefe an die Philipper, an Philemon, an die Kolosser, an die Epheser,* Regensburger New Testament series. Regensburg, 1974.

Schweizer, E. *Der Brief an die Kolosser.* Evangelisch-Katholischer Kommentar z. NT. Zürich–Köln–Neukirchen, 1976. This is the fullest, most recent commentary.

Stuhlmacher, P. *Der Brief an Philemon*. Evangelisch-Katholischer Kommentar z. NT. Zürich–Köln–Neukirchen, 1975. The first volume in a new interconfessional commentary series (EKK).

STUDIES IN THE EPISTLES

Bauckham, R. J. 'Colossians 1:24 Again: The Apocalyptic Note', *EQ* 47, 1975, pp. 168–70.

Beasley-Murray, G. R. 'The Second Chapter of Colossians', *Review and Expositor* 70, 1973, pp. 469–79.

Beasley-Murray, P. 'Colossians 1:15–20: An Early Christian Hymn Celebrating the Lordship of Christ', in *Pauline Studies, Essays Presented to F. F. Bruce*, ed. D. A. Hagner and M. J. Harris (Exeter/Grand Rapids, 1980), pp. 169–83.

Benoit, P. 'L'hymne christologique de Col. 1, 15–20' in *Christianity, Judaism and Other Greco-Roman Cults. Studies for Morton Smith at Sixty*, ed. J. Neusner, Part i, Leiden, 1975, pp. 226–63.

Carr, W. 'Two Notes on Colossians', *JTS* 24, 1973, pp. 492–500.

Crouch, J. E. *The Origin and Intention of the Colossian Haustafel*. Gottingen, 1972 (on this title, see W. Lillie, 'The Pauline House-Tables', *ExpT* 86.6, 1975, pp. 179–83, and D. Schroeder, 'Lists, Ethical', *Interpreter's Dictionary of the Bible. Supplementary Volume*, Nashville, 1976, pp. 546f.).

Egan, R. B. 'Lexical Evidence of Two Pauline Passages', *NovT* 19, 1977, pp. 34–62.

Francis, F. O. and Meeks, W. A. *Conflict at Colossae*. (Society for Biblical Literature Publication) Missoula, Montana, 1973. This is an edited reprint and translation of some of the key contributions to an understanding of Colossians.

Hendricks, W. L. 'All in All. Theological Themes in Colossians', *South Western Journal of Theology* 16, 1975, pp. 23–35.

Hollenbach, B. 'Col. II. 23: Which Things lead to the Fulfilment of the Flesh', *NTS* 25, 1979, pp. 254–61.

Hooker, M. D. 'Were there False Teachers in Colossae?' in *Christ and Spirit in the New Testament. Studies in Honour of C. F. D. Moule*, ed. B. Lindars and S. S. Smalley. Cambridge, 1973, pp. 315–31.

Hopkins, Keith. *Conquerors and Slaves*. Sociological Studies in Roman History, vol. 1 (Cambridge, 1980). The chapter (written with P. J. Roscoe) "Between Slavery and Freedom: On Freeing Slaves at Delphi" has some interesting background material to the situation in Philemon (see the commentary, p. 146).

Ladd, G. E. 'Paul's Friends in Colossians 4:7–16', *Review and Expositor* 70, 1973, pp. 507–14.

Lamarche, P. 'Structure de l'épître aux Colossiens', *Biblica* 56, 1975, pp. 453–63.

Lane, W. L. 'Creed and Theology: Reflections on Colossians', *Journal of the Evangelical Theological Society* 21, 1978, pp. 213–20.

McCown, Wayne. 'The Hymnic Structure of Colossians 1:15–20', *EQ* 51, 1979, pp. 156–66.

Manns, F. 'Col. 1, 15–20; midrash chrétien de Gen. 1, 1', *Revue des sciences religieuses* 53, 1979, pp. 100–10.

Moir, I. A. 'Some Thoughts on Col. 2, 17–18', *Theologische Zeitschrift* 35, 6, 1979, pp. 363–65.

Moule, C. F. D. '"The New Life" in Colossians', *Review and Expositor* 70, 1973, pp. 481–93.

O'Brien, P. T. 'Col. 1:20 and the Reconciliation of All Things', *Reformed Theological Review* 33, 1974, pp. 45–53.

O'Neill, J. C. 'The Source of Christology in Colossians', *NTS* 26, 1979, pp. 87–100.

Overfield, P. D. 'Pleroma: A Study in Content and Context', *NTS* 25, 1979, pp. 384–91.

Pollard, T. E. 'Colossians 1. 12–20: A Reconsideration', *NTS* 27, 1981, pp. 572–75.

Reicke, B. 'The Historical Setting of Colossians', *Review and Expositor* 70, 1973, pp. 429–38 (Reicke's argument for dating the letter in Paul's Caesarean captivity is elaborated by J. A. T. Robinson, *Redating the New Testament*, London, 1976, pp. 60ff.).

Schweizer, E. 'Christianity of the Circumcized and Judaism of the Uncircumcized—the Background of Matthew and Colossians' in *Jews, Greeks and Christians: Religious Cultures in Late Antiquity*. Festschrift for W. D. Davies, ed. R. G. Hamerton-Kelly and R. Scroggs, Leiden, 1975.

— 'Christus und Geist im Kolosserbrief' in *Christ and Spirit in the New Testament* (see above under Hooker), pp. 297–313.

— 'Zur neueren Forschung am Kolosserbrief (seit 1970)' in *Theologische Berichte* 5, Zürich, 1976, pp. 163–91. (A survey of recent studies on Colossians from 1970 to 1974.)

— 'Versöhnung des Alls, Kol. 1,20' in *Jesus Christus in Historie und Theologie*. Festschrift for H. Conzelmann, ed. G. Strecker, Tübingen, 1975, pp. 487–501.

— 'Christ in the Letter to the Colossians', *Review and Expositor* 70, 1973, pp. 451–67.

Trudinger, L. P. 'A Further Brief Note on Col. 1:24', *EQ* 45, 1973, pp. 36–8.

Walter, N. 'Die "Handschrift" in Satzungen Kol. 2:14', *ZNTW* 70, 1979, pp. 115–18.

Weiss, H. 'The Law in the Epistle to the Colossians', *CBQ* 34, 1972, pp. 294–314.

Wengst, K. 'Versöhnung und Befreiung. Ein Aspeckt des Themas "Schuld und Vergebung" im Lichte des Kolosserbriefes', *Evangelische Theologie* 36, 1976, pp. 14–26.

INTRODUCTION

to

Colossians

INTRODUCTION TO COLOSSIANS

1. THE CITY AND PEOPLE OF COLOSSAE

Colossae lay in the valley of the Lycus river, a tributary of the Maeander, in the southern part of ancient Phrygia which would be located in the west of modern Turkey. As the town was situated on a main trade route from Ephesus to the east, it is not surprising that ancient historians refer to it in their descriptions of the military movements of such generals as Xerxes and Cyrus. When Herodotus tells how the army of Xerxes was stopped in its march on Greece, he speaks of Colossae as 'a great city of Phrygia' (*Histories* vii.30.1). A century later, the chronicler Xenophon described it as 'a populous city, both wealthy and large' (*Anabasis* i.2.6). Its commercial importance was due largely to its place as an emporium of the weaving industry. The wool was gathered from sheep which grazed on the slopes of the Lycus valley, and dyed. The name 'Colossian' was used of a particular colour (*colossinus*) of dyed wool (Strabo, *Geogr.* xii.8.16; Pliny, *Hist. Nat.* xxi.51).

But the importance of Colossae diminished in Roman times, largely because the city's neighbouring centres, Laodicea and Hierapolis, had expanded and grown more prosperous. The elder Pliny (*Hist. Nat.* v.145) in describing Phrygia places Colossae among 'its most famous towns' (*oppida . . . celeberrima*), but he has in view towns which had known greatness in past times, and the third city mentioned alongside Hierapolis and Laodicea was Apamea (Dibelius–Greeven, p. 4).

Laodicea, situated to the west of Colossae, became under Roman rule the seat of Roman administration (Cicero, *Att.* v.21). Hierapolis, on the north side of the Lycus river valley, was also an important city, notable for its healing waters (Strabo, *Geogr.* xiii.4.14). See M. J. S. Rudwick and E. M. B. Green, 'The Laodicean Lukewarmness', *ExpT* 69 (1957–8), pp. 176–8, and W. M. Ramsay, *The Cities and Bishoprics of Phrygia*, vol. i, Oxford, 1895, pp. 208–34. At the beginning of the Christian era, Strabo (*Geogr.* xii.8.13) apparently could describe Colossae as only a 'small town' (Gr. *polisma*), though there is some textual uncertainty arising from the fact of a lacuna in Strabo's text after the word for 'small towns', and it is open to question whether Strabo intended to include Colossae in the listing of 'small towns' which follows.

Parts of the Lycus valley, especially Laodicea, were destroyed by earthquake in A.D. 60–1, according to Tacitus (*Ann.* xiv.27), but Colossae is not mentioned. Orosius, however, later (*Hist. Adv. Paganos* vii.7.12) comments that 'in Asia three cities, Laodicea, Hierapolis, Colossae, fell by earthquakes'. *Cf.* Eusebius, *Chronicle*, p. 215, who dates this destruction in the ninth or tenth year of Nero.

Laodicea was restored without outside assistance, but Colossae never regained its place, and it is likely that it suffered further seismic damage (a frequent hazard in those parts) and was never rebuilt (Lohse). There is, however, some inscriptional and numismatic evidence of Colossae's continuance as a Roman city with its officials well into the Christian centuries (*Inscriptiones Graecae ad Res Romanas Pertinentes* iv.870). See D. Magie, *Roman Rule in Asia Minor*, Princeton, 1950, pp. 127, 986 (cited by J. L. Houlden, p. 119). The present-day site is uninhabited and not yet excavated (*cf.* S. E. Johnson, 'Early Christianity in Anatolia' in *Studies in New Testament and Early Christian Literature*, ed. D. E. Aune, Leiden, 1972, p. 185).

At the time when Paul lived, the commercial and social importance of Colossae was already declining. What effect this depression might have had on the Colossian townspeople, or the Christians among them, we have no means of knowing. What does seem certain is that, in Lightfoot's words, 'Colossae was the least important church to which any epistle of St Paul is addressed' (*Commentary*, p. 16).

When Paul wrote to the Christians living at Colossae, the city's population consisted mainly of indigenous Phrygian and Greek settlers. But Josephus (*Ant.* xii.147–53) records the fact that Antiochus III in the early part of the second century B.C. had brought two thousand Jews from Mesopotamia and Babylon and settled them in Lydia and Phrygia. Colossae in Paul's day was thus a cosmopolitan city in which diverse cultural and religious elements met and mingled.

On the Jewish side, we can appreciate something of the influence which persisted since the immigration of the Jews in the second century B.C. Grave inscriptions found at Hierapolis show how well Jews had become part of the Asian culture (see E. Schürer, *Die Geschichte des jüdischen Volkes*, Leipzig, 4th edn. 1909, vol. iii, pp. 17f.); and in 62–61 B.C. an order of the Roman governor

Flaccus forbad Phrygian Jews from sending twenty pounds of gold from the region of Laodicea as part of the Jerusalem temple tax (Cicero, *Pro Flacco* xxviii.68); and this has led to the computation, on the basis of the weight and value of the head-tax, of a Jewish male population of 11,000 in the district of Laodicea.

The religious scene in Phrygia is one in which several characteristic elements are known to have been present. The cult of Cybele, the great mother-goddess of Asia, flourished (Strabo says that all Phrygia worshipped her: see G. Showerman, *The Great Mother of the Gods*, Chicago, 1901, pp. 71ff. for the data which show that Phrygia was the centre of the worship; and cf. Franz Cumont, *Les religions orientales dans le paganisme romain*, Paris, 1929, pp. 43ff.). This cult was originally a nature rite tied in to fertility customs and leading to excessive joy and ecstasy. Under the name of Hera-Atargatis sacrifices were offered to her with 'noisy and ecstatic joy' (John Ferguson, *The Religions of the Roman Empire*, London, 1970, p. 19), according to Lucian's descriptions of the festival at Hierapolis (*The Syrian Goddess*, pp. 49–60). But ascetic practices were also part of this religion, and one suggestion has been to see in Paul's allusion to 'severity of the body' (2:23) and circumcision (2:11) a reference to initiatory rites and mutilation practices, familiar from this cult.

In an atmosphere of syncretism it is easy to see how other cults could be practised and merged with existing religious ceremonies. The worship of Isis was widespread in the world of Paul's day (see R. E. Witt, *Isis in the Graeco-Roman World*, London, 1971, p. 131: 'It was natural enough . . . that Isis as she became a pancosmic figure should fuse with the primordial Divine Mother of Asia Minor'); and the oracle shrine of Apollo at Claros contains an inscription which contains the same verb as occurs in Paul's text (2:18) used of the Colossian 'mystery' (Apuleius xi.23: see M. P. Nilsson's discussion in *Geschichte der griechischen Religion*, vol. 2, Munich, 1961, p. 476.)

The possible influence of syncretistic Judaism in Asia Minor is seen in the cult of Mēn Ascaenus who was, according to Strabo, the chief god of Pisidian Antioch. The cult was immensely popular during the Empire (J. Ferguson, *op. cit.*, p. 217) and offered a healing cult with a strong element of enthusiastic personal religion. The god was variously known as Apollo, Dionysus and Asclepius, but one fragmentary inscription begins with the name 'Ouio' which may be taken as a version of Yahweh. Monotheism was an important tenet in this religion, and one inscription (given in Cumont, *op. cit.*, p. 227, n. 54) proclaims 'one God in the highest, great heavenly Mēn, great power of the immortal God'. The cult of the 'Most high God' (*hypsistos theos*) was related in the Isis-worship with the divinity's control of the 'elements of the world' (Isis is *elementorum omnium domina*, Apuleius xi.5); and this ascription raises the most interesting problem of ancient Phrygian religion: the question of the *stoicheia*, which is Paul's word in 2:8, 20.

A fuller treatment of this enigmatic Greek phrase 'the elemental spirits of the universe', as *RSV* renders, will be reserved for later. At this point we may notice that the manifestations of the four simple 'elements' of which the ancients thought the universe to be composed, fire, earth, water, air, were treated by the religion of Mithraism as divinities in their own right (see Franz Cumont, *The Mysteries of Mithra*, New York, 1956, p. 116). Probably the origin of this process of deification is to be traced to Iranian (Persian) sources as Cumont argues (*op. cit.*; this is accepted by J. Lähnemann, p. 92), and it is interesting that inscriptions which depict the Mithraic conflict and victory often portray the character wearing Phrygian caps. This is part of the evidence which shows that Iranian cosmology and astrology were linked with the redemption-mystery of the religion of Mithras and came early to the Asia Minor region; and this also was in the background of the religious life of the Colossians at the time when Paul wrote to them.

J. Lähnemann sums up the situation in a sentence: The Judaism in the towns of the Lycus valley is to be seen in the setting of a hellenistic culture-merging in which the rigorism of Phrygian religion was joined with Iranian religious elements and with characteristics of a wisdom-teaching taken from the mystery cults (*Der Kolosserbrief*, Gütersloh, 1971, p. 104).

This background has a bearing on the rise of the teaching which came to assault the church at Colossae. As we shall observe, the nature of the teaching is composite and was made up partly of Jewish elements and partly of ideas belonging to the world of hellenistic religious philosophy and mysticism. Colossae was a cultural centre where this syncretism might well have been expected; so it is not surprising that it was the Colossian congregation in a city partly Jewish-oriental and partly Greek-Phrygian that became the target of an assault in the name of a syncretistic 'fancy religion'.

2. THE CHURCH AT COLOSSAE

The Christian gospel was introduced to Colossae during Paul's ministry based in Ephesus. According to Acts 19 : 10 Paul exercised a preaching ministry in the capital city of proconsular Asia with a result that 'the whole population of the province of Asia, both Jews and pagans, heard the word of the Lord' (*NEB*). This description must mean that, while he was based in Ephesus during a period of two or three years (so Ac. 19 : 10; 20 : 31), and 'at the zenith of his labours' (according to the record in Acts: see E. Haenchen, *The Acts of the Apostles*, Oxford, ET 1971, p. 558), he sent out his representatives to carry the message to outlying cities and districts in the province. The letter to the Colossians itself affirms that Paul was not personally responsible for evangelistic work in the Lycus valley region eighty miles or so from Ephesus. In two places (1 : 4; 2 : 1) there are indications that Paul had not, at the time of writing, visited the church nor any Christian communities in the area including Laodicea. His hope to meet them personally may have been realized later, if the request of Philemon 22 was made good in the fulfilled desire he had to be released from prison and to visit Philemon.

The most likely person to have carried the good news of Christ to Colossae was Epaphras. He was a native of that city (4 : 12: he is described as 'one of yourselves'), and stood in a special relation to the believers there as well as to the apostle (4 : 13). Tribute is paid to him (1 : 7) as a 'faithful minister of Christ' who as Paul's personal delegate had evidently evangelized the Lycus valley district and later had come to visit Paul in his captivity. Indeed, he had, either voluntarily or because of his arrest by the authorities, shared Paul's imprisonment (Phm. 23), and so was not free to return to the congregation when the letter was sent. It was entrusted to Tychicus as its bearer (4 : 7, 8). He is commissioned to carry also the news of the apostle's prison experience and to bring some encouragement to the Colossian church over the detention of their leader, Epaphras. From him the Colossian Christians had 'heard and understood the grace of God in truth' (1 : 6, 7), and it is only natural that they were concerned about their pastor's well-being, especially since he would not be returning along with the delegation (Tychicus, Onesimus) which brought the letter. Other members of the Colossian church included Philemon and his family (Phm. 1, 2) including Archippus

(4:17) and his fugitive slave Onesimus (4:9 Phm. 11) who is to be welcomed as a fellow-believer and new church member (Phm. 16, 17).

3. THE OCCASION OF THE LETTER

When Epaphras came to seek Paul in his imprisonment, he was able to report that the Colossian church was responding well to apostolic instruction, both in growth (1:6) and in determination to stand firm in the faith (2:5–7). The tenor of these verses and others has suggested to some interpreters, notably H. J. Holtzmann (*Kritik der Epheser – und Kolosserbriefe*, Leipzig, 1872) and C. R. Bowen (*JBL* 43 (1924), pp. 189ff.), that the Colossian church was a young community, only recently established at the time of Paul's writing to them. Bowen's appeal is especially made to some eighteen verses (1:4, 5, 6, 7, 8, 9, 21f., 23; 2:1f., 5, 6, 7; 3:7f., 9f.) in which, he maintains, there are at least fourteen direct allusions to the Colossians' conversion. He concludes: 'All this is the language of fresh and vivid reaction upon that happy event . . . at the time the letter is written the Colossian church has been in existence only a period of weeks or of months at most' (p. 190).

This inference of the church's being of recent foundation is a matter which cannot really be proved. But it is a matter of some consequence to be able to envisage the situation in the Colossian church which led to Paul's writing to them. And this raises several questions, which are still being actively debated. Epaphras brought news to Paul about a threat to the church's faith. This called for his intervention, couched in the plain warnings of 2:4, 8 and 2:16. The first question is, is the nature of this false teaching such as would appeal to a newly-formed church? Then, what can we say about the speculative and practical issues involved in this Colossian 'heresy'? There is another matter which concerns the dating of the epistle, which in part is settled by our answer to the question, where was Paul in captivity? (4:3, 18). To which part of his apostolic career does this 'epistle from prison' belong? But there is also the matter of the epistle's genuineness, since if the false teaching is patently later than Paul's time or if his answers presuppose a line of reasoning which is different from what we know of his theology in the accepted epistles, then the inference will be that this epistle comes out of a post-Pauline era.

The issues are, however, not of equal importance. For an understanding of the letter far more depends upon what we can make of the nature of the Colossian errorists' teaching than upon the matters of Paul's imprisonment and the epistle's date and authenticity.

4. THE THREAT TO FAITH AND THE COLOSSIAN CRISIS

Perhaps quite unconsciously the church at Colossae was being exposed to a false teaching which Paul regarded as a denial of his gospel which Epaphras had brought to them. Part of the occasion of his letter may be traced to the presence of this threatened danger and the need to rebut the error which lay at the heart of what Paul describes as a strange aberration of the apostolic kerygma. The letter to the Colossians is thus 'Paul's vigorous reaction to the news of the strange teaching which was being inculcated at Colossae' (F. F. Bruce, *Commentary*, p. 165). But, as H. Chadwick has shown, Paul's defence of the apostolic faith goes hand in hand with an apologetic statement of that faith to the intellectual world of his day ('All Things to All Men', *NTS*, 1 (1954-5), pp. 270ff.). In this sense his letter to the Colossians is one of the earliest Christian 'apologies', or defensive statements of the faith over against its rivals that we possess.

Nowhere in the letter does Paul give a formal definition of the teaching, and its chief features can be detected only by piecing together and interpreting his positive counter-arguments. There are, however, some crucial passages where he seems to be actually quoting the slogans and watchwords of the cult and these form invaluable clues in any attempt to understand the nature of what was being advocated at Colossae. These citations will enable us to build up a sort of 'identi-kit' picture of the teaching against which Paul sets his face. The verses in question are:

1 : 19 For in him all the fullness of God was pleased to dwell
2 : 18 insisting on self-abasement and worship of angels
2 : 21 'Do not handle, Do not taste, Do not touch'
2 : 23 rigour of devotion and self-abasement and severity to the body

And the allusions to 'elemental spirits of the universe' (2:8, 20) pick up terms which were being advocated as an important part of the strange theosophical cult.

Even from this short list we are able to see that the threat to apostolic faith and life was both academic and practical. Part of the teaching was related to a theological issue and centred on the question of the meaning of religion. W. Warde Fowler in his *The Religious Experience of the Roman People*, London, 1911, p. 8, quotes a description of religion (from Ira W. Howerth) which aptly exposes the core of the problem: 'the effective desire to be in right relations with the Power manifesting itself in the universe.' The answer suggested in the incubus which the teachers at Colossae were laying upon the church ran along these lines, if we assume that their interpretation of the universe was gnosticizing (see for an admirable statement of the basic tenets of gnosticism, J. Ferguson, *The Religions of the Roman Empire*, London, 1970, pp. 128–31). God's fullness is distributed throughout a series of emanations from the divine, stretching from heaven to earth. These 'aeons' or offshoots of deity must be venerated and homage paid to them as 'elemental spirits' or angels or gods inhabiting the stars. They rule men's destiny and control human life, and hold the entrance into the divine realm in their keeping. Christ is one of them, but only one among many.

The other question was intensely practical. How may a person prepare himself for a vision of heavenly realities as part of his rite of passage into a knowledge of the divine mysteries? The reply was given in terms of a rigorous discipline of asceticism and self-denial. Abstinence, especially from food and drink; observance of initiatory and purificatory rites; and possibly a life of celibacy and mortification of the human body (2:21, 23)—all these exercises and taboos were prescribed as part of the regimen to be accepted if the Christians at Colossae were ever to gain 'fullness of life' (2:10).

In brief compass, this is the sketch or 'cartoon' boldly brushed onto the canvas in deft strokes by the verses mentioned above. As the key-terms are more closely examined, it is possible to fill in more detail and to add colour and distinctiveness to this first-century scientology.

5. THE COLOSSIAN PHILOSOPHY

Two terms are used to identify the false teaching introduced at Colossae. They are 'philosophy' (2:8) and 'forced piety' (2:23,

NEB). The latter term (Gr. *ethelothrēskeia*) is not easily translatable and of the various possibilities (see the commentary) we prefer the rendering 'self-devised religion'. We may enquire about the elements which went to make up this teaching. G. Bornkamm in an essay dedicated to this theme ('Die Häresie des Kolosserbriefes', *ThLZ* 73 (1948), cols. 11ff., reprinted in *Das Ende des Gesetzes. Paulusstudien*, Munich, 1961, pp. 139ff.) calls attention to the background drawn from a 'history-of-religions' study of the main terms which Paul 'borrows' from the cult at Colossae. These catchwords, when set against this background, are paralleled by profuse examples of terms found in astral, theological and demonological concepts which, in turn, are derived from Persian-Chaldean astrology, oriental-hellenistic mysteries and gnostic speculation (*loc. cit.*, pp. 141f.). These are far-ranging categories, which can best be subdivided under the chief terms which Paul employs: the *stoicheia*, the cult of angel-veneration and the advocacy of 'humility' as part of 'severity to the body'.

(*a*) The *stoicheia* (2:8, 20). The basic meaning of *stoicheia* is 'objects which stand in a row or which form a series' (*cf.* G. H. C. Macgregor, 'Principalities and Powers: The Cosmic Background of St Paul's Thought', *NTS* 1 (1954–5), pp. 21f.). The most natural example of these objects is letters of the alphabet, which stand together in a line to make continuous writing. From this idea it is an easy step to reach the notion of 'elements of learning', or, as we say, ABC, meaning rudiments or basic principles. This is the sense of Hebrews 5:12: 'the elementary truths of God'.

The term 'elements' was also applied by the Greeks to the physical substances which compose the totality of the world (*cf.* 2 Pet. 3:10, 12), and the common view (voiced by Empedocles, born about 490 B.C., and later elaborated by Plato, Aristotle, and the Stoics: see G. E. R. Lloyd, *Greek Science after Aristotle*, London, 1973) was that there were four 'elements'—earth, fire, water, air—as the 'root of all things'. The Ionian philosophers who were based in Miletus challenged this by emphasizing the importance of a 'living spirit' which, they believed, suffused all nature, and 'air' or 'breath' was thought of as a life-giving force (so Anaximenes). Such a development points in the direction of a divinizing of the upper regions which are thought to contain 'air in motion' and to be immortal and divine. This notion is developed by the Pythagoreans. Diogenes Laertius (third century A.D.) preserves a very interesting passage, attributed to Alexander Polyhistor (first century B.C.) who in turn derived it from a Pythagorean contemporary of Plato (fourth century B.C.)1, which contains several arresting features which are roughly parallel with the Colossian cult. (E. Schweizer draws attention to the passage in Diogenes Laertius, viii.24ff., in his study 'Die "Elemente der Welt". Gal. 4, 3.9; Kol 2, 8.20' in *Verborum Veritas*, Wuppertal, 1970, pp. 257ff.)

In this statement of Pythagorean beliefs (*cf.* F. M. Cornford, *Greek Religious Thought From Homer to the Age of Alexander*, London, 1923, pp. 67f.) we may pay particular notice of the use made of the *stoicheia* which are described as the constituent parts of the universe (viii.25). The 'upper air' (Gr. *aithēr*) is distinguished from the lower air (Gr. *aēr*) (*cf.* G. E. R. Lloyd, *op. cit.*, p. 59), and it is the former which holds the sun, moon and stars. They are treated as gods (viii.27) and with their existence is bound up human destiny since the gods determine man's lot by 'fate' (Gr. *heimarmenē*).

After a section which deals with the relation of the human soul and body, the discussion makes a distinction between the 'pure' souls and the 'impure' souls (viii.31). The former are escorted by Hermes to the upper region of the divine, while the latter are detained in chains. The 'atmosphere' around the earth is filled with spirit-powers which influence both men and nature, and these 'demons' or 'heroes' are to be reverenced (viii.33) and the soul kept purified.

This passage is worth extended treatment because its terminology matches strikingly the prescriptions and rituals found at Colossae. But the fundamental issue is that it offers a parallel to the *stoicheia* in the twofold use of the term in the letter to the Colossians. Part of Paul's reply to the false teaching is to insist that all the parts of creation are both created and sustained (1:16, 17) by the cosmic Christ; and he opposes the faith in Christ to the veneration paid, in the cult, to non-human powers which were thought to rule men's lives (2:8). Paul's answer, on the double front, is to assert the headship of Christ (1:18; 2:10) and to neutralize the power of these *stoicheia* as immortal lords of creation, existing in their own right, and as astrological tyrants who laid claim to control men's lives as the playthings of fate.

To the very real problem of man's relation with the cosmic powers in the first century, represented by the cult of astrology, one answer was given in terms of a placating of the star-deities and a purification by ascetic practices. These 'regulations' (*cf.*

2:2c) held out the possibility for a person to escape the mesh of inevitability and to break from imprisonment in 'matter' and ascend to the higher regions of 'spirit'. In the cult of Isis, the goddess is hailed as greater than fate and as liberator of men and women from 'necessity' (i.e. astrological bondage). The hope was held out, in these cults (whose presence in the Lycus valley may well be presupposed, as we have seen), to 'short-circuit the stars' (in the vivid expression of W. W. Tarn and G. T. Griffith, *Hellenistic Civilisation*, London, 3rd edn. 1952, p. 351), and to obtain liberty from the power exerted by the *stoicheia*.

These are the choices of interpretation open to us in reference to Paul's phrase. On the one hand, Paul is regarding the false system as 'elementary teaching' practised either by Jewish or pagan ritualists and he dubs it as obedience to the '*stoicheia* of the world' in the sense that it is materialist at heart and exclusively tied to this world and so infantile. By contrast, Paul's gospel invites men to accept the freedom of Christ and to remain no longer in a kindergarten stage of religious taboos and restrictions (so Moule). On the other hand, Paul is branding this cult as false because it consciously paid deference to the powerful spirit-intelligences which held men prey and which needed to be placated. Many reasons are forthcoming to support the second interpretation (*pace* G. Delling's insistence in *TDNT* vii, p. 670, that the phrase has no connection with the star-gods and must be given a neutral connotation):

(*i*) The tenor of other polemical parts of the letter indicates Paul's belief in Christ's victory over demonic agencies (2:15) and the Christian's freedom from them (2:20).

(*ii*) Only this view explains his repeated insistence that the divine 'fullness' dwells in Christ, and not in these cosmic forces (1:19; 2:9). They, on the contrary, owe their existence to him (1:15-20; 2:10).

(*iii*) The references to circumcision in 2:11, and to calendrical and dietary observance in 2:16 are more likely to link up with particular cultic practices based on the control of the heavenly bodies and the call to abstinence (see later) and are not associated with distinctive Jewish elements. An exception may be the observance of the Sabbath (see E. Lohse, *TDNT* vii, p. 30) but even this 'Jewish' term may be linked with spirit-forces in the cosmos (see Schweizer, *loc. cit.*, p. 256). G. Delling (*loc. cit.*, p. 685) concedes that the meaning of *stoicheia* in Colossians 2 is

different from the use in Galatians 4:8–10 where it is usually taken
to refer back to Judaizing legalism. However, the relapse of the
Galatian Christians to 'the weak and beggarly elements' (Gr.
stoicheia) more probably means a return to the gods of paganism
from which they had been converted (4:8–10). Paul can hardly
mean that they were relapsing to simplistic forms of religion and
that the effect of a superstitious evil-eye of bewitchment (3:1) was
calculated to lead them to an uncomplicated faith. Moreover, the
observance of special days mentioned in Galatians 4:10 is
probably, as in Colossians 2, to be taken as a respect paid to the
planets as controllers of nature and human life (so Bornkamm,
loc. cit., p. 148) to which the Galatian Christians were formerly
enslaved (Gal. 4:3).

(*iv*) E. Percy (*Die Probleme der Kolosser – und Epheserbriefe*, Lund,
1946, p. 167) has argued cogently that Paul sets the *stoicheia* in
direct antithesis to Christ (2:8) and this suggests that 'for him
the contrast lies . . . between this age ruled by spirit-forces and
Christ. It is the contrast between Greek and early Christian
understandings of existence'.

(*v*) The practice of asceticism was encouraged by these teachers
(2:20–3) as part of their discipline. It is likely that such was a
preparatory exercise intended to overcome hostile spirit-powers
and to induce a trance-like visionary experience (2:18). See the
commentary on this verse.

(*vi*) 'Worship of angels' (2:18) must be related to the cultus,
and the homage paid to these heavenly orders suggests that it is
part of the same 'philosophy' or theosophical system that venerated
the deities which inhabited the stars, according to popular
hellenistic belief. This startling innovation came about mainly
because of the advent of oriental astrology and occultism which
'with its accompanying astral religion and dominant fatalism, lay
like a nightmare upon the soul' (P. Wendland, 'Hellenistic Ideas
of Salvation in the Light of Ancient Anthropology', *AJT* 17
(1913), p. 345) of first-century man. The vacuum (caused by
disillusion over the collapse of the Homeric gods who were like
magnified men and women on Mount Olympus: see the texts
drawn from Hesiod in F. M. Cornford, *Greek Religious Thought*,
pp. 19ff.) was quickly filled with an all-embracing fatalism. Men
who came under the spell of star-worship were made to feel that all
things were ruled by 'fate'. The particular conjunction of the
stars or planets under which a person was born was of decisive

importance and settled irretrievably his destiny. Hence the central place of the heavenly bodies in popular hellenistic religion was established once the astrologers had capitalized on this yearning for a 'religion' to fill the void (*cf.* R. S. Barbour, 'Salvation and Cosmology: the Setting of the Epistle to the Colossians', *SJT* 20 (1967), pp. 257–71).

(*vii*) In the Jewish tradition represented by Philo and such literature as *The Testament of Solomon*, the *stoicheia* are seen as astral powers which are malevolently disposed to men. This is clear in *Test. Sol.* viii.2ff., xviii.1ff., where *stoicheia* and *kosmokratores* ('world rulers', demonic agencies, as in Eph. 6:12) stand together. See G. H. C. Macgregor, *loc. cit.*, p. 22, and J. Lähnemann, *op. cit.*, pp. 91f.

Our conclusion is that Paul's evidence suggests that the Colossian 'philosophy' was concerned to give a prominent place to angelic orders as custodians of human destiny. In current hellenistic thought this was closely related to the stars and their patron deities. But Paul will have none of this in his insistence that all cosmic powers are dependent upon the pre-existing Christ who entirely fills the universe and leaves no room for competing agencies, since they are defeated by him and subservient to him. He alone gives meaning to the universe which coheres in him (1:16, 17); and so he alone gives meaning and purpose to life (2:10).

(*b*) The tantalizing allusion in 2:18 to the 'worship of angels' looks at first glance to support the notion that the Colossian cultists were Jews with a highly developed and unorthodox angelology. Evidence for an important place accorded to angels is now forthcoming from Qumran (*cf.* G. Vermes, *The Dead Sea Scrolls in English*, Harmondsworth, 1962, pp. 75f.) and some commentators (e.g. Bornkamm, *loc. cit.*, p. 150, and Houlden, pp. 195f.) draw attention to the influence of the aberrant form of Judaism seen in Elchasai, a Jew who practised rites and customs such as baptism, circumcision and sabbath observance but in a highly individualistic way and by adopting accompanying beliefs which were patterned on the Jewish-Christian Ebionites, (see J. Daniélou, *The Theology of Jewish Christianity*, London, 1964, pp. 64–7). He too had a strongly developed doctrine of angels.

Another variation of the idea of Jewish practices underlying Paul's phrase is offered by F. O. Francis ('Humility and Angelic

Worship in Col. 2:18', *ST* 16 (1962), pp. 109–34; *idem*, 'Visionary Discipline and Scriptural Tradition at Colossae', *Lexington Theological Quarterly* 2 (1967), pp. 71–81). He argues that Paul's opponents appealed to Exodus 19, which is used in Hebrews 12 as a foil to advance the idea of worshipping in heaven with the angels (12:22, 28). Colossians 2:17 presents a contrast, shadow/ substance, which plays a decisive role in Hebrews. But Francis' view that the Colossian errorists stressed a sharing in heavenly worship *led by angels* is contradicted by 2:23 (see the commentary and the counter-arguments against Francis of N. Kehl, *ZKTh* 91 (1969), pp. 389f.).

The final suggestion is that this phrase speaks of a place given to the angels as mediators between heaven and earth. In hellenistic philosophy the angels or heavenly beings were closely associated with the stars or the demonic and irrational forces which control man's life on earth (see G. Kittel, *TDNT* i, p. 86). The 'worship of angels' is best taken, then, as part of the apparatus of veneration paid to these astral powers which hellenistic man feared as a ruler and arbiter of his fate. There was need to placate such spirit-powers and overcome them by seeking the protection of a stronger deity. Paul's gospel repels all suggestion that these 'angels' are worthy of reverence because, as demonic forces, they have been conquered and neutralized by Christ on his cross (2:15) and in his risen life, in which the Colossians have a share (2:20).

(*c*) There was another tenet championed by the innovators at Colossae. They evidently held a dualism which separated the high God from creation and taught that to attain to God man must be delivered from the evil influence of material things. This 'liberation' in later gnostic religion was achieved along two quite diverse routes, one starting from the premise that the human body in its appetites, instincts and desires is evil (since it is part of matter) and is to be kept on tight rein; the other treating the body as indifferent to religious interests and so opening the door to libertinism.

One path to salvation was (as we have indicated) asceticism, which summoned the devotee to a life of abstinence and self-punishment. Paul preserves the actual wording of the slogans which were being advocated at Colossae (2:21, 23) and retorts that such denials as 'don't handle' (or possibly, 'don't engage in sex relations'; see Schweizer, *loc. cit.*, p. 258); 'don't taste' wine; 'don't touch' food (*cf.* 1 Tim. 4:1–4), are of no value to counter 'the indulgence of the flesh'. That is, when these ascetic practices are used simply to prepare an initiate to enter a trance-like state and thereby to gain a vision of heavenly things (2:18), they serve only to inflate him with pride and fill him with vain knowledge and so bolster his 'flesh', that is, his unrenewed ego, which is puffed up by this experience.

Coupled with these ascetic practices was a code which several scholars take to be influenced by Jewish legalism, with its observances of the sabbath, feast-days and new moon celebrations (2:16), possibly the practice of circumcision (2:11) and Jewish dietary laws (2:21f.). Various suggestions have been made to place these practices in a cultural milieu. J. B. Lightfoot drew a comparison between these restrictions and the taboos and practices of the Essenes; and more recently the Qumran texts from the Dead Sea area have shown that similar religious observances and calendrical details were highly regarded among the Essene monks in that community. But it is doubtful if Essenism had penetrated to the Lycus valley. There is a singular absence of debate over the Mosaic law in the Colossian controversy, whereas it remains true that Qumran beliefs and practices represent a body of religious discipline 'which is more legalistic than the legalists' (E. Haenchen, *The Acts of the Apostles*, p. 260, n. 3).

Interesting also is the suggestion made by T. W. Manson in 'The Problem of the Epistle to the Hebrews' (in *Studies in the Gospels and Epistles*, ed. M. Black, Manchester, 1962, pp. 252ff.) of a link between the prohibitions in Colossians and the type of heresy countered in the epistle to the Hebrews. He concludes a discussion of the comparison between what we know of the Colossian heresy and the outline of the argument in Hebrews (chiefly the supremacy of Christ and the opposition to dietary restrictions in 13:9) with this statement: 'I therefore think that the Epistle to the Hebrews may have been sent to the Churches of the Lycus Valley to meet the same peril as is combated by Paul's to the Colossians' (p. 254). This supposition may now be strengthened if we rely on more recent studies in the Epistle to the Hebrews which see it as opposing not simply Judaic ideas but gnosticizing tendencies. And this raises at its acute point the issue of the type of Judaism which underlies the aberrations practised—or at least entertained—by a section of the Colossian community. The focus of interest is in chapter 2:16–23, especially the verses which deal with abstentions from food and drink and (possibly) sex, and which advocate a rigorism under the discipline of 'self-abasement' and 'severity to the body'.

The type of Judaism reflected in these verses is a matter for continuing discussion. Clearly it is not the orthodox Judaism of the Palestinian rabbis, nor is it indubitably a sectarian wing of Essenism or Qumranism. A body of scholars prefers to speak of a 'Jewish Gnosticism' which combined with Christian elements to form the substance of the Colossian heresy (so W. G. Kümmel, *Introduction to the New Testament*, London, 1965, p. 240) or 'a Jewish or Judaistic gnosis, most thoroughly infected with Iranian ideas' (so Bornkamm, *loc. cit.*, p. 150) or a 'a kind of "theosophy"—in this instance, a "gnostic" type of Judaism or a Jewish type of "gnosticism" ' (Moule, p. 31).

The principal argument in favour of an incipient or proto-gnosticism in existence at Colossae (see R. McL. Wilson, 'Gnosis, Gnosticism, and the New Testament' in *The Origins of Gnosticism. Messina Colloquium, 13–18 April 1966*, Leiden, 1967, pp. 511–27 for the propriety of this term) and refuted in our letter, is found not only in the polemic against an angel cult but in Paul's attitude to a dualistic system. The latter takes us to the heart of the gnostic world-view. We are hindered in our effort to press back behind Paul's words to what must have given rise to them in the Colossian church. Clearly there was a practice of angelic worship (2:18) and Paul goes out of his way to accentuate the teaching on cosmic reconciliation, with no part of the universe unaffected (1:15–20) and no hostile power unsubdued (2:15). The angelic super-beings are reduced to impotence and are led in triumph. Some transcendental engagement between Christ and an enemy is envisaged, and peace is proclaimed after the armistice is declared (1:20).

What is the type of dualism implied here? S. Lyonnet (in 'Saint Paul et le Gnosticisme. L'épître aux Colossiens', in *The Origins of Gnosticism*, Leiden, 1967, pp. 538–51) insists that it is a moral tension, not an ontological gulf, which sets Christ in opposition to his rivals. Evil spirits are not mentioned as such, but their existence is implied. What may be the case is that it is Paul who has set these angelic powers against Christ and has given them the character of rivals to him, because he cannot tolerate any lasting dualism between good and evil (see for this understanding of the universal reconciliation in 1:15–20 and 2:15, R. P. Martin, 'Reconciliation and Forgiveness in the Letter to the Colossians', in *Reconciliation and Hope*, ed. R. Banks, Exeter, 1974). Then these powers have been invested with a demonic character by Paul since he cannot envisage any rivalry to Christ which does not spring from an antagonistic source. Dualism, however, took on a practical form at Colossae. This would account for the rigoristic ethical code, which practised a scrupulous observance of ceremonial (2:16) as well as a negative turning away from natural habits (2:21-3). Probably what underlay both forms of the cult was a desire for purification, a regimen of abstinence and obedience which would fit the devotee for a trance-like vision (2:18) and the progress of his soul to the ethereal region in an ecstasy. Evidence for this set of purificatory rites is widespread through the hellenistic mystery religions; and Diogenes Laertius (viii.33) clearly describes the Pythagorean belief that the soul must be purified. 'Purification is by cleansing, baptism and lustration, and by keeping clean . . . from all pollution, and abstaining from meat . . . and other abstinences prescribed by those who perform mystic rites in the temples.' This is a remarkable statement, containing many of the key-terms in Paul's chapter (2:11, 12, 16, 21-3).

We may summarize concerning this part of the error. Evidently Paul had to face tendencies and teaching at Colossae which set God and the world in some sort of opposition. God was distanced and made remote; the world was spurned and the human body held in contempt and its physical appetites held on unnaturally tight rein. Possibly some teachers had argued from the premise of a dualism between God and matter that asceticism should be replaced by its opposite. The trend would then flow towards libertinism. If matter has no relation to God (the argument ran), then the material body has no relation to religion. Therefore, a man can indulge his body without restraint or conscience.

To be sure, there is no explicit reference in this epistle to an antinomian strain. But it may well be in the background and explain Paul's vehement and stringent moral warnings in 3:5-8.

CONCLUSION

The soil of Phrygia was fertile ground for the luxuriant germination and growth of strange religious practices. The synagogues had a reputation for laxity and openness to speculation drifting in from the hellenistic world. In the Colossian church we appear to be in touch with a meeting-place where the free-thinking Judaism of the dispersion and the speculative ideas of Greek mystery-religion are in close contact. Out of this interchange and fusion comes a syncretism, which is both theologically novel (bringing Christ into a hierarchy and a system) and ethically conditioned (advocating a rigorous discipline and an ecstatic visionary reward). On both counts, in Paul's eyes, it is a deadly danger to the incipient church.

6. PAUL'S RESPONSE

Having surveyed the main outline of the false ideas which had been introduced to the Colossian church, we should pass on to observe the various ways in which Paul rebuts the theosophical teaching and praxis. It is probably more adequate if we leave the detailed discussion to the body of the commentary, where the Pauline teaching may be seen and studied in context. But a summary statement of the apostle's main positions is needed.

(a) Paul's main insistence is made in his christological teaching. For him the chief danger in this Colossian aberration is that it cuts a man off from union with Christ, the Church's head (2:19) and so from the source of spiritual life and access to God. The error is both theoretical (in demoting Christ to a rank of one mediator among many) and practical (in awakening religious uncertainty that casts a doubt on his sufficiency to impart 'fullness of life'). Both aspects are handled in Paul's assertions in 2:9, 10.

The polemical setting explains the insistence Paul gives to the cosmic and reconciling role of the Church's Lord, especially in the impressive diptych of 1:15–20. Here the two sides of Christ's office are fully described. He is both cosmic agent in creation (1:15–17) and the reconciler through whom God restores harmony between himself and his creation (1:18–20). No loophole is left for any intruding aeon to come between God and Christ on the one hand, or between Christ and the world and the Church on the other. In him (and not in any spirit or angel or other intelligence) the totality of the divine fullness dwells, at the pleasure of God (1:19). This encourages the security of the Church, which is assured thereby of fullness of life in him (2:9, 10).

The comprehensiveness of his reconciling work is such as to include even those alien powers which the hellenistic world

thought of as hostile to man. The risen Lord is both their creator
and ruler. He engineered their coming into being (1:16) in the
beginning; and by his victory over death he has taken his place as
'the head' or ruler over all cosmic forces, angelic and demonic
(2:10). In the new beginning which is marked by his resurrection, he takes his rank as the pre-eminent one (1:18), having
gained the victory over all the evil powers which first-century
man most feared (2:15).

In a paradoxical way the syncretistic theological teachers not
only cast a role for Jesus Christ which demoted him from his
pinnacle as God's image and Son; they seem to have doubted the
reality of his manhood also. Yet this was part of their general
understanding of God and the world. In their view, God was remote and inaccessible except through a long chain of intermediaries. Jesus Christ was one of these, but he was sufficiently
related to God to share the divine abhorrence of any direct contact
with matter. To the gnostic mind God was pure spirit, and the
world stood over against him as something alien and despicable.
On this assumption, the character of God as creator is imperilled
and redemption is expressed in terms of an ascent of the soul to
the higher world. Bound up with this attitude to the present
world and human history is a denial of any serious value to be
attached to Jesus' death and, indeed, a devaluing of his historical
existence.

Hans Conzelmann has recently expressed the dilemma facing
the Pauline churches in the light of these gnosticizing denials in
the following way.

> If faith loses its connection with its historical fixed point, the death
> of the man Jesus, then its object, the exalted One, becomes a mythical
> figure. The redeemer is separated from the creator. The locus of faith
> then is no longer the world, but a fantasy world, which is the product
> of the subjective mind.
> (*History of Primitive Christianity*, Nashville, ET 1973, p. 72.)

Although Conzelmann's statement is a general description of the
dangers confronting primitive Christianity, it admirably describes
the Colossian situation. Paul attacks that situation on several
fronts. He is emphatic on the historical reality of Jesus' incarnation (1:22, 2:9, 11). He locates redemption in the cross where his
blood was shed (1:20) after his sufferings (1:24). The cosmic
work of Christ is thus grounded in historical existence, since the

aim of his reconciliation was to unite heaven and earth (1:20);
and any teacher who denies a real incarnation and a factual
redemption in the interests of a mythical schema is branded as the
victim of his own delusion (2:18).

(b) In taking up these positions Paul's appeal is made to
apostolic tradition, which is set in antithesis to 'human tradition',
mentioned in 2:8, 22. The key-verses here are 2:6, 7. Paul is
reflecting on the past experience of the readers' Christian standing.
From Epaphras they had learned of God's grace (1:7) and he in
turn came to their city as Paul's proxy and missioner. What he
taught was the 'gospel' and this was certified as 'the word of
truth' (1:5), that is, it carried the ring of truth as a God-given
message. The Colossians had accepted it as such and had been
drawn to 'faith in Christ Jesus' (1:4).

Paul can therefore express his deep gratitude to God for this
ready reception and cordial acceptance of the saving word. Now
(in 2:6) he recalls this in the statement that the Christ they had
received as Lord was the Christ of apostolic proclamation. It was
no human tradition they had assented to; rather they had been
'taught' the true word and had begun to build their lives on
Christ, to take root in the soil of divine truth and to bear fruit in
Christian living (1:6). They had come to know God's grace 'as it
really is' (1:6) and not in reliance on any human tradition.

There is a subtle play on words here, which it is difficult to see
in the English version. It is the contrast Paul has in view between
acceptance of 'human tradition' (Gr. *paradosis*, 2:8) and 'teaching' (Gr. *didaskalia*, 2:22) and the obedience to apostolic tradition,
represented in 2:6: 'as you received' (Gr. *parelabete*: the complementary verb is 'what was handed on to you'—*paradidonai*—as in
1 C. 11:23, 15:3; Gal. 1:9–14) and 2:7: 'as you were taught'
(Gr. *edidachthēte*). It is the stark contrast between a man-made
religion, both cleverly contrived (2:4, which suggests 'tricked out
in persuasive language', so W. Bieder, *Die kolossische Irrlehre und
die Kirche von heute*, Zürich, 1952, pp. 62ff.) and laying claim to a
kind of wisdom but false and ineffectual (2:23) and the true
word which is entrusted to the apostolic preachers and which
centres in Christ, the mystery and revelation of God (2:2; 4:3).

(c) Paul's final rejoinder was conveyed in essentially practical
terms. He addresses himself to the effect of the cultists' regimen on
daily living. The Colossian propagandists made much of dietary
taboos and ascetic practices. Paul sees these as a threat to the

Christian's charter of freedom in Christ, already secured in him by his death and risen life. The call he sounds is one to a new quality of Christian living, unencumbered by false inhibitions and man-made regulations (2:22). These prescriptions and rules belong to the shadows (2:17). He asks, why remain in the dismal half-light of fear and uncertainty when the sun is high in the sky, filling the world with light? Seek a life which draws on Christ's own risen power (3:1–3), as those who share an inheritance in light (1:12) with all God's people, since you have died with him to those agents of demonic powers which tried to get rid of him on the cross (2:20). Have no dealings with their taboos based on a pretended authority since that authority has been once-for-all broken. And do not compromise or forfeit your Christian liberty (2:8) by surrendering to a specious philosophy which is deceptive and to a type of religion which can only be branded as man-made, and therefore fake (2:23).

For Paul the essence of 'religion' is Christ, and the mainspring of morality is a death-and-resurrection experience (signified in a believing response in baptism) in which the old nature dies to self and sin, and the new nature is received as a gift from God (2:11–13; 3:9–12). It is that new humanity, which is Christ-living-in-his-body, the Church, which provides both the sphere in which Christian morality is defined and also the motive-power by which Christians are able to live together in the one family of God. This has been called the *koinōnia* motive (in A. M. Hunter's phrase in his *Interpreting Paul's Gospel*, London, 1954, pp. 104, 118) by which is meant that Paul's ethical norms are found by following the call, 'Act as members of Christ's body.' His counsels in chapter 3 of our epistle include a teaching on the true self-discipline as well as a much fuller statement of what life is to be like among Christian men and women in their church relations and in contemporary society, who are called into the 'one body' (3:15) with love giving coherence to all the ethical qualities which characterize that new life-style (3:11, 12).

7. THE PLACE OF PAUL'S IMPRISONMENT

Of the collection of four epistles which are known as 'imprisonment epistles', three letters stand together. Colossians 4:7f. and Ephesians 6:21f. speak of Tychicus as a bearer of the two epistles, and there are indications of 'the most extensive verbal contact' between the two letters at this point (so Dibelius–Greeven, on Eph. 6:21, 22). Moreover, Tychicus had as his companion on the journey to the Lycus valley Onesimus, who is mentioned in the note to Philemon as returning at what is presumably the same time (Phm. 12). So this 'covering letter' is brought into the same orbit as Colossians–Ephesians. The place of Archippus adds a confirming feature. He is addressed in Colossians 4:17 and also in the list of recipients (in Phm. 2). On the other hand, there is nothing in Philippians which suggests a dating at the time of these epistles, if we are to judge from the memoranda of proper names and travel plans.

A further observation is of some importance. Paul's future, as reflected in Philippians, was full of uncertainty and anxious fore-boding (see the introduction to Philippians (NCB, 1976), pp. 74–80, 107f.). His life was in the balance (1:20ff., 30; 2:17) and he had no way of predicting which way the decision would go, though he hoped for a release on pastoral (1:24–6) and theological grounds (2:24) rather than trusting to any favourable turn in his legal position as a prisoner. Indeed, on the latter score, he can contemplate his fate as a martyr for Christ (1:21, 2:17).

The other three prison epistles show none of this apprehensive-ness and alarm for the future. The tone of Colossians is calm and even; there is nothing to compare with the perturbation of spirit suggested in Philippians. If these two letters belong to the same captivity, we are forced to imagine that Paul's situation worsened considerably in the interval between the two letters, suggesting that, if the imprisonment is identified with the one recorded in Acts 28:30, Colossians (but not Philippians) may well belong to the earlier phase of the two year detention at Rome. This is the traditional view.

(a) Roman Imprisonment

The basis for the identification of Paul's place of confinement with Rome appears to be laid as early as the time of Eusebius' *Church History*. He records (ii.22.1) that Paul was brought to Rome and that 'Aristarchus was with him, whom also somewhere in his epistles he suitably calls a fellow-prisoner'. That elusive reference is to Colossians 4:10. This mention of Aristarchus matches the reference in Acts 27:2 where the companion of Paul is specifically singled out. Other pointers which seem to indicate a placing of Colossians in the Roman imprisonment are:

(*i*) Paul's stay in Rome and his confinement 'without restraint' (Eusebius' term, borrowed from Ac. 28:30) suggests a freedom of conditions which would make practicable both letter-writing (possibly requiring the presence of a scribe: see commentary on 4:18) and the companionship of friends (4:7–17).

(*ii*) These names link up with similar lists in Philemon (23, 24) and bring into the picture the case of Onesimus. He was a fugitive slave who had sought asylum in Paul's presence. It is argued that a runaway slave, fearful of being caught and punished, would seek the anonymity of the imperial city in whose shadows he could safely disappear from public notice.

(*iii*) No other imprisonment recorded in Acts seems a viable alternative. At Philippi (Ac. 16:23–40) he was in the gaol for one night only. At Caesarea (Ac. 23:33–26:32) he was held for two years (Ac. 24:27) but had no prospect of an early release, suggested by the request of Philemon 22, and no easy-going conditions which would make it possible for friends to visit him and stay by his side. Nor is the setting at Caesarea at all likely to have provided an outlet for evangelistic opportunity, such as he refers to in Colossians 4:3, 4 (so A. Wikenhauser, *New Testament Introduction*, London, 1958, p. 418). Finally, Caesarea is not a likely refuge for a slave on the run and seeking an inconspicuous hiding-place.

(*b*) Caesarean Imprisonment

The case for this identification has never been strong, although its advocates in recent years have included some weighty names: E. Lohmeyer (*Meyer Kommentar*, ix, 2, 13th edn, Göttingen, 1964, pp. 14f.), W. G. Kümmel (*Introduction to the New Testament*, London, ET 1966, p. 245), and B. Reicke ('Caesarea, Rome, and the Captivity Epistles', *Apostolic History and the Gospel, Essays Presented to F. F. Bruce*, eds. W. W. Gasque and R. P. Martin, Exeter, 1970, pp. 277–82). For the latest treatment in favour of this theory see J. J. Gunther, *Paul: Messenger and Exile*, Valley Forge, 1972, pp. 98–112. The main evidence is the presence of several hellenistic Christians at Paul's side in Caesarea (which matches the data in Phm. 23f.; Col. 1:7; 4:7–14). This is the inference Reicke draws from Acts 20:4, 16 (*cf*. Ac. 24:23) and the likelihood is that Onesimus would seek Paul's protection in such congenial company. Reicke further suggests that Paul intended to visit Colossae on his way as a prisoner to Rome, once he had uttered the fate-laden words, 'I appeal to Caesar' (Ac. 25:11), thus quashing all local proceedings against him. Other pieces of data appealed to are more tenuous, *viz.* that Philemon 9*b*: 'now also a prisoner' indicates that Paul had been arrested only shortly before and so considers his imprisonment to be a new situation. In fact, he had been arrested in Jerusalem and later transferred to Caesarea where he spent two years (A.D. 59–61).

Almost certainly decisive against this position is that such a small city as Caesarea could hardly have been the home of active missionary work requiring the presence of a number of Paul's helpers of Gentile origin (Col. 4:3, 11), as Kümmel grants (*op. cit.*, p. 245); and in this concession he tacitly admits that Caesarea 'cannot be said to have been the centre of vigorous Christian propaganda' (J. Moffatt, *Introduction to the Literature of the New Testament* 3rd edn, Edinburgh, 1918, p. 169) as in Colossians 4:3, 4, where Paul has freedom to speak. Lohse, for whom the question is really an academic one, since he finds the epistle to reflect a post-Pauline situation, accepts this criticism of the Caesarean theory but attaches little importance to it since, in his view, Paul's captivity is described in idealized terms as what the author regarded as a 'typical·picture' (*Commentary*, p. 167). Nor is there any hint in the record of Acts that Paul contemplated an early release once he had asked for his case to be remitted to Rome.

(c) Doubts Over a Roman Captivity Dating

(*i*) The distance between Colossae and the place of Paul's imprisonment is a factor to be reckoned with since certain journeys have been made prior to the letter (Epaphras and Onesimus have come to Paul) and others are contemplated (Tychicus and Onesimus will return). The question is one of feasibility, whether it is likely that these journeys across land and sea, some 1,200 miles one way, are envisaged by the casual way in which Paul refers to them.

(*ii*) Would Onesimus have risked his safety and been able to evade the watchful eye of the police throughout such a long voyage from Colossae to the imperial city in order to bury himself in Rome?

(*iii*) If Epaphras (Phm. 23) has been arrested and is a prisoner in Paul's cell at Rome (though Paul's word is *synaichmalōtos*, fellow prisoner of war, not *desmios*, the normal word for prisoner;

however, see Col. 1:7) on what ground was action taken against him in this pre-Neronian period? And the same goes for Aristarchus (Col. 4:10), who is also called 'my fellow-prisoner'.

(*iv*) If Paul's hopes of a release from prison are granted, he is expecting to visit Colossae (Phm. 22). But this prospect entails a revision of his earlier resolve to turn his face westwards to Spain (Rom. 15:28) in the conviction that his missionary and pastoral work in the eastern Mediterranean sector was completed (Rom. 15:23f.). While there is no reason to charge Paul with inconsistency here and we must allow room for a change of plans, it needs to be noted that if Colossians comes out of Rome, a shift of missionary strategy is required. This is a substantial argument against a locating of Paul's imprisonment both at Caesarea and Rome (A. Wikenhauser, *New Testament Introduction*, pp. 418f.). Implicit also in this reading of Paul's plans for the future is the acceptance of the tradition which derives from Eusebius (*HE* ii.22.2,3) that Paul *was* released after the two years of detainment in Rome. But this is by no means certain, as G. Ogg has shown in his study, *The Chronology of the Life of Paul*, London, 1968, ch. 21.

Furthermore, Paul's hopes of an *early* release (which seems implied in the wording of Phm. 22) are to be followed by a journey to Colossae; but this is a strange request—'prepare a guest room for me'—when he knows he has to undergo a mammoth sea and land trip before he can reach Philemon's home. So we are faced again with the question of distance (*cf.* Houlden, *Commentary*, p. 139). This factor has led to a third possibility, based on the assumption that Paul was held in confinement at Ephesus, and that some of his so-called 'prison epistles' come out of this time of his life and missionary career. One of the fullest discussions of this possibility is given by G. S. Duncan, *St Paul's Ephesian Ministry*, London, 1929.

(d) An Ephesian Detention

The enforced confinement of Paul at or near Ephesus is an inference to be drawn from a series of connected and cumulative facts. They are:

(*i*) The portrayal of 1 Corinthians 15:32 which speaks of Paul's enduring a life-and-death struggle at Ephesus. This is a puzzling verse which is best taken to mean that Paul was exposed to the danger of being condemned to the arena and that if men (i.e. his enemies) had had their way he would have perished; but

that he was delivered from this fate, perhaps by his Roman
citizenship. 2 Corinthians 1:8–10 is thought to relate either to the
same harrowing experience or to a later crisis, perhaps set in an
outlying part of the Asian province (so Duncan, *op. cit.*, ch. 14).
Romans 16:3f. speak of Paul's exposure to peril and his rescue by
Prisca and Aquila. And Romans 16:7 mentions his fellow-
prisoners. It is a very possible view that the sixteenth chapter of
Romans was written to the church at Ephesus (see the impressive
list of reasons for this, displayed by Gunther, *op. cit.*, pp. 78f.).

(*ii*) There is the extra-biblical witness. A local tradition mentions a watchtower in Ephesus which is known as Paul's prison.
In the Marcionite prologue to Colossians, there is an ascription:
'The apostle already a captive writes to them from Ephesus'
(*apostolus iam ligatus scribit eis ab Epheso*). There is also the apocryphal story of Paul and the lion in the Ephesian arena (see
M. R. James, *The Apocryphal New Testament*, Oxford, 1953,
p. 292). But the value of these traditions is very limited, though
not to be passed over (*cf.* Duncan, *op. cit.*, p. 70).

(*iii*) Evidence of imprisonments other than those recorded in
Acts is forthcoming in 2 Corinthians 11:23 and Clement of Rome
(A.D. 96) mentions seven imprisonments. Moreover, several
passages in the extant Corinthian letters which *ex hypothesi* come
out of a period of Paul's conflict in Ephesus are suggestive of his
deep troubles (in addition to 1 C. 15:32; 2 C. 1:8–10 mentioned
earlier, there are 1 C. 4:9–13; 2 C. 4:8–12; 6:4, 5 and 11:23–5).

If we grant the possibility of such a captivity, it becomes a
reasonable exercise to test whether we can place Colossians more
satisfactorily in this period of Paul's life, *viz.* during his extended
stay at or near Ephesus, from the autumn of A.D. 54 to the late
summer of A.D. 57. For this dating, consult Ogg, *op. cit.*, pp. 134–8.
Whether we can be more precise and define the occasion of Paul's
enforced disengagement from his active missionary work in Asia
depends on a number of other factors. The most imaginative
putting together of the data is that undertaken by Duncan (*op.
cit.*, pp. 111ff.) who attributes the imprisonment of Paul to a
direct consequence of the Demetrius riot (Ac. 19:23–41). That
disturbance is suggestively connected with the festival in honour
of the goddess Artemis, probably to be dated in the late spring in
the year A.D. 57. This would link up with the notice in 1 Corinthians 16:8; in A.D. 57 Pentecost fell in May. The presence of a
crowd of people in Ephesus for the Artemisia would give Paul a

real opportunity for his mission work, and he may have this in view in 1 Corinthians 16:9. If the riot occurred earlier than the Artemisia, since Demetrius may have forestalled Paul's exploiting of the opportunity to preach against Artemis (Ac. 19:26f.: so Ogg, p. 137), we can understand how his plea in Colossians 4:3, 4 (using the same imagery of an open 'door') would express a deep and poignant meaning and explain his discomfort at being in confinement at a crucial season of the year.

If this identification is a guide to Paul's time in prison or at least under restraint, there is another historical factor which may account for his collision with the authorities. The social anarchy which followed the assassination of Junius Silanus, the proconsul of Asia, in October A.D. 54, lasted for several years; in fact, according to Tacitus, *Annales* xiii.33, Publius Celer, one of the assassins, remained in the province until A.D. 57. It may well be that, in a time of stress and confusion, Paul's Roman citizenship and standing were ignored as the authorities yielded to popular pressure and placed him in custody. Then this custody—a form of *libera custodia* similar to his confinement in Rome, as recorded in Acts 28:16, 30—explains the paradox of both the allusion to his 'bonds' (4:18) and the comparative freedom of social intercourse which Paul enjoys, as reflected in the epistle. It also throws some light on his prospect of early release (in Phm. 22) and his concern that Tychicus and Onesimus will inform his friends at Colossae what has transpired at Ephesus (4:7, 9)—a sentence which gives the impression that there has been a new turn of events (possibly a prospect of immediate release) which will gladden their hearts (4:8).

Let us now enumerate the arguments which point in the direction of a setting of Colossians in the period of Paul's Ephesian ministry.

(1) The proximity of Ephesus to Colossae is a decided point in favour of this hypothesis. Onesimus is just as likely to have sought refuge in metropolitan Ephesus as in far-away Rome.

> He would make for the nearest town. . . . He would want to go far, but Ephesus, of which he must have known and heard not a little, would surely be his limit. He could go the whole distance by foot. He would not need to be at the expense or risk the exposure of embarking on board a ship. He would have been more or less familiar by hearsay with Ephesus, the greatest city of Asia, while none of his fellows are likely ever to have been in Rome.

(B. W. Robinson, 'An Ephesian Imprisonment of Paul', *JBL* 29 (1910), p. 184)

(2) The request made in Philemon 22 now becomes more realistic, since Paul's captivity while short and sharp had none of the legal indictments of his arrests in Jerusalem, Caesarea or Rome. He can therefore await with confidence his release once his Roman citizenship is known (*cf.* his experience at Philippi) or once social order in the province is restored.

(3) The personnel surrounding Paul in his confinement are satisfactorily accounted for on this theory. As C. R. Bowen concludes after a citation of the data ('Are Paul's prison letters from Ephesus?' *AJT* 24 (1920), pp. 112–35, 277–87 [p. 132]):

> Of the ten companions of Paul named in these letters, four (Timothy [Ac. 19 : 22], Aristarchus [Ac. 19 : 29], Tychicus [Ac. 20 : 4; 21 : 29], Luke [from Ac. 19 : 21 the narrative proceeds with more attention to detail which may denote Luke's presence at Ephesus during the final stages of Paul's ministry there: *cf.* Duncan, *op. cit.*, p. 156]) seem quite certainly to have been in Ephesus with Paul, three (Epaphroditus, Epaphras, Onesimus) could have been there much easier than in Rome, the other three could have been there as easily as in Rome, while for no one of the ten is there *any evidence* (save inference from these letters) *that he was in Rome*, at least in Paul's time.

(Italics in the author's quotation.)

(4) C. R. Bowen (*JBL* 43 (1924), pp. 189ff.) has offered as an independent support the impression he has received from the text that Colossae had only recently been evangelized when Paul wrote to the church there. If there is substance in this claim that the congregation was newly formed, this would be an extra argument for locating the letter in the period between Acts 19 : 10 and Paul's subsequent imprisonment in the region around Ephesus.

(5) Counter-arguments from the development of Paul's theological themes are not conclusive, and we cannot categorically say that his christological and ecclesiological thinking was possible only at what happened to be the end of his life. Enforced interruption of his missionary activity (at whatever place) and the catalyst of the Church's threatened danger from false teaching would be enough to set his mind to work, and his 'prison christology' in Colossians is a plausible extension of his earlier thought in 1 Corinthians (see F. F. Bruce, 'St Paul in Rome: 3. The Epistle to the Colossians', *BJRL* 48 (1965–6), p. 280).

(6) A. F. J. Klijn (*An Introduction to the New Testament*, Leiden, 1967, p. 116) has indicated that the only argument against an 'earlier' dating of our epistle is the fact that the letter states in 1:6, 23 that the gospel has been preached in the whole world. But clearly this is a polemical statement of the apostle, intended to show the universality of his proclamation in contrast to the heretics' esoteric message. He probably has more than just his personal ministry in mind; this is a statement which attests the genuineness of the apostolic preaching in general and is his way of rebutting the cultists' claim by his appeal to accepted Christian teaching throughout the churches. Moreover, there is another objection. If these verses were not true in A.D. 54–7, how could they be validated only a few years later on a Caesarean or a Roman imprisonment dating? The logical conclusion is that the epistle emanates from a period well after Paul's death and represents the apology of his disciples in his name and urged on by a love for their master (*amore Pauli*, in the later phrase). This is a conclusion drawn by several modern scholars who appeal, among other considerations, to this claim to Paul's apostolate as universally acceptable (Lohse, *Commentary*, p. 167; E. Käsemann, *Essays on New Testament Themes*, London, 1964, pp. 166f.). While this understanding of a 'Pauline' composition is defensible in respect of an encyclical, impersonal epistle of catholic proportions like Ephesians, which holds up Paul's ministry to some sort of veneration (Eph. 3:1–5), it is hardly justified on exegetical grounds for Colossians, an epistle which does not even give Paul the title of apostle after 1:1 and is addressed to a congregation with closely defined needs.

Our conclusion is that this apostolic letter belongs to that tumultuous period of Paul's life, represented in Acts 19–20, when for a brief space his missionary labours were interrupted by an enforced spell as a *détenu* near Ephesus. Epaphras came to bring him news of troubles on the horizon at Colossae; and our epistle is the reply, as Paul used both the occasion of this news and the language used in the description of the Colossian 'error' to formulate a statement of the gospel which intricately combines three elements; the terminology of the cult, the accepted teaching current in his mission churches, and his own response (*currente calamo*) to a pressing need.

His answer, couched in epistolary form, met a species of false teaching which increasingly in future years was to afflict the Church. The Pauline gospel and Greek thought (in a hellenistic-

Jewish dress) were here engaged in a struggle; and the letter to the Colossians 'thus represents the first confrontation of Christianity with a trend against which it was to be forced to defend itself for centuries to come' (Klijn).

There is some evidence to show that, while Paul's letter may have held the gnosticizing tendency at Colossae in check for a while, the Pauline gospel did not take permanent root in Roman Asia. It is open to speculation why this should have been. We can surmise that, since Paul left Ephesus (Ac. 20:1) at a critical time in his life when he had faced both pastoral problems at Corinth and outside opposition from the authorities (cf. 1 C. 15:32; 2 C. 1:8ff.) he was in no mood to return to the province and so lost the opportunity of further instructing the churches in Asia Minor. See G. Ogg, *The Chronology of the Life of Paul*, London, pp. 135f. Some scholars (e.g. H. Conzelmann, *Die Apostelgeschichte*, Tübingen, 1963, pp. 114f.; E. Haenchen, *The Acts of the Apostles*, Oxford, 1971, p. 588) think that Paul's departure from Ephesus was more like an expulsion or an escape at considerable risk to his life. He had no wish to expose himself to renewed dangers when he returned after a visit to Macedonia (Ac. 20:13–16). So he remained in the harbour of Miletus and summoned the elders to meet him there. Luke's account of the speech he gave (20:18–35) is full of fear and foreboding, and there is an ominous hint that all is not well in the Asian churches (20:29f.).

This defection is attested in several strands of the New Testament literature. Acts 20:29f. may be Luke's apology for Paul's ministry (Haenchen, p. 596), if we are correct in assuming that at least one purpose of his writing was an anti-gnostic defence (cf. C. H. Talbert, *Luke and the Gnostics*, Nashville, 1966). More certain is the witness of the pastoral epistles, ostensibly addressed to Timothy at Ephesus (1 Tim. 1:3) and directed against false teaching of a speculative (1 Tim. 1:4; 6:4, 20) and practical (1 Tim. 4:3; 2 Tim. 2:18) character which has observable links with the Colossian error. The polemical section in Romans 16:17–20 may be relevant too, if it was addressed to the Ephesian church (cf. W. Schmithals, 'The False Teachers of Romans 16:17–20', in *Paul and the Gnostics*, Nashville, 1972, pp. 219ff.; cf. the Johannine epistles with their combating of docetic heresy, a theme picked up in Ignatius' correspondence addressed to communities in western Asia Minor). To such aberrations the Pauline school replied with the epistle to the Ephesians (see

R. P. Martin, *ExpT* 79 (1967–8), pp. 296ff.). All these pointers indicate how the Asian congregations failed to grasp the essential Pauline gospel, and were largely lost to the gnostic heresy in subsequent years after the sending of the letter to the Colossians (see W. Bauer, *Orthodoxy and Heresy in Earliest Christianity*, Philadelphia, 1971, pp. 233ff.).

8. THE AUTHENTICITY OF THE LETTER

So far we have assumed that the epistle is a genuine composition of Paul, written by him or at his dictation and sent out in his name. This view, of course, does not exclude the possibility that Paul incorporated other material into his letter, and there is considerable evidence to show that almost certainly 1:15–20 and very possibly 2:13–15 had an independent existence as pre-Pauline liturgical passages which Paul inserted at crucial points in his letter. For an extended treatment of these sections in the light of Paul's redaction of traditional and liturgical elements in a *Vorlage*, see R. P. Martin, 'Reconciliation and Forgiveness in the Letter to the Colossians' *Reconciliation and Hope*, ed. R. Banks, Exeter, 1974: (*cf.* B. Vawter, *CBQ* 33 (1971), pp. 62–81).

The tradition that Colossians is authentically Pauline stands on good ground. The later Church fathers accepted it (Irenaeus, *Adv. Haer*, iii.14.1; Tertullian, *De Praescr. Haer.* vii; Clement of Alexandria, *Strom.* i.1) and there was no dispute over its authorship in the earlier decades, even if the allusions to the letter in the earlier part of the second century are 'both dim and dubious' (Moffatt, *Introduction*, p. 154). Marcion included it in his canonical list, and it found a place in the Muratorian canon. The letter itself confirms this, with Paul's name appearing both at the beginning (1:1) and the end (4:18) of the letter, though this item cannot be pressed since Paul's name appears (albeit in a different context) in Ephesians (3:1).

(a) Doubts Expressed Because of the Epistle's Teaching

The first substantial denial of Paul's authorship came in 1838 with the publication of E. T. Mayerhoff's *Der Brief an die Kolosser*, Berlin. He rejected the letter mainly because of its alleged dependence on Ephesians. This view has recently been championed by F. C. Synge, *Philippians and Colossians*, London, 1951, pp. 51–9,

who takes Ephesians to be genuine and Colossians a pale and in-
adequate imitation which at key-points obscures by its lack of
'style and sentiment and grandeur' the model on which it is
based and which is more directly borrowed from Ephesians. In
other words the author of Colossians, at those places where his
thought runs parallel to Ephesians, expresses himself in such a way
as to show that he is improvising and imitating: and doing it
poorly.

Mayerhoff also believed that Colossians was full of non-Pauline
ideas; and in this belief he was accompanied by F. C. Baur and
the Tübingen school, who cast doubt on the apostolic authorship
on the ground that this epistle did not reflect the conflict between
Jewish Christianity and Gentile Christianity which was the hall-
mark of the apostolic age, and that the letter's christology belonged to a much later period of Church history when classical
gnostic influences had begun to exert themselves (see for Baur's
position W. G. Kümmel, *The New Testament: The History of the
Investigation of its Problems*, London, ET 1972, pp. 135f., 167).

Both these arguments are to be questioned. The relationship of
the two 'prison epistles', manifestly close, does not warrant
Synge's theory (which is more recently supported by J. Coutts,
'The Relationship of Ephesians and Colossians', *NTS* 4 (1957–8),
pp. 201–7). Recent investigation by A. F. J. Klijn (*Introduction*,
Leiden, 1967, pp. 101–2, 208–17) leads to the conclusion that
neither epistle is directly dependent on the other. Moreover, the
tortuous syntax of the passages which Synge appeals to (e.g.
2:16–20) is more likely to be explained as Paul's use of the actual
terminology used by the errorists. Synge's case would have been
strengthened had he appealed rather to such places as 2:14 which
is tautologous or 2:23 where the text looks as if it has suffered in
transmission. In 2:14 we may possibly trace Paul's revision of a
piece of traditional material. Thus the phrase 'which was contrary to us' is best regarded as a Pauline gloss on the preceding 'the
certificate which stood against us'. See the commentary.

The heresy combated in the letter is not the fully developed
gnosticism of the second-century systems but a proto-gnostic
syncretism which may well have arisen in the apostolic age (seen
most obviously at Corinth, as E. von Dobschütz as early as 1904
was quick to recognize [see a quotation from him in Kümmel, *op.
cit.*, p. 314] and recently demonstrated with thoroughness by
W. Schmithals, *Gnosticism in Corinth*, Nashville, ET 1971) and for

which there are parallels in heterodox Judaism in the Phrygian diaspora.

More serious objections to Paul's authorship have been launched in an attempt to drive a wedge between Colossians and the Pauline 'capital epistles' (*Hauptbriefe*) of Romans, 1 and 2 Corinthians, and Galatians. Part of this argument turns on some postulated differences of terminology. For instance, it is argued that the term 'body of Christ' is used differently in 1 Corinthians-Romans, where its usage is figurative of the Church, from Colossians, in which the author speaks of the body as a cosmic reality as well as a description of the Church (1:18, 24; 2:19; 3:15) of which Christ is the head. But the ecclesiological sense predominates and there are clear adumbrations of Paul's Colossian teaching in his second Adam typology; and the emphatic cosmic dimension of Christ's headship may well have been evoked by Paul's partial agreement with and partial correction of the false teaching on this theme. At 1:18 he has apparently transformed an existing tribute to Christ as the universe's Lord (current in hellenistic circles) into a statement of ecclesiology based on redemption and a subjugation of the cosmic powers (2:10). See the commentary.

The teaching on baptism is held to be different in the two sets of documents. In Romans 6:1-4 the baptismal experience is described with a strongly moral emphasis and is set in a future eschatological frame, whereas Colossians lacks this eschatological tension and presupposes that baptism points back to a completed and fully 'realized' salvation. But his judgement overlooks the meaning of 3:1-4 (see the commentary). Some contemporary scholars (Marxsen, Käsemann, Lohse) submit that the epistle belongs to the era of post-Pauline 'early catholicism', on the following grounds: (1) the transformation of 'hope' from an existential and anticipatory posture into a present possession and a settled virtue; (2) the part played in the epistle by baptismal confession; and (3) the use of tradition embodied in the apostolate, which gives evidence of the first signs of a doctrine of apostolic succession in the case of Epaphras who (in 4:12) is treated as successor to Paul, like the presbyters in the pastoral epistles.

Each of these arguments is worthy of comment, since they are offered, in current discussion, as compelling reason for abandoning the apostolic authorship of the letter.

(1) The nature of 'hope' in this document has been investigated by G. Bornkamm, 'Die Hoffnung im Kolosserbrief—Zugleich ein

Beiträg zur Frage der Echtheit des Briefes' in *Studien zum Neuen Testament und zur Patristik*, Berlin, 1961, pp. 56–64. The essential elements of Bornkamm's conclusions may be read in H. Conzelmann, *An Outline of the Theology of the New Testament*, London, ET 1969, pp. 314f. The former discussion is based on the description of hope as 'prepared for you' in the heavenly sphere (1:5) in the context of 1:3–8. 'Hope' is regarded as signifying not the subjective experience of the Christian (like 'faith', 'love') but the content of the whole gospel as a present, inviolable possession (Bornkamm, p. 64), 'the content of the good news as such; faith and love have their ground in this content' (Lohse). Hope is a present reality for the Christian (1:27); and it is the deposit of the faith which the Colossians have received as part of the divine economy' (1:25) entrusted to the apostle and which presents a doctrinal position from which they must not depart (1:23). So, it is 'hope which is hoped for' (*spes quae speratur*) rather than the normally accepted Pauline meaning of 'hope by which something is hoped' (*spes qua speratur*) (Rom. 4:18; 5:5; 8:24f.). The latter use of the term is either couched in an eschatological setting as the believer's hope of the parousia and the resurrection of the dead (1 Th. 4:13, 5:8; Gal. 5:5), or has an existential reference to his present life of tension between the poles of 'already . . . not yet' (Rom. 8:20f., 12:12), 'the tension-filled dialectical reciprocity between death and life', set between the now and the future—a tension which is lacking in this epistle (Bornkamm, p. 62).

It is true that 'hope' does carry this special meaning in Colossians, occasioned (we may believe) by the need to show that the Church's trust in the gospel is secure 'in the heavenly world' where Christ's lordship was in dispute. It is not to be lost by compromise with the heretics. However, Bornkamm's denial of a temporal aspect of hope in this epistle (p. 62) overlooks the eschatological dimension and the hope of the Lord's parousia which appear in one important section (3:1–4). The present hour (4:5) is one of opportunity as Christians live 'between the times' of the two advents; and the prospect of future reward and judgement is held out (3:24–4:1).

(2) The appeal which the author makes to the Church's traditional teaching, especially the baptismal *homologia* has also been used to indicate a post-Pauline development. This is the argument of E. Käsemann, 'A Primitive Christian Baptismal Liturgy', *Essays on New Testament Themes*, London, 1964, especially

pp. 159–68. He maintains that the author of the epistle has taken over a pre-Christian hymn (1:15–20) and employed it to his purpose by setting it within the framework of a Christian 'confession of faith' (homology) by flanking it with baptismal motifs (1:13, 14, which, however, he found already connected with the hymnic period, p. 153) and a pastoral admonition to remain true to the faith (1:21ff.). The purpose of the author's Christian use of the hymn is to combat heresy by a confession of the faith shared by the community. 'By reminding the community of its baptismal confession, the writer calls it to order and makes it proof against false teaching which obliterates the frontiers of these spheres of (heretical) influence' (p. 166). The writer adds one strengthening factor as he appeals not only to the confession of faith but also to the apostolic office as guardian of the truth.

> The apostolate expounds the truth of the Gospel, as the confession of faith fixes it. We may justly doubt whether it is in fact Paul who is relating confession and apostolate . . . and making the apostolate . . . the explication of the confession. This is the voice of the sub-apostolic age (p. 167).

The merit of Käsemann's treatment is that, as with his study of Philippians 2:5–11, he has addressed himself to the question of the 'life-setting' of the hymn in 1:15–20. His understanding of the hymn presupposes two ideas. First, he takes it as axiomatic that the primary purpose of the passage which had an existence independent of and prior to its inclusion in the letter is *not* to combat the Colossian heresy (*loc. cit.*, p. 164). As Ch. Masson (*L'épître aux Colossiens*, p. 107) puts it, the purpose of the citation of the hymn is not as a rebuttal of heresy but in praise of Jesus Christ. The hymn is an aretalogy, and its content as such has no eye on the situation in the Lycus valley, though its use by the apostolic writer is clearly related to his purpose. But that purpose cannot be discerned in the hymn on its own but only in the application which he makes by quoting it and setting it in a neighbouring context.

Secondly, the surrounding context of 1:12–14 gives substantial support to the view that the hymn was part of a baptismal liturgy. The several lines of demonstration may be summarized: (*a*) the motifs of 'beloved', 'sonship' (1:13) and God's approval (1:19) pick up the ideas expressed in the synoptic accounts of Jesus' baptism (Mk 1:11 and par.). See G. Bornkamm, 'Das Bekenntnis im Hebräerbrief', *Studien zu Antike und Urchristentum*, Munich, 1959, pp. 188ff. (*b*) The verbs 'to deliver' and 'to transfer' (1:13) are placed in contrast and in a context which suggests a release from the domain of evil powers (Ac. 26:18) and a transference to the realm of God's Son. This suggests an occasion in the life of a new convert when this experience was memorably actualized, *viz.* baptism, as the assurance of forgiveness (1:14) was vividly given. (*c*) Terms also suggesting a baptismal motif are 'light', 'share', 'inheritance' (1:12), and denote by a powerful imagery the passing over to a new domain of lordship (Käsemann, *loc. cit.*, p. 160, who uses the exact phrase, 'in den neuen Herrschaftsbereich'). (*d*) When the teaching of 1:12–20 is set alongside that of 2:9–15 the points of contact are numerous, with the main emphasis falling on the renunciation of an old allegiance and the acceptance of a new obedience. The middle term is an act of 'putting off' (2:11) by which the Lord stripped himself of his spiritual enemies (2:15) and overthrew their control of him; similarly the Lord's follower, in baptism, abandons his old way of life and 'puts on' a new life, as a new set of clothes (Gal. 3:27). This is precisely Paul's call in 3:8–11 as he issues the summons, Put on the new man, Christ, whose image (cf. 1:15) is being renewed in the lives of his people.

This close interrelation of ideas makes it almost certain that the author is drawing upon a liturgical pattern familiar to his readers (see further R. P. Martin, 'An Early Christian Hymn (Col. 1:15–20)', *EQ* 36 (1964), pp. 195–205). So much may be willingly conceded to Käsemann's argument. It is less persuasive when he proceeds to conclude that the author of the epistle has taken over both the introit (1:12–14) and the hymn without modification (see E. Lohse's critique, 'Christologie und Ethik im Kolosserbrief', in *Apophoreta*, ed. W. Eltester, Berlin, 1964, p. 164) and that these modifications do not represent the author's response to the Colossian heresy. The following commentary will show the likelihood that the epistle's editor has utilized an early hymn and suitably redacted it for his purpose to emphasize (*a*) the eschatological/salvific teaching of an original cosmological tribute, and (*b*) the application of the cosmic victory of Christ to his readers' lives. If these two considerations are borne in mind, it must be granted that this type of citation and application, set in a baptismal frame, is exactly Paul's manner of joining soteriology and ethics, as in Philippians 2:5–11. So J. Jervell, *Imago Dei*, Göttingen, 1960, pp. 218ff. There is no valid reason why the two passages should not be placed on the same level of 'occasion', i.e. both use an independent piece of liturgy and fit it into a paraenetic framework as a call to live as members of Christ's body. In both instances a pastoral situation lies in the background, with moral problems pressing on Paul's mind at Philippi (2:1–4) and doctrinal issues uppermost at Colossae (2:8–10).

(3) W. Marxsen's insistence (in *Introduction to the New Testament*, Oxford, ET 1968, pp. 177f., 184f.) that Epaphras' position holds the key to a placing of the epistle in the stream of early Christianity is ingenious but hardly compelling. In his view 1:7 means that 'Epaphras is recognized by Paul as a fellow-servant who works in the church "in place of" the apostle' (p. 178). This interpretation is decided by the better reading 'on *our* behalf', and it is suggested that Epaphras stood in a special relationship to Paul and the Church. This may well be so, but it scarcely merits the conclusion that 'Paul' rests his rebuttal of the error on the basis of 'apostolic succession' or orthodoxy transmitted to Epaphras. A later hand would have exulted in Paul's apostolate (as in Eph. 3:20; 3:1–10) but that emphasis is singularly lacking in this epistle (*cf.* R. H. Fuller, *A Critical Introduction to the New Testament*, London, 1966, p. 63: 'Epaphras . . . is a fellow-labourer rather than a successor to the apostle').

(b) Doubts Engendered Because of the Epistle's Style and Word Usages

An intermediate position on the question of authorship is taken by Masson (*L'épître aux Colossiens*) who postulates an authentic Pauline letter (consisting of 1:1–4, 7f.; 2:6, 8f., 12*a*, 16, 20f.; 3:3f., 12, 13*a*, 18–22*a*, 25; 4:1–3*a*, *b*, 5–8*a*, 9–12*a*, 14, [15], 17f.) which has been interpolated with additional material by the author of Ephesians. Following Holtzmann's lead initially, but travelling by a different road he concludes: 'In its actual form it [Colossians] is a revision and development of the primitive epistle of Paul to the Colossians by the author of Ephesians who, publishing both letters under Paul's name, has related them closely together one to the other' (*op. cit.*, p. 86). A similar view, that Paul wrote a version of Colossians which was subsequently worked over by the author of Ephesians and it was he who added expansions (e.g. 1:15–20; 2:8–23) was offered by P. N. Harrison, 'Onesimus and Philemon', *ATR* 32 (1950), pp. 271–4. But this theory has been virtually ruled out by Kümmel's criticisms

(*Introduction*, p. 244). E. P. Sanders (*JBL* 85 (1966), pp. 28–45) has tried to show the textual foundation for such a view as a side-issue of his form-critical study of the epistle. But our doubts over this method are considerable since, where few external controls are available, it must remain a subjective exercise to separate out a genuine Pauline basic document from a canonical text and to regard the residue as editorializing accretions, inserted by a later hand (so W. Michaelis, *Einleitung in das NT*, Bern, 2nd edn, 1954, p. 215, criticizing Masson).

Our knowledge of how Paul's letters were composed is limited (see W. G. Doty, *Letters in Primitive Christianity*, Philadelphia, 1973, ch. 2). This epistle witnesses indirectly to the use of an amanuensis (4:18), though O. Roller doubts this on the ground that no amanuensis is named, as in the case in Romans 16:22 (*Das Formular der paulinischen Briefe*, Stuttgart, 1933, pp. 9ff.). But this is unlikely: *cf.* G. J. Bahr, 'The Subscriptions in the Pauline Letters', *JBL* 87 (1968), pp. 27–41. We cannot say whether Paul gave liberty to a secretary (Timothy? 1:1) to write up the final letter from his rough draft, taken down by dictation. For this possibility see G. J. Bahr, 'Paul and Letter Writing in the Fifth Century', *CBQ* 28 (1966), pp. 465–77. On that assumption, however, the unusual literary style of the epistle could be explained, along with the presence of some terms not found elsewhere in Paul. This is P. Benoit's hypothesis ('Rapports littéraires entre les épîtres aux Colossiens et Ephésiens', in *Neutestamentliche Aufsätze*, Regensburg, 1963, pp. 21f.). There are 28 words not found elsewhere in Paul, and 34 other words not represented elsewhere in the New Testament. These rare words, moreover, are largely technical or quasi-technical terms, which Paul may well have borrowed from his opponents, especially if he is quoting their actual language or using phrases suitable in debate. In addition he does incorporate the hymnic period (1:15–20) where a proportion of the special vocabulary is found. The evidence of these *hapax legomena* is not decisive, as Lohse candidly notes (*Commentary*, p. 86) and insists attention should be paid 'to determining what significance in subject matter should be assigned to the differences which are indicated in the comparison of the vocabulary of Colossians with that of other Pauline letters'.

Finally, the absence of some of the characteristic Pauline stylistic features especially in the use of particles (*cf.* Moffatt, *Introduction*, p. 154) may be set down to the nature of the letter as a document embodying distinctive material in a liturgico-hymnic style and containing traditional material of a didactic nature related to a specific occasion. Colossians is a type of pastoral letter different from 1 Corinthians or Philippians. This is Percy's contention: *Die Probleme*, p. 43.

The argument that the style of Colossians is non-Pauline needs some inspection. Percy (*op. cit.*, pp. 36ff.) concludes from an examination of the stylistic features (pp. 18–35) that there is no ground for denying Pauline authorship. Lohse, *Commentary*, p. 91, grants that arguments from language and style are inconclusive in settlement of the issue; he regards the theology of Colossians as decisively non-Pauline (*cf.* his essay 'Pauline Theology in the Letter to the Colossians', *NTS* 15 (1968–9), pp. 211–20).

CONCLUSION

While it is a polemical document, the Colossian letter is not written in a combative style, as is Galatians (Gal. 4:20; 5:12). Paul keenly felt his pastoral responsibility for the churches of Galatia (Gal. 1:6; 4:12–20). But this letter, addressed to a congregation he knew only at a distance—a fact which may account for the omission of 'my brothers' as a frequent term in the indisputed epistles, as E. Schweizer has observed ('Zur Frage der Echtheit des Kolosser- und Epheserbriefes', *ZNTW* 47 (1956), p. 287)—is by contrast more dispassionately reasoned and detached. It 'pursues its course like a quiet stream without going off in a diversion' (Jülicher, quoted by Kümmel, *Introduction*, p. 244). This special occasion required the conscious use of a specialized vocabulary, partly drawn from the cult's teaching which Paul was confronting, and gave Paul's scribe a simpler task to compose in a more leisurely, systematic and reflective style.

The several strands of evidence suggest that Paul's vocabulary and style as well as his use of rare and unusual terms may well be accounted for by the special circumstances of the background and purpose of this letter. To a degree Colossians stands out in the Pauline corpus as a specimen of his correspondence addressed to a church he did not know at first-hand and written to combat the threat of false teaching. When these features are recognized, it may be affirmed that there is no serious obstacle in the way of an acceptance of apostolic authorship.

ANALYSIS OF COLOSSIANS

PAUL'S LETTER
TO THE COLOSSIANS

1. **Paul** is introducing himself to a Christian community to which he is personally unknown (2:1) and for whose founding he was not personally responsible (1:4, 7–9). This fact explains several features in the opening greeting. For one thing it very probably accounts for the title of **apostle of Christ Jesus** which he applies to himself. There is no evidence that his apostolic authority had been challenged at Colossae (as at Corinth or among the Galatian congregations). But we do know that Paul wrote the letter because he felt it incumbent to expose and refute a false teaching which had intruded into the church's life at Colossae (e.g. 2:4, 8). So it was equally needful that he should establish his credentials as an authorized teacher right at the outset. This he does by the use of the term **apostle,** which was conferred upon him according to the divine purpose with special application to his mission to the Gentile churches (see Eph. 3:1ff. for a clear statement of Paul's apostolate as it was understood by the Gentile congregations). As apostle he had authority both to teach (*cf.* 1 Tim. 2:7) and to deal pastorally with the congregations under his charge (2 C. 13:10). This 'right' he now claims.

Yet Paul is not alone. The title apostle is his prerogative as ambassador of the exalted Lord (1 C. 9:1; Gal. 1:15f.) and this epistle knows no other apostolic figure except Paul (Lohse). But he valued the support of his trusted colleague and collaborator **Timothy.** Of all the men who were associated with Paul's mission none held such an esteemed place as Timothy. The tributes paid to him (1 Th. 3:2; 1 C. 4:17; Phil. 2:19ff.) show the worth Paul placed on him, and how he regarded him as almost an extension of his own personality. Paul mentions him in the superscription because he would show them he is not alone in his imprisonment.

There may be a deeper reason. Paul will have to confront head-on the false claims of the Colossian 'heretics' and he will need to rebut their denial of apostolic preaching. To have Timothy's name alongside his own and to give him some standing as **our brother** (meaning that he was evidently well known in the mission churches of Asia Minor) would be a useful buttress to his own teaching office and a denial in advance that the following letter was simply an expression of his own ideas.

2. The custom of ancient letter-writing practices was to introduce both writer and reader with their names, followed by a greeting, usually of peace. Paul takes over this literary form but adds some distinctively Christian features. We have noticed one of these: the announcement of his office as Christ's plenipotentiary and messenger.

Now he resorts to equally theological language to describe the recipients of his letter. It is remarkable that the word 'church' is not found in the praescript, but this is not unique as we see from its omission in Romans, Philippians, and Ephesians. In those cases as here the replacement term is **saints,** while Ephesians adds also the thought of **faithful** though it lacks the noun **brethren.** No great distinction turns on this omission of the term 'church' since 1 C. 1:2 shows how Paul used the title 'called to be saints' as a pastoral amplification of those who made up 'the church of God' (*cf.* 2 C. 1:1). Indeed, if we would enter Paul's mind as to the meaning of the concept of the 'church', there is no better entrée than to study what he envisaged as the calling of 'saints'.

To take the Greek word *hagioi* as a separate noun here is preferable to regarding it as an adjective agreeing with **brethren.** The latter construction would give the translation: 'to the holy and faithful brethren'. It is better to retain the meaning of *hoi hagioi* as a definite class of people, *viz.* God's holy ones. Conceivably this class includes the angels as holy ones *par excellence* (as possibly in 1:12) but that idea is excluded by the geographical location which follows. The term in this setting means God's holy people, chosen by God and appointed to his service.

There are two aspects in the biblical picture of this choice and call of God, addressed first to Israel and then renewed to the Church of Jesus Christ. Israel was summoned to separate itself from other peoples (Num. 23:9; Ps. 147:20). Also, the nation was called into covenant-relationship with Yahweh by which it was pledged to allegiance and service in the world (see Exod. 19:5, 6; Lev. 19:1, 2; Dt. 7:6, 14:2). At Qumran this covenant-union was pronounced in the sect's description of itself as 'the people of the saints of the Covenant' 1QM x.10, Vermes p. 136) pledged to live in obedience to God's will. The Church is successor to Israel in these respects, *viz.* it consists of those summoned to break with evil as men and women renewed in holiness of life (e.g. 2 C. 7:1) and as called to a life of dedication in the service of Christ the Lord (e.g. Rom. 6:22).

Paul's opening greeting also matches the need of the situation at Colossae. Lohmeyer (*Kommentar*, p. 18) is probably correct when he remarks that 'no other letter of Paul so disregards the historical particulars', but there is no denying the appropriateness of surnaming his addressees 'holy people and faithful brethren' at the head of a letter which repeats constantly the theme of stead-fastness in the face of false teaching (1:23; 2:6, 7). This accords with Paul's practice of praising his churches before dealing pastorally with their deficiencies and needs.

The customary greeting in ancient letters in the Greek world was *chairein* (as in Jas 1:1; *cf.* Ac. 15:23, 29; 23:26). In Paul's hand this becomes the freshly minted Christian salutation of **grace** (*charis*). It is a tribute to God's concern for and care of men who are in need of a restored relationship with God. It is his love expressed in the forgiveness of sins (so Masson); and it is not surprising that its complement is given as **peace.** Again 'peace' was a familiar term of literary convention (*cf.* Dan. 3:31 LXX [4:1]; Simon ben Kosebah's letter to Jeshua ben Gilgolah expresses the greeting of 'peace'). Paul takes it up and gives it a rich theological content. It expresses the friendship of God extended to men in Christ (Rom. 5:1) and issuing in the salvation of the whole person. It is thus comparable with the Hebrew *šālôm* (see *TDNT* ii, pp. 414 f.) but more meaningful since its avail-ability in human experience signalizes the dawn of a new age, the fulfilment of eschatological salvation which the coming of Jesus Christ has brought (Lk. 2:14). The fuller attribution of this bless-ing to 'the Lord Jesus Christ' as well as to **God our Father** (as in most Pauline letters) is added by several textual authorities to conform to Paul's usual practice.

REASONS FOR PAUL'S THANKFULNESS 1:3–8

Paul's custom is to express thanksgiving to God in the preamble to his letters. This practice follows a literary convention in the letter-writing habits of the first century, though in Paul's case the distinctively Christian elements are prominent. One such feature is the address to God as **the Father of our Lord Jesus Christ.**

Another noteworthy aspect of Paul's opening epistolary thanks-givings is the way in which he seeks occasion to congratulate his readers on their Christian state and quality (Galatians is the exception, for obvious reasons). In the case of the Colossian church, Paul knew of their response to Christ only indirectly through his delegate and missioner, Epaphras (v. 7), yet he still expresses unbounded confidence that their initial commitment to his preaching would continue without hindrance. This is an important function of the Pauline thanksgivings, detected by Paul Schubert (*Form and Function of the Pauline Thanksgivings*, Berlin, 1939), who observes that the opening theme of the apostle's thanks to God describes the 'epistolary situation' of the following letter. So here Paul's gratitude for his readers' firm and growing faith is also a call to them to remain loyal to the apostolic message which his representative brought to them.

3. We always thank God. Paul's custom is to oscillate between 'I' and 'we', with no apparent change of meaning. See 1:23ff. which begins a section in the first person singular. Even when he uses the 'we' form, it is still Paul the individual who is speaking but with a consciousness of apostolic authority (*cf.* 2 C. 13:5-10 for a similar section).

the Father of our Lord Jesus Christ. Judaism invokes God as Father in its liturgy, both collective and private (see G. Schrenk, *TDNT* v, pp. 978-82). But 'the spirit of true faith in the Father' is found in the fuller understanding of God's name and nature made known in his Son. The title of God as the Father of Jesus opened up a new era in religious history, and gave to Christians an intimacy and warmth in their approach to him.

when we pray. Paul's thanksgivings take the form of prayers of intercession (v. 9).

4. Because we have heard. Now he proceeds to recall all the reports which have reached him via Epaphras who 'has made known to us your love in the Spirit' (v. 8).

The Colossians' experience is summed up in a threefold way, corresponding to a formula (which is arguably pre-Pauline; so A. M. Hunter, *ExpT* 49 (1937-8), pp. 428f.) found in 1 C. 13:13: 'so faith, hope, love abide, these are [the well-known] three'. The sequence is slightly different here, but it seems clear that there was in the early Church a handy compendium of Christian qualities which was made up of 'faith, hope, love' (e.g. 1 Th. 1:3; 5:8; Rom. 5:1-5; Gal. 5:5, 6; Eph. 1:15, 18; 4:2-5, Heb. 6:10-12, 10:22-4; 1 Pet. 1:3-8, 21, 22 and Barn. i:4; xi:8; Polyc., *Phil.* iii:2, 3).

In certain gnostic circles a fourth member ('knowledge') is

found and some scholars think that Paul took over this quartet and reduced it to three parts as an anti-gnostic polemic (E. Stauffer, *TDNT* i, p. 710, n. 78), but this is speculative.

Paul's use of the pattern in this passage is formed by a concern to celebrate the Christian experience of his readers. Naturally, then, he begins with their **faith in Christ Jesus;** the name of Christ Jesus signifies the sphere rather than the object or content of the faith; it points to 'the realm in which "faith" lives and acts' (Lohse). If this is so, it is Paul's way right at the head of the letter of focusing on the exalted *Kyrios* as the giver of new life to his people who live under his lordship. It is that theme which Paul will argue out polemically in the later chapters.

love which you have for all the saints. For Paul it was ever the case that 'faith' proved its reality by 'working through love' (Gal. 5:6). He has little to say about man's response to God in love; the more appropriate term for that response is faith. 'Love' as here suggests the practical expression of care and concern within the Christian brotherhood (Gal. 5:13*b*, Phm. 5). **All the saints** refers to the entire family of believers, perhaps in a wider sense than just the Colossian congregation and the neighbouring churches of the Lycus valley.

5. because of the hope laid up. It is not easy to relate this clause to what precedes (see Moule). But the general sense is clear. Paul's confidence is that, as they have received the message of **hope** as part of the apostolic kerygma, they will not willingly surrender it. The inference is that the false teachers at Colossae were intending to rob them of this aspect of the Christian message, possibly by denying any future dimension of Christian salvation (see Introduction pp. 34f). Paul recalls to his readers the importance of this teaching which was part and parcel of **the word of the truth,** i.e. the true gospel or, with *tou euangeliou* taken in apposition to *tēs alētheias* (so Masson), 'the true word which is the gospel'. A contrast with false teaching seems clearly in view.

6. the whole world. One of the characteristic features of Paul's exposition of 'his gospel' is its universality. This is, for Paul, a sign of its genuineness and of God's seal of approval. The message which the Colossians **have heard before** (v. 5) (at the time of Epaphras' initial evangelism) and **which has come** to them takes in a wide constituency. Its appeal is unrestricted, in contrast to a gnostic limitation of their message to 'initiates' of special discernment.

bearing fruit and growing plainly refers to the progress of the Pauline message. The phrase is drawn from the Old Testament, though there it is used literally of human reproduction (Gen. 1:22, 28) or Israel's population increase (Jer. 3:16; 23:3). In Paul's description **the gospel** is almost personified and likened to a force which conquers the world (Masson).

If W. L. Knox (*St Paul and the Church of the Gentiles*, Cambridge, 1939, p. 149, n. 5) is correct in calling attention to the gnostic use of these verbs (in Irenaeus, *Adv. Haer.* I. i.3, 4; xviii.1; xxi.5) as background here, Paul may be boldly appropriating *their* terms which the Colossian heretics used to stress that further development beyond 'simple faith' was needed. They may have picked up the metaphor from Mk 4:8. At all events, Paul puts the idea to good use, and congratulates his readers that their faith is alive and growing under the ministry of *his* gospel.

the day you heard looks back to Epaphras' mission (4:12, 13) which may be placed historically in the period of Paul's Ephesian ministry (Ac. 19:10).

[You] **understood the grace of God in truth,** i.e., the message of God's grace 'as it truly is', 'untravestied' (Moule). Alternatively, Paul's Greek phrase *en aletheia* is to be taken in reference to the previous mention of the gospel (Lohse). Verse 6 then corresponds to verse 5, and both attest that the Pauline message is God's truth, not man-made, and that it centres in the pledge of his grace, i.e. it sets men free from superstition and bad religion. Paul is again in a polemical mood, castigating the heretical version of the Christian message which had gained currency at Colossae.

7. The teacher he authorized to bring the gospel to them was Epaphras, **our beloved fellow-servant.** Himself a native of Colossae (4:12) he had evangelized in Colossae and was now with Paul either as a colleague (if **fellow-servant** is to be construed metaphorically as a 'slave of Christ') or as a fellow-prisoner with Paul if 4:10 describes him also, as Phm. 23 does. The accent now falls on Epaphras' trustworthiness as **a faithful minister of Christ** and as Paul's authorized representative.

on our behalf is based on the superior textual evidence of important early and well-distributed authorities, and the sense of the verse requires that Paul is commending Epaphras as a valued colleague who represented his gospel in the mission to the Lycus valley. For that reason the Colossians ought not to give heed to a version of the Christian faith which appeared later in time than

Epaphras' preaching (verse 5: you have heard it *before*, i.e. when Epaphras first came on the scene) and which carries none of the insignia or apostolic endorsement which Epaphras' mission had. He is a trustworthy **minister** (Gr. *diakonos*, just like Paul, 2 C. 11:23) and one through whose ministry they had come to faith (1 C. 3:5). Paul stresses repeatedly the prime qualification of reliability in his associates (4:7, 9) as evidence which supports the identity of his apostolic authority and the work of his colleagues in his name. When the Colossians **learned** the gospel (a rare phrase in Paul) from his delegates, it was as though they had learned it from him (*cf.* 1 C. 4:17).

8. your love in the Spirit completes the circle which was started at the beginning of the thanksgiving (v. 4). The report which Epaphras had brought back from Colossae was enthusiastic and reassuring to Paul. The community was thriving and progressing. They cherished a warm affection for Paul, and this gave him a good rapport with a congregation he did not know personally (2:1). He would now have to admonish them in a no-nonsense fashion by setting them on their guard against the presence of false teachers in their midst (2:4, 8).

PAUL'S PRAYER 1:9–11

The observation of Paul Schubert ('All Pauline thanksgivings have either explicitly or implicitly a paraenetic [= hortatory] function', *op. cit.* p. 89) applies equally well to Paul's intercessions for his churches. In the verses of this section we overhear Paul in his prayerful concern for the Colossians. But these words are, in the best sense, public prayers intended to encourage and stimulate the recipients of his letter to do the things for which the apostle prays.

9. from the day we heard of it refers back to the day when the Colossians first heard the good news from Paul's representative and accepted its message (v. 6). Epaphras had brought a glowing report of the Colossians' initial response and continuing loyalty to the apostolic gospel (vv. 7, 8). Paul is gladdened by this bulletin, and expresses his joy in his prayers (v. 3).

These few verses (vv. 9–11) give the content of his prayer which is directly based on the report of verses 6–8. Many of the thoughts in the earlier section (e.g. 'bearing fruit and growing') are picked up in the prayer vocabulary of the later verses.

**knowledge of his will . . . spiritual wisdom and under-
standing.** It is possible that Paul is boldly appropriating terms
which were used by the Colossian false teachers in their endeavour
to entice the rank and file of the Church. Paul is aware of their
'beguiling speech' (2:4) which for him would be never more
seductive or dangerous than when it offered attractive promises of
a deeper understanding of divine truth. It may be that Paul takes
over these terms and disinfects them by his own additions.
Knowledge (Gr. *epignōsis*) is directly related to God's will, and
this knowledge on its Old Testament–Jewish background is
always connected with practical obedience. Heretical *gnōsis* was
speculative and theoretical; Paul opposes this with a promise that
it is knowledge of God which shows itself in obeying his commands
and serving him in a realistic down-to-earth fashion (for example,
see *TDNT* iii, pp. 57–9).
Similarly **wisdom** (Gr. *sophia*) and **understanding** (Gr. *sunesis*)
are qualified by the adjective rendered 'spiritual'. This is no
courtesy reference, but it should be given its full value as an allusion
to the aid which the Christian may call upon as he seeks the help
of the Holy Spirit. The adjective *pneumatikos* is notoriously difficult
to interpret. See E. G. Selwyn, *The First Epistle of St Peter*, London,
1947, pp. 281–5, who translates the text here: 'sanctified by the
Spirit and influenced by grace'.
wisdom for Paul, as for the Old Testament writers, is also
intensely practical and related to life. Its possession 'shows to the
Christian the direction in which he is to go and the standards by
which he should regulate his actions' (Masson). The third moral
term is **understanding** which again has application to concrete
situations in life when there is need to have a 'clear vision of what
needs to be done in each instance' where a moral decision is
required (again drawing on Masson). In the Old Testament
tradition, wisdom and insight are joined to an understanding of
God's will; and it is striking that these three qualities appear in
the list of gifts which belong to the men of Qumran who live under
the direction of the Spirit of truth: 'understanding, intelligence
. . . and (a spirit of) mighty wisdom' (1 QS iv.3). For Paul these
are gifts embodied in Christ (2:2f.) and granted as the *charismata*
of the Spirit. They stand in direct contrast to the counterfeit claims
made by the heretics (2:23).

10. The effect of these moral dispositions is seen in the type of
life-style to which they lead the believer. Three areas are covered

in the ethical guidelines which Paul lays down: **a life worthy of the Lord** is the first. The call to live 'worthily' is a favourite Pauline moral incentive, with a variety of standards suggested by him, e.g. 1 Th. 2:12; Phil. 1:27; Rom. 16:2 and Eph. 4:1. In each case Paul is appealing to his converts to rise to the level of their profession as Christ's people.

fully pleasing to him renders a noun (Gr. *areskeia*) found only here in the New Testament. In secular Greek it normally, though not exclusively, carries a bad connotation, *viz.* seeking to please another out of motives of personal gain or advantage. Here it is a different sense: adopt every kind of pleasing attitude (W. Foerster, *TDNT* i, p. 456) presumably in the Christian's relationship to God or the Lord (Jesus). F. F. Bruce translates: 'so as to satisfy Him in all things'.

The third is the summons of growth: **bearing fruit in every good work and increasing in the knowledge of God.** Probably the two participles are to be held together and related to the source of progress in maturity. Then the call is to yield fruit in every good deed (by benevolence) and so increase (in influence upon others) by an ever-deepening knowledge of God. In this way the request of the earlier part of the verse ('filled with the knowledge of his will') is answered in the Colossians' increasing influence on their community. That influence may be taken in one of two ways: either by the lives of the Christians which produce the Spirit's harvest of goodness described in Galatians 5:22f., or by the evangelistic work of the community which is designed to bear fruit in the expansion of the church as the 'knowledge of God' is made known to those outside the fellowship. It is not easy to decide between these views, especially as Paul uses the same metaphors 'bearing fruit' and 'work' for both personal piety and congregational evangelism. But the choice is not a vital one, since for him the quality of Christian living goes hand in hand with the corporate witness of the church.

11. One advantage of taking the preceding verse to refer to the individual's growth in grace by cultivating the Spirit's fruit is that Paul's thought then smoothly continues to take in other specimens of that fruit, notably **patience** and **joy** (Gal. 5:22f.).

Otherwise it is more logical to think that Paul has the church in mind in his desire for the congregation's strengthening. **Strengthened with all power** means 'in virtue of the power which belongs to God as he has revealed himself to men' (Moule).

The goal of this prayer is that the church may not fail under attack or discouragement to carry out its missionary mandate. Probably the most disquieting feature was the presence of incipient heresy which has diverted the Colossians from their mission to the world. Paul would recall them to this priority.

endurance and **patience** are two requisites of Christian character needed in the face of hardship and opposition. If a distinction is drawn between the two terms, 'endurance' is used in relation to adverse circumstances, while 'patience' is the virtue needed when trying persons tax our self-control (so J. Horst, *TDNT* iv, p. 384, *cf. id.* p. 587). The two nouns are put together in 2 C. 6:4ff.; 2 Tim. 3:10; and both words are used often in an eschatological context, that is, to describe the virtues which believers need when they enter upon a conflict with evil powers at the end-time. No such special sense is required here. The pressure of evil forces which would make them dispirited comes rather from their particular situation at Colossae. Whatever the specific cause, it is characteristic of Paul to add in the note of **joy.** 'Joy' also stands in the list of Galatians 5:22f. and illustrates the Christian's attitude to life's trials. In this context Paul's intention in writing to the Colossians is to equip them for their struggle with false doctrine.

CHRISTIAN EXPERIENCE AND
THE CHURCH'S LORD 1:12–20

At first sight it looks as though Paul's prayer for the Colossians is continuing in an expression of thanks to God on their behalf (v. 12), or even that he is calling for a thankful spirit to abound in them (*NEB marg.*). But neither impression can be supported. If his prayer ended with a thanksgiving, this would be uncharacteristic of Paul who 'never closes the intercessions in his letters with thanksgiving or with a summons to it' (so Lohmeyer and Lohse). Instead, we should regard verse 12 as beginning a new section, with the Greek participle (rendered **giving thanks**) having the force of the imperative mood. It is Paul's call to his readers, who are addressed in the second person plural, as most modern editors agree against the translation adopted by *RSV*. His readers are directly described as 'made fit to share the heritage of God's people in the realm of light'.

12. The verse is full of Old Testament echoes. **To share in the**

inheritance of the saints recalls the promise, first made to Abram (Gen. 13:14–17) and renewed to the Jewish people (Num. 26:52ff., 34:2, 13; Dt. 32:9; Jos. 19:9), that they would possess their inheritance as the tribes were apportioned the land of Canaan by lot. The saints are the people of God under the old covenant (see on 1:2).

Paul boldly appropriates these images and uses them in reference to the Church of the new Israel. Believers in Christ have come into a richer heritage. They are in the company of 'God's holy ones **in light**'—a phrase which, in view of 1QS xi.7f., can only mean the angels. They have their hope secure in God's presence where the angels live. Paul is reflecting on his thought in 1:5, and looking forward to a polemic against the cult of angels, which the deviationists at Colossae were evidently practising (2:18). At a single blow he dispels this veneration of the angelic powers by assuring the Colossians that they have attained a place shared by the angels (3:1).

13. A further elaboration of the present possession of the Church. Two aspects are covered. Negatively, God has rescued us (a change to first person, as Paul widens the scope of his recital of Christian experience) from the **dominion of darkness** where evil powers hold sway (Lk. 22:53) and where Satan's authority is exercised (Ac. 26:18). On a positive side, God has **transferred us to the kingdom of his beloved Son.** Paul's verb (*metestēsen*) refers to a removal or migration of a people, as when Antiochus III transported several thousand Jews to Asia Minor in the early part of the second century B.C. (Josephus, *Ant.* xii.149). This migration, however, is a spiritual movement as Christians gain admittance to the kingdom of Christ, i.e. the fellowship of Christ's people in the Church.

Several commentators (C. F. D. Moule, E. Schweizer *Neotestamentica*, Zürich, 1963, pp. 293–316, 323–9) detect a veiled polemic in the way Paul proceeds to explain the process by which this 'transference' was made. Gnostic teachers may well have suggested that entry into Christ's kingdom could be accomplished automatically and instantly, with a present resurrection to new life in baptism guaranteeing an immediate immortality here and now. To counter this distortion Paul goes on to stress that the middle term between deliverance and the new life in the Church is 'redemption' which consists in the experience of forgiveness.

14. In whom we have redemption looks back to its antecedent in Christ the 'beloved Son', a title peculiarly significant in the context of Jesus' baptism (Mk. 1:11, etc.). John the Baptist proclaimed a baptism of forgiveness (Mk 1:4, 5). With E. Käsemann ('A Primitive Christian Baptismal Liturgy', *Essays on New Testament Themes*, London, ET 1964, pp. 149-68) we suggest that Paul's allusion in the present experience of 'redemption' expressed as the forgiveness of sins is to baptism, when the Colossian readers forsook the old life in **the dominion of darkness** and entered the realm of light (1:12). Forgiveness is essentially a moral response to the gospel, and Paul emphasizes this to check any wrong-headed notion of a non-moral salvation.

15-20. The polemical cast of the previous verses would lead us to suspect that Paul will continue this appeal to Christian experience with a view to showing how false and misleading these gnostic ideas of salvation really are. This understanding of the background is the key to unlock several mysteries in these stately verses. We may set down a series of propositions which can then be tested in the light of the detailed study of the indicated verses. For a short discussion of the form and background of these verses, see *Excursus* on pp. 61-6.

(*a*) The passage is generally believed to be hymnic in literary character, and can be arranged in three strophes or stanzas. Schweizer's arrangement is one of the latest attempts at versification, and probably the best. He divides the passage into the following parts:

Strophe i (1:15-16) consists of three lines which hail the cosmic Christ as Lord of creation, as the one who brought the universe into existence, who is its rightful 'soul' or sphere, and who guides its destiny.

Strophe ii (1:17-18*a*) partly repeats the thought of his pre-existent activity. Then it goes on to assert that Christ acts as a unifying principle which holds the universe together. As such he is its head. Notice that the leadership is of the universe, in the pre-Pauline draft of the hymn (see below).

Strophe iii (1:18*b*-20) celebrates the triumph of this cosmic Lord who embodies the divine 'fullness'. God's plan is executed through him who marks a new beginning of world history as the risen one and who is God's agent in bringing the universe into harmony with the divine purposes (reconciliation).

(*b*) It will be seen from the above outline that certain parts of the text have been omitted. By these omissions it is possible to secure a 'hymn' of perfect symmetry, with each stanza consisting of three lines and with a discernible rhythmical pattern. Now it is claimed that the additional parts represent Paul's additions to a hymn which was in circulation prior to his writing the Colossian letter. He has taken over an already existing hymn and 'edited' it by the addition of those extra lines. A parallel example to this procedure is seen in Philippians 2:6–11 where it is highly likely that precisely this same process of redaction has occurred.

The 'extra' phrases are added for emphasis, as he wished to stress certain points which an existing piece of Christian liturgy, conceivably used at baptism and celebrating Christ as cosmic Lord and giver of new life to the world, did not exactly do. The additions are:

(*i*) The lines describing the 'all things' which were created in Christ are an eloquent expansion of the cosmic powers which owe their existence to him:

> visible and invisible,
> whether thrones or dominions,
> or principalities or authorities (v. 16)

Here Paul fastens on the very spiritual powers which we know were being used at Colossae to suggest that they needed to be placated. Paul declares that they derive their existence from Christ and they owe their obedience to him who has subjugated them (2:10, 15).

(*ii*) At verse 18, Paul inserts the two Greek words (*tēs ekklēsias*) in a way which shows that they are a later insertion by him. The original hymn proclaimed that Jesus Christ was the head (or ruler) of the cosmic body. Paul alters this to emphasize that he is ruler of *his* body, the Church. The reason for this change may well be that Paul effectively rebuts the false idea that Christ's body is to be identified with the world and that he permeates it in a crassly pantheistic way.

(*iii*) Verse 20 contains two enlargements hypothetically given by Paul as he took over the hymn. He wished, first, to spell out in the clearest possible way the universal scope of Christ's lordship. The hymn declared that God has reconciled 'all things' to himself through Christ. Paul amplifies the embrace of 'all things' (*ta panta*) to include 'whether on earth or in heaven'. More significantly, he interprets the reconciliation to mean a moral process undertaken by Christ's deed on the cross. There 'he made peace' at the cost of his own self-sacrifice offered in his blood. This one

phrase is Paul's way of enunciating the rationale of cosmic reconciliation. His reason for so doing—in a way which is unique in
Paul, both in language and thought—is to ensure that the reconciliation, while affecting cosmic relations, shall not be thought of
as a physical miracle that merely changed the state of the universe
outside of man. By inserting a reference to the cross (as in Phil.
2:8) and by enlarging on the peace-making work of Christ as well
as by expanding that reference in 1:21, 22 in clearer terms to include his readers, he has anchored the work of Christ in an historical
event. He has highlighted the moral effect of the gospel which
brings salvation from evil and has safeguarded it from distortions
which would make 'salvation' an automatic or inevitable process.
Above all, he has placed the 'theology of the cross' at the crucial
point of the hymn, and transformed a hymn in praise of the cosmic
Lord of creation into a song of redemption which centres in
Christ's atonement as Saviour of the Church.

   15, 16. He is the image of the invisible God expresses
succinctly the New Testament teaching about Christ's person and
place. It repeats the familiar conviction shared by all the biblical
writers that God is spiritual and invisible (Jn 1:18, 4:24; 1 Tim.
1:17, 6:16) and unknown except for his self-revelation. That self-
disclosure is seen supremely in his Son, Jesus Christ (2 C. 4:4-6)
who 'embodies' the character of God. **Image** (Gr. *eikōn*) stands
for two ideas: representation and manifestation (Lightfoot). The
really significant point to observe, however, is that in ancient
thought *eikōn* was believed not only to be a plastic representation
of the object so portrayed, but was thought in some way to partici-
pate in the substance of the object it symbolized. 'Image is not to
be understood as a magnitude which is alien to the reality and
present only in the consciousness. It has a share in the reality.
Indeed, it is the reality' (H. Kleinknecht, *TDNT* ii, p. 389). Thus
Christ as God's image means that he is not a copy of God, 'like
him'; he is the objectivization of God in human life, the 'projection'
of God on the canvas of our humanity and the embodiment of the
divine in the world of men (*cf.* Masson, p. 98, n. 1). The description is revelatory, more than ontological. It tells us what Christ
does (to reveal God) rather than what he is in himself.

   However, a rudimentary ontology is not lacking in the phrase
first-born of all creation, for it is clearly Paul's purpose in
appealing to this hymn to show the primacy of Christ over all
orders of creation (so *NEB*). 'First-born' cannot therefore mean

that he belongs to God's creation; rather he stands over against God's handiwork as the agent through whom all spiritual powers came into existence (v. 16). He is Lord of creation and has no rival in the created order (see N. Turner's discussion, which prefers the rendering, 'Archetype of all creation', in his *Grammatical Insights into the New Testament*, Edinburgh, 1965, pp. 122–4).

Paul is indebted to some ideas in hellenistic Judaism. Jewish thinkers speculated about wisdom which was given a quasi-personal status as 'created before all things' (Prov. 8:22; Sir. 1:4) and present with God from all eternity (Wis. 9:9). She (the Hebrew noun for wisdom is feminine) shares the divine throne (Wis. 9:4) and she exists before heaven and earth (Aristobulus, according to Eusebius, *Prep. Ev.* vii.14.1). Most strikingly, Philo calls this partner in God's handiwork both logos and wisdom, 'the first-born son' (*prōtogonos huios: Conf. Ling.* 146; *Agric.* 51; *Som.* i.215).

Similarly, wisdom in Philo's thought is the instrument 'through whom the universe came into existence' (*Fug.* 109), and it is clear that Paul's hymnic quotation in verse 16 says the same in regard to this pre-existent Christ. He is creation's 'artificer' (Wis. 8:6) and the universe is created 'in' him in the further sense that heaven and earth are 'joined': a similar function is attributed to the divine word in Sirach 24:5f. and Wisdom of Solomon 18:16. And, as we shall see from verse 20 of the present passage, this is perhaps the meaning of 'reconciliation' in the pre-Pauline version of the hymn.

However, interpreters agree that there is no precise parallel in Jewish speculation concerning wisdom to the assertion that **all things were created** (a perfect tense in the Gr. *ektistai* 'in order to express the creation's continuing existence' [Lohse]) . . . **for him.** The final part in the verse states that Christ is creation's goal (lit. 'to him' as the final end towards which the whole creation is moving). No Jewish thinker ever rose to these heights in daring to predict that wisdom was the ultimate goal of all creation. Yet this is Paul's claim as he anticipates the finale of the hymn (in verse 20) which hails the crucified Lord as the great unifier of heaven and earth.

17–18a. Three lines of the hymn bring the first main section to its close with these majestic statements concerning the cosmic Christ. **He is before all things** as pre-existing all of creation and so Lord of all the created order. **In him all things hold together,**

i.e. he is the sustainer of creation. Probably here the thought is indebted to Proverbs 8:30 where wisdom is hailed as God's *'āmôn* (*RSV* 'master workman'). R. B. Y. Scott ('Wisdom in Creation: the *'Āmôn* of Proverbs viii. 30, *VT* 10 (1960), pp. 213–23) argues for the translation, 'a living link or vital bond', suggesting that wisdom is regarded as a principle of coherence between Yahweh and his world. This is precisely the sense of the Greek verb in verse 17: 'all things cohere (*sunestēken*) in him'.

The third line of the strophe **He is the head of the body** forms a fitting climax to the first part of the poem. The headship is seen primarily over the entire cosmos (see E. Schweizer, *TDNT* vii, pp. 1074ff.). For 'head' (Gr. *kephalē*) meaning 'ruler' (in the sense of Heb. *rôš*) see S. F. B. Bedale, 'The meaning of *kephalē* in the Pauline Epistles', *JTS* ns 5 (1954), pp. 211ff. Paul reinterprets the cosmological statement to give it sharper point by his addition of the phrase 'of the church' (see above). It is Paul's way of declaring the present rule of Christ over the world because he has already received headship in the Church of his body.

18b–20. With this new stanza a fresh background is to be sought. There are no immediate parallels in Jewish thought except the descriptions of wisdom as 'the beginning' (Philo, *Leg. All.* i.43; cf. Prov. 8:22). The correspondence of verse 18*b*, *c* with the opening of the Bible's story might lead us to anticipate that the second part of the hymn would hail Christ as a second Adam, the founder of a new race of men. Adam was God's image (Gen. 1:26f.) and God's son or king of paradise. He was the beginning of the old order, doomed to sin and death and decay. Christ is the second man, whose coming marks a new beginning as a new segment of humanity is brought into existence. **The beginning** and **first-born** are reminiscent of Genesis 49:3 (LXX): 'Reuben, you are my *first-born*, my strength and the *beginning* of my children', where the same Greek terms *prōtotokos*, *archē*) are used. This combination suggests, as Lohse remarks, that the first-born is the founder of a people (as in Rom. 8:29).

The new Adam as God's Son and image reflects the divine glory in a unique way. **In him all the fullness of God was pleased to dwell** represents a straightforward rendering of the Greek sentence, but its meaning is open to question. Does the statement personalize the concept of 'the fullness of God' and make it the subject of the verb 'was pleased to dwell'? So Moule, with some hesitation on the score that the personification may be too violent to be credible. But Käsemann (*loc. cit.* pp. 158f.) has no such hesitation, since he believes that the entire thought is gnostic and that 'all the fullness' (*plērōma*) relates to the new aeon (or gnostic emanation) which has become incarnate in the Redeemer. 'Thereby the All is "reconciled", its conflicting elements are pacified . . . in that they have found their Lord' to whom they submit.

The other main possibility is that the implied subject is God, or God in all his fullness. A later verse in the epistle (2:9) corresponds with this thought, and if the purpose of the present section of the hymn is to assert that God expressed all his saving and reconciling activity in Jesus (i.e. the christology is functional rather than metaphysical), this is the sense required. Also, it leads to a smoother transition to the next verse, where clearly it is God who reconciles all things by the blood of Christ's cross. For a discussion see G. Münderlein, 'Die Erwählung durch das Pleroma', *NTS* 8 (1961–2), pp. 264–76, and J. G. Gibbs, *Creation and Redemption*, Leiden, 1971, pp. 99ff.

20. to reconcile to himself (i.e. God) **all things.** This is a notable *crux interpretum* in systematic theology. What kind of universal reconciliation is envisaged as a completed fact? Answers range from a universalistic inclusion of all men in the purpose of God's redeeming enterprise, even extending that to include the devil and his angels (so Origen) to a more limited scope of the word 'reconcile' with the intended sense of reconciliation through subjugation and a forced admission on the part of these rebellious spiritual powers that God in Christ has robbed them of their status (so Percy, Bruce). Paul's purpose in this line of the hymn has probably a more defined objective. We should find the key in the phrases which are quite possibly his own additions to the original hymn: **whether on earth or in heaven.** He is intent on rebutting any idea that part of the universe is outside the scope of Christ's reconciling work; and especially he stresses that there is no alien power or hostile spirit-force which can work havoc against the Church. The assurance is distinctly parallel with Romans 8:38, 39, and its rationale comes later in 2:15. There Christ's victory on the cross effectively overcame every evil agent and rendered it powerless. In that sense all evil powers are 'reconciled' and restored to the place under their rightful head (2:10) from which they broke loose to become rebels against the divine purpose. Christ's achievement in **making peace** on the cross shows how his atonement reached even those malevolent forces and secured for them a place in God's design for the universe in which, at the last, there should be no discord (Eph. 1:10).

Again we may trace Paul's hand in the last line which pinpoints the place in the reconciliation: **making peace by the blood of his cross.** By this vivid phrase he has ensured that the reconciliation centres in his theology of the cross. This is his counterblow to gnostic redemption and reconciliation which works by non-moral fiat and automatic process. Reconciliation for Paul, on the contrary, does not work like, to use a gnostic image, a magnet put in heaven and drawing those who are brought into its magnetic field irresistibly after it. The effect of Christ's death is the effect of a deed of love bringing its fruit in a human life which is touched by it (E. Schweizer, *The Church as the Body of Christ*, Richmond, Virginia, 1964, p. 70).

EXCURSUS:
THE LITERARY FORM AND BACKGROUND OF COLOSSIANS 1:15–20

The history of the 'form analysis' of the passage begins with E. Norden (*Agnostos Theos*, Berlin, 1913, pp. 250ff.). Before him scholars such as Fr. Schleiermacher ('Über Koloss. 1, 15–20'. *TSK* 5 (1832), pp. 497–537), A. Deissmann (*Paulus*, Tübingen, 1911, p. 75) and J. Weiss (*Christ the Beginnings of Dogma*, London, 1911, pp. 84ff.) had noted the unusual character of the verses and had classified the piece as an example of a 'solemn confession' and 'a kind of dogmatic hymn'. Norden, however, broke new ground in that he subjected the verses to close inspection and sought to find in them, on the double ground of form and content, 'undoubtedly old traditional material' which he thought came originally from Jewish circles influenced by Greek ideas. The evidence for the latter description was the use of a Stoic formula with emphasis on 'all' (in 1:16f.) and the division of the cosmos into 'things seen and things unseen', which may show a Platonic influence.

Later comment on this section of the epistle carried the observations of Norden considerably farther, chiefly because it was apparent that the meaning of verses 15–20 could be adequately seen only in the context of the preceding and following verses.

Lohmeyer in his commentary of 1930 described the section
1:13-29 as 'the order of a primitive Christian worship service',
which opens with a thanksgiving prayer (1:12) and which in turn
follows directly upon an intercession for the assembled congregation
(1:11). All the thanks and intercession have a basis in what
Lohmeyer called 'the hymnic development of the "Word of God",
as that "word" is fulfilled in Christ, in the Church, and through
the apostle himself'. It is natural, therefore, that we should expect
a statement concerning Christ at this point, and this expectation
is confirmed by the style and the contents of the verses which
follow 1:12.

Since 1930 the conclusion, stated by Käsemann, that 'the
hymnic character of Col. 1:15-20 has long been recognized and
generally acknowledged' ('A Primitive Christian Baptismal
Liturgy', *Essays on New Testament Themes*, London, 1964, p. 149)
has been widely shared. But it remains equally obvious that no
agreement has been attained on the exact way in which the lines
should be versified, and how much (if any) of the existing text
belongs to (*i*) a non-Christian gnostic hymn; (*ii*) a pre-Pauline
Christian tribute; and (*iii*) Paul's own redactional work. See a
recent discussion on 'The Colossians Hymn and the Principle of
Redaction' by B. Vawter, *CBQ* 33 (1971), pp. 62-81. This is
perhaps the most observable feature in the recent debate over the
place of 1:15-20 in the Colossian letter. In the course of a survey
of discussion covering the last 130 years up to 1963, H. J. Gabathuler, *Jesus Christus, Haupt der Kirche—Haupt der Welt*, Zürich,
1965, writes that the discoveries of two strata in the hymn, i.e. a
pre-canonical version which has been worked over by the author
of the epistle, and the supposition that the author did not quote
the hymn as he received it, but corrected it—these are the 'basic
results of the investigation' of the hymn's form (*op. cit.*, pp. 139,
167). Added to this complexity is the question whether the pre-
Pauline (or, more precisely, pre-redactional, on the assumption
that the epistle comes out of a later Pauline school) version of
the passage is cast in a liturgical framework and played a part in
the Church's worshipping life as a baptismal confession. See
Käsemann's essay.

Literary criticism has also moved beyond Norden in seeking to
demonstrate that the passage is a self-contained unit with a more
complex construction than he was content to allow. Norden
divided the passage into two strophes, corresponding to verses

15–18*a* and 18*b*–20. This is perhaps the simplest way in which verses can be arranged under the two heads of (*i*) Christ and creation; and (*ii*) Christ and the Church. Attempts (notably by Masson in his commentary) to arrange the text in five strophes on a supposed metrical basis or Lohmeyer's arrangement of 1:13–20 into a pattern of 7 + 3 + 7 + 3 lines have not commended themselves.

The combined evidence of stylistic peculiarities (such as the repetition of words and phrases in verses 16, 20); the presence of identical words (e.g. 'first-born' in verses 15 and 18, coming in the same place in each hypothetical stanza); the use of constructions such as the *hoti*-clause in verses 16 and 19; and the incorporation of the formula 'from . . . through . . . to' (as in Rom. 11:33–5)—all these data show that we are reading a piece of carefully composed writing, set in a poetic mould and designed to be read as a self-contained whole and not as a series of unrelated statements.

Further proof of the 'hymnic' character of the passage is seen in the close correspondence between the two stanzas with matching phrases and terms. This was shown by J. M. Robinson, 'A Formal Analysis of Col. 1, 15–20', *JBL* 76 (1957), pp. 270–87. In order to secure a hymn with a semblance of symmetry it was necessary for him to delete from the existing text a number of phrases and to construct a putative first draft of the composition; and then he proposed that the author of the epistle in taking over the hymn has both supplemented the original and drastically reinterpreted the meaning of the words. The reasons why the author would wish to edit and enrich the original text are discussed in the commentary. While there is still debate as to the legitimacy of this method of interpretation, most modern commentators accept that Paul's additions (or those of the redactor) are to be seen in the following two ways. First, 'the church' is added in verse 18*a*, a procedure which turns a cosmological statement that Christ is the head of the body, i.e. the universe, into a christological and ecclesiological one, 'he is the head of the body, the church'. Secondly, Paul's theology of the cross is seen in the addition of 'making peace by the blood of the cross' (v. 20). By this addition he has safeguarded the meaning of reconciliation and shown its intimate connection with redemption and forgiveness as moral considerations are introduced.

These arguments, which are partly literary and partly based on content, are further extended by Schweizer in several studies ('The Church as the Missionary Body of Christ', *NTS* 8 (1961–2),

pp. 1–11; 'Die Kirche als Leib Christi in den paulinischen Antilegomena', *ThLZ* 86 (1961), cols. 241–56. Both these articles also
appear in the author's collection of essays, *Neotestamentica*, Zürich,
1953). He offers a new analysis of the verses by arranging them
into three triplets and suggesting that these three strophes com-
prise the three aspects of creation, preservation, and redemption.
Some adjustment of the text is needed to arrive at a perfectly
formed and balanced set of stanzas, and there is some lingering
doubt that his 'middle strophe' (vv. 17–18*a*) can be made to act as
a bridge between the first (vv. 15, 16) and the last (vv. 18*b*–20)
stanzas. But as an endeavour to see the passage as a whole the
version of Schweizer's is probably the best that has been proposed.
Cf. J. Lähnemann, *Der Kolosserbrief*, p. 38; R. G. Hamerton-
Kelly, *Pre-existence, Wisdom, and the Son of Man*, Cambridge, 1973,
pp. 168–74.

Later attempts at periodization have not taken the discussion
much farther. E. Bammel ('Versuch zu Col. 1:15–20', *ZNTW* 52
(1961), pp. 94f.) suggests that the key factor is an elaborate
chiasmus throughout the whole piece (as distinct from finding a
specimen of chiasmus in verses 16*c* and 20, which most interpreters
do), but this destroys other literary clues such as the presence of
parallel phrases in verses 17 and 18. It also means that verses
17–18*a*, 20 which contain teaching vital to the hymn are left un-
attached to the main structure as a pendant. This is a formidable
weakness, noted by Houlden (*Commentary*, pp. 157–62), who opts
for this view. Suggestions to revert to a two-strophe analysis (e.g.
P. Ellingworth, 'Colossians 1. 15–20 and its Context', *ExpT* 73
(1961–2), pp. 252f.) or to oppose the virtual consensus that the
words 'the church' in verse 18*a* did not belong to the original
form of the hymn (as N. Kehl does, *Der Christushymnus der Kolosserbrief*, Stuttgart, 1967, pp. 93ff.) have not commended themselves,
though Lohse (*Colossians*, pp. 44f.) accepts a two-stanza division,
with 'Pauline' additions in verse 18*a* and 20.

The history of interpretation of the form and meaning of this
hymn has been written by H. J. Gabathuler, *Jesus Christus, Haupt
der Kirche—Haupt der Welt*, Zürich, 1965. The latest discussions are
those by R. Deichgräber, *Gotteshymnus and Christushymnus in der
frühen Christenheit*, Göttingen, 1967, pp. 146–52 and Kehl, *op. cit.*,
pp. 28–51. J. G. Gibbs, *Creation and Redemption*, Leiden, 1971,
pp. 94ff. also considers the literary setting of the passage but
accepts 'no single reconstruction [as] fully persuasive' (p. 99).

More unanimity has been reached that this section is a non-Pauline composition, taken over by him or the author of the letter. The chief argument against Paul's authorship is the evidence of the unusual terms and constructions rather than the employment of a unique style (*cf.* Kehl, *op. cit.*, p. 51). There are about ten or twelve non-Pauline expressions (Masson, p. 106) and many of the hymn's ideas are not attested in Paul's other writings. But this argument has not persuaded everyone (*cf.* Gibbs, *op. cit.*, p. 96f.).

However, the position which Käsemann adopts that the hymn is pre-Pauline because the author of the letter has taken over an existing gnostic tribute has been challenged in several ways. His dependence on the gnostic myth of the First Man has been criticized (*cf.* Kehl, *op. cit.*, pp. 78ff., 87, 104, who points to Philo and the Jewish Wisdom literature as sources for the notion of pre-existence without recourse to the *Urmensch* idea: *cf.* F. B. Craddock, 'All Things in Him', *NTS* 12 (1965–6), pp. 78–80). His regarding certain key terms in the hymn (e.g. 'image', 'first-born', 'reconcile') as original gnostic language has come under scrutiny as the more probable source of the first two terms is seen to be hellenistic Judaism (*cf.* A. Feuillet, *Le Christ Sagesse de Dieu d'après les épîtres pauliniennes*, Paris, 1966, pp. 166–72, 189–91); Lohse, *Colossians*, p. 45 *et passim*) and the term 'reconcile' is shown to be uniquely Christian. This brings us to the statement of an emerging consensus that the background of the hymn is neither gnostic *simpliciter* (i.e. with closest parallels in the Hermetic literature) nor rabbinic Judaism (a proposal submitted by C. F. Burney, 'Christ as the *ARCHE* of Creation', *JTS* 27 (1926), pp. 160–77, and accepted by W. D. Davies, *Paul and Rabbinic Judaism*, London, 2nd edn 1955, pp. 150–2, 172: see the criticism here by Gabathuler, *op. cit.*, pp. 28f.) but a gnosticizing trend within hellenistic Judaism mediated through the Phrygian synagogues and picking up ideas which are found in the Wisdom literature (*cf.* Lohse, *op. cit.*, p. 46).

Paul is evidently laying under tribute a hymnic confession of faith, perhaps originally cosmological in its purport and later edited by him to make it conform to his purpose, which was known to and used by the Colossian congregation. It may well have been part of their baptismal liturgy which proclaimed the Christian's entrance upon new life through obedience to the cosmic Lord as a heavenly aeon. The significant thing is what Paul does with the hymn, both by his adaptation of it to set forth a theology of the cross, and his use of its baptismal teaching to recall his readers to the apostolic faith in the sole supremacy of Christ and his present victory over all spiritual powers (*cf.* 2:10, 15, 20). The final version of the hymn represents a possible corrective of a pre-Pauline statement of cosmology. In Paul's hands its character has been changed and its purport transformed. 'It has nothing to say about Christian cosmology . . . but rather something about ecclesiology and mission' (Gabathuler, *op. cit.*, p. 8: cited by J. Reumann, who discusses the modern ecumenical debate centred on this passage in *Christ and Humanity*, ed. I. Asheim, Philadelphia, 1970, especially pp. 106ff.).

APPLICATION TO PAUL'S READERS 1:21–3

21. And you. These words stand in an emphatic position in Paul's Greek sentence just as they do in the English translation. There is a close link with the foregoing, as though Paul wished to make it clear that Christ's universal, cosmic reconciliation also had a personal application to his readers. Indeed some interpreters (e.g. Schweizer) see a Pauline polemic here directed against all speculation and theoretical interest. He centres his theology in the cross (v. 20c) and now he insists that reconciliation must not be thought of in terms of physical or metaphysical events which guarantee salvation in an impersonal way. Rather reconciliation for Paul has meaning only in terms of human relationships.

Reconciliation presupposes estrangement. Paul now describes in some detail the human need. The Colossians were once **estranged** (i.e. continuously and persistently out of harmony with God, as Paul's periphrastic Greek puts it; *cf.* Eph. 4:18). They too were **hostile** enemies **in mind** which is the seat of man's intellectual life seen as enslaved by his 'flesh' (Gr. *sarx*) or unregenerate life (see J. Behm, *TDNT* iv, pp. 966f.). A third part of the description turns to expose the practical effect of the Gentiles' alienation. They were opposed to God's will by their **evil deeds,** a term which suggests a combination of idolatry and immorality, as in Romans 1:21–32. On every count they stood in desperate plight and in dire need of God's restoring grace.

22. The wonder of Paul's message is that God in Christ has taken action on behalf of those estranged and disadvantaged Gentiles. **He has now reconciled** seems to refer to Jesus Christ in view of the phrase **in his body of flesh by his death,** but it is

better to see God as the implied subject of the verb in the light of
verse 20 and the Pauline teaching elsewhere (e.g. 2 C. 5:18, 19).
The latter view may be defended by a preference for the alternative reading (*apokatēllagēte*, a passive indicative in the second
person plural, attested by P⁴⁶ and B) in place of a reading which
gives the active meaning of the verb, as in *RSV*. Some punctuation
changes are needed with the P⁴⁶ reading (see Moule, p. 72) but it
has the merit that it allows us to take God as the author of the
reconciliation. Then, we would submit that the words **in his body
of flesh by his death** are Paul's afterthought, supplied to demonstrate that the reconciliation of the Church is accomplished only
at the cost of a true incarnation (against a docetic understanding
of Jesus' historical life) and a realistic death (against a gnostic
interpretation which glossed over his death as unreal). The phrase
is heavily loaded with polemical overtones.

The phrase **body of flesh** looks cumbrous within the syntax of
the verse. An exact parallel to it is found in the Qumran literature
(1QpHab ix:2: 'And they inflicted horrors of evil diseases and
took vengeance upon his [*scil.* the wicked Priest] body of flesh').
See K. G. Kuhn, 'New Light on Temptation, Sin, and Flesh in the
New Testament', in *The Scrolls and the New Testament*, London, ed.
K. Stendahl, 1958, p. 107. But it is just the right expression needed
to underline the cost of the redemption in personal terms. It speaks
impressively of Jesus' identity with men and his submission to
death in a human body. The verse is a tilt at gnosticizing tendencies prevalent in the Colossian heresy.

**in order to present you holy and blameless and irre-
proachable before him. To present** translates an aorist
infinitive (Gr. *parastēsai*) which may look back to God's good
pleasure in verse 19 or else represent a reason for or a result of
Christ's reconciliation of men to God. His design is to bring about
a moral transformation expressed in the formation of Christian
character. This character is known by its intention to please God
and to live a life consistent with the profession which the believer
makes. The language may be drawn from the Old Testament,
either ceremonial (Ex. 29:37f. LXX, used of sacrifices in the
Jewish cult; *cf.* I Pet. 1:19) or eschatological–juridical (promising
that at the day of judgement no sentence of condemnation will be
brought against God's people). The last term **irreproachable**
(Gr. *anenklētos*, literally, 'not to be called to account') may well fit
in with the forensic sense of the verb **to present,** i.e. to bring

another person into court (Lohse). Then, reconciliation means
that no charge will henceforth be placed against the Christian
since he is declared **blameless** and 'innocent in his sight' (*NEB*).

23. Yet this new status he enjoys is never allowed to excuse
careless living or to contribute to a false security. **Provided that
you continue in the faith** sounds a needful warning, which
prevents Christian salvation from being seen as an experience
inalienably guaranteed and certified as a once-for-all transaction,
regardless of subsequent conduct on the part of the believer. This
would be a timely caution at Colossae where the peril of drifting
from **the faith** (i.e. the apostolic gospel) was real. **The hope of
the gospel** is that 'faith' expressed in other words.

Instead the call is to be **stable and steadfast.** These are
metaphors of strength and security drawn from the picture of a
house (*cf.* Matt. 7:24–7). The Qumran community saw itself as
God's house (1QS v:6; vii:17; viii:7f; ix:5f; 1QH vi:25–7; vii:8f.
See the comments by R. J. McKelvey, *The New Temple*, Oxford,
1969, p. 52). The New Testament writers often pick up this thought
(1 C. 3:10f., 17; 1 Tim. 3:15; Eph. 2:20; 1 Pet. 2:4–10; *cf.* Mt.
16:17–19). The summons to steadfastness (Gr. *hedraioi* is the
adjective) is needed in time of discouragement and stress (1 C.
15:58) and reappears in Christian vocabulary when the church
has to meet the attacks of heretics (Ignatius, *Eph.* x:2: 'Be steadfast in the faith'; Polycarp, *Philippians* x:1: *firmi in fide*).

The claim of Paul's gospel to be the authentic message is
attested by its universal appeal. **Preached to every creature
under heaven** does not mean that every individual has heard the
message. It states rather the universal scope, with no class or group
excluded. This is an obvious counterblast to the heretical restriction of their secret doctrine to a select coterie of interested persons
(Masson). Paul announces his own stake in this gospel, thrusting
himself to the fore as its minister.

The title **minister** (Gr. *diakonos*) is found in 1 Corinthians 3:5
where it is used of the individuals who helped the Corinthians to
faith, *viz.* Paul and Apollos. It is a broader term than 'apostle'
which Paul uses of himself at Colossians 1:1. Some recent interpreters (Käsemann, Lohse) see in the ascription of the title
'minister of the gospel' to Paul a sign that the sub-apostolic age is
looking to Paul as the guarantor of the apostolic office. In that way
a later generation is putting in a bid for the validity of the Pauline
gospel because of its apostolic authority. But this reading of the

situation fails because the key-term 'apostle' is missing, and there may be a sufficient reason why Paul uses a title shared by others (1:7; 4:7), including Christ himself (Rom. 15:8). That reason is to associate Epaphras and Tychicus who are called 'ministers' (in 1:7; 4:7) with the Pauline statement of the gospel, and so to defend the former's pastoral leadership at Colossae at a time when it was apparently under fire. Equally needful will be Paul's endorsement of Tychicus' standing in the apostolic circle, since he is to deliver the letter and presumably to back it up with oral instructions. These men are one with Paul's ministry, and trusted fellow-workers.

PAUL'S MINISTRY TO THE CHURCHES 1:24-2:5

24. Now I rejoice. The personal note, already sounded in verse 23, is continued here. The theme of Paul's ministry is the transition to a fuller discussion of the subject. Possibly Paul had need to defend his ministry against insinuations at Colossae that his sufferings showed that his claims to leadership were spurious (as in 2 C. 10–13). The entire section which follows is a sustained statement of 'apology' in which he proves how integral his work is, as a divine commission, to the full discharge of God's plan among the Gentiles. The key lies in 2:4 with its warning to set the readers on their guard against those who would mislead them and turn them away from the Pauline gospel.

The section as a whole divides into three parts:
(*i*) Paul's ministry to the Gentiles (1:24, 25)
(*ii*) Paul's message (1:26–9)
(*iii*) Paul's call to the Colossian church (2:1–5).

The gladness of the apostle's opening remark is explained by the reason he gives for his **sufferings**. They are **for your sake** (*cf.* Eph. 3:1, 13). What that means is spelled out in the following words which have occasioned a great deal of discussion. Three possibilities are in the field to give a satisfactory explanation of **in my flesh I complete what is lacking in Christ's afflictions for the sake of his body, that is, the church.**

First, the most unlikely view (given by H. Windisch, *Paul und Christus,* Tübingen, 1934, but largely abandoned by all recent scholars) is that Paul saw his sufferings as completing the unfinished saving work of Christ. This would be in denial of the other places in this letter (e.g. 2:13f.) where Christ's death and resurrection are sufficient to remove all sins and promise full forgiveness (*cf.* 1:14). Moreover, Paul never speaks of Christ's afflictions (Gr. *thlipseis*) as having redemptive or vicarious power.

Secondly, if we are guided by Philippians 3:10, we might have here an allusion to Paul's passion mysticism by which he thought of himself as having special communion with the Lord in his dying and resurrection. In some way, he declares, this mystical union confers a benefit on the churches. But this is improbable in view of the time factor referred to in the text (Paul suffers and hopes to complete the deficiency of the sufferings of Christ). It should be recalled that Paul suffers, not as a private individual but as an apostle to the Gentile churches (*cf.* R. Yates, 'A Note on Col. 1:24', *EQ* 42 (1970), pp. 88–92).

The third view draws upon the Jewish background of the 'afflictions of the Messiah' (Heb. *ḥeb^elô šel mašîaḥ*). See SB i, p. 950. This is the expectation in apocalyptic Judaism that as a prelude to the end-time which will herald the coming of an anointed ruler God's people will be called upon to suffer (as women labour in childbirth, Mk 13:8 and par.). God sets a limit to these sufferings and prescribes a definite measure for the afflictions which the righteous and the Jewish martyrs are required to endure (1 Enoch xlvii).

Paul takes over this notion and bends it to his purpose. In his life of service to the Gentile churches he is called upon to represent his people as a martyr figure and to perform a vicarious ministry (2. C. 1:6); and in this way he completes the still deficient tally of sufferings which God's new Israel has to endure before the end of the age. **In my flesh** refers to his bodily sufferings (Gal. 6:17, 2 C. 4:10), but 2 C. 12:7 (the thorn in the flesh) may be just as close a parallel.

his body, that is, the church is one of Paul's favourite designations of the congregations which he was summoned to serve in the Graeco-Roman world. The origin of the phrase 'body of Christ' is much discussed (see J. A. T. Robinson, *The Body*, London, 1952, pp. 55ff.); the most likely suggestion is that Paul's conversion experience in which the risen Christ's words identified him with his people (Ac. 9:4 and par.) set the apostle on the track of the unity of Christ and the Church under the imagery of the head-body.

25. of which I became a minister (Gr. *diakonos*, as in v.

23). In the Gentile communities Paul was known as a 'minister' (as in 1 C. 3:5). The source of that appointment is traced to **the divine office** (Gr. *oikonomia*; *cf.* 1 C. 9:17). He describes himself in 1 Corinthians 4:1 as one of 'the stewards (Gr. *oikonomoi*) of the mysteries of God.' The deep meaning of the ministerial term he applies to himself is seen in the use of the word *oikonomia* in Ephesians. In Ephesians 1:10, 3:9 it is translated 'plan' and is used of God's saving purpose for the world. At Ephesians 3:2 'the stewardship of God's grace that was given to me for you' praises the high dignity of Paul's mission to be a minister to the Gentile congregations in Asia Minor and marks him out in a special way as apostle to the Church in an ecumenical sense. The Colossians are involved in this ministry (**for you**); hence a transferred honour accrues to them as they stand in the shadow of that service to which Paul has been appointed (so Masson, followed by J. Reumann, '*Oikonomia*-terms in Paul in comparison with Lucan *Heilsgeschichte*', *NTS* 13 (1966–7), pp. 147–67 [163]). Paul is effectively on the defensive, both answering the charge that his ministry was self-devised, and repelling any idea that the Colossian readers stood outside the circle of his interest and pastoral ministry.

26. As a commissioned servant of both the gospel (seen as a universal message) and the Church (seen as a world-wide body) Paul had a chief task. This was 'to fulfil the word of God' by a territorial ministry (as in Rom. 15:19) and to extend the influence of the saving message. What that message was is now elaborated in a kind of digression (Dibelius–Greeven). It was **the mystery hidden for ages and generations** (or 'from the ages', the aeons or spiritual rulers of this world-order in a mythological sense, as 1 C. 2:7f.).

but now made manifest to his saints. The parallel in 1 C. 2:7–10 shows the same scheme which Paul uses elsewhere (Rom. 16:25f.) of 'once hidden . . . now revealed'. And there are several Qumran parallels to the idea of a special revelation of divine truth (1QpHab vii:4f; 1QH iv:27f.). The interest in these references is that they also contain the equivalent (in Heb. *rāz*) of Paul's word **mystery.**

The term 'mystery' has always, in the biblical literature, to be defined by its context (see G. S. Hendry in Richardson's, *A Theological Wordbook of the Bible*, London, 1950, pp. 156f.). In the present setting it speaks of 'the inclusion of the Gentiles as well as the Jews in the divine purpose of salvation' (Hendry); and the token of the fulfilment of this purpose is that Christ has made his presence known to these non-Jewish people. The full significance of this fact is seen in Ephesians 2:11–22 where the Gentiles' former condition as a disadvantaged and 'lost' people is described. **Now** (which marks the turning point in salvation history to include the world) they are the recipients of the divine revelation which ensures that, since Messiah's purpose in reconciling men to God included them, they have a place in the divine scheme as God's **saints,** i.e. believers (1:2) who have entered into an inheritance formerly reserved for Israel as Yahweh's holy people.

27. among the Gentiles . . . this mystery, which is Christ in you, the hope of glory. At a deeper level the Gentiles are assured of God's provision. He chose (literally 'wished', 'desired') to make known to the non-Jews the wonder of his purpose which embraces them. We may compare the saying of Rabbi Aqiba (*'Ăbôth* iii.15): 'Beloved are Israel for they were called children of God; still greater was the love in that it was made known to them that they were called children of God.' So the Gentiles too are assured of God's interest in them and care for them. The token of that regard is the presence of Christ 'among' them (*RSV* **in,** Gr. *en*). The Greek may mean either, but it is better to see Paul's meaning as the pledge of Messiah's presence among the Gentiles, so confirming their salvation. It is an anticipation of the restoration of man's lost 'glory'. This is a trace of Paul's teaching of the two Adams. What the first Adam lost in Paradise (his 'glory' *cf.* Rom. 3:23) is regained by the new Adam, Christ and his people, made up of believing Jews and Gentiles. *Cf.* M. Black, 'The Pauline Doctrine of the Second Adam', *SJT* 7 (1954), pp. 170–9.

28. Now follows a short statement of Paul's method as an apostle. There are three related terms which he uses: **proclaim . . . warning . . . teaching.** The first verb is the simple term 'to announce' and refers to Paul's declaration of the fact of Christ's presence among the Gentiles. This is the revelation specially committed to his charge, as in Ephesians 3:1–3; it is defined in Ephesians 3:6 in terms of the Gentiles' share alongside Israel in the new humanity created in Christ (Eph. 2:15).

warning (Gr. *nouthetein*) is a word belonging to New Testament pedagogy. Sometimes it has a general character of instruction given to new Christians (Ac. 20:31; *cf.* 1 C. 10:11) and sometimes it is specifically related to the training of children in the Christian family (Eph. 6:4). Paul uses the term chiefly of a ministry of admonition, criticism and correction, whether by himself, as at Corinth (1 C. 4:14f.), or by church leaders, as at Thessalonica (1 Th. 5:12; *cf.* v. 14). At least one reference is to the disciplining of those who espoused heterodox beliefs (Tit. 3:10), and it may well be that this is the background for the verse in Colossians as a shaft aimed at the false teachers, though 3:16 shows how the word can be more generally used of congregational edification.

teaching (Gr. *didaskein*) plays a more significant role in this epistle. It is used 'in a pastoral and ethical sense as a function of Christians in their mutual dealings' (in 1:28; 3:16). So writes K. H. Rengstorf (*TDNT* ii, p. 147). This is true, but 2:7 gives another side of the picture in which Paul's interest lies in the teaching the Colossians had received, presumably from Epaphras. Perhaps 1:28 also, as it relates to Paul's own ministry, carries a more authoritative tone, and speaks of his instruction 'in all wisdom' as an apostolic teacher in the Gentile churches, a function reflected in 1 Tim. 2:7. Either his claim to the possession of 'wisdom' may betray his polemical stance, or else he opposes the Colossian errorists who were boasting of their superior and secret wisdom.

Paul did not restrict his ministry to a select group in the Church. He aimed to **present every man** (three times repeated) **mature** (Gr. *teleios*, another heretical watchword, used of the 'initiated') **in Christ.**

29. The cost of Paul's ministry is described in some bold terms: **I toil, striving** (Gr. *agōnizomenos*) **with all the energy.** These word pictures are very graphic. 'I toil' is found in some contexts which refer to Paul's manual labour (as a *skēnopoios*, a leather-worker, see E. Haenchen, *The Acts of the Apostles*, Oxford, ET 1971, on Ac. 18:3). (See 1 C. 4:12; 1 Th. 2:9; 2 Th. 3:8; *cf.* Ac. 20:34.) In the present verse, however, the verb is figurative and powerfully denotes the intense concern of Paul in his pastoral attitudes and actions.

An even stronger term follows. **Striving** is sometimes employed to describe physical conflict (Jn 18:36: 'my servants *would fight*', RSV). In other places it denotes the athletic contest of the Greek games (1 C. 9:25: 'every athlete'). This is the literal sense, and it is claimed equally for the present verse by V. C. Pfitzner, *Paul and the Agon Motif*, Leiden, 1967, p. 110, in the light of 2:1 where the noun *agōn* appears. But a metaphorical sense in both verses is more probable and Lohmeyer's view that Paul writes these terms in conscious awareness of his fate as a martyr does not commend itself. If *Philemon* belongs to the same prison experience, Paul in that note is confidently awaiting his release (Phm. 22).

In his ministerial labours Paul strained every moral sinew in an exertion which, however, was energized by divine help. *RSV* is more a paraphrase here: literally, 'according to the energy which he actively and powerfully makes to operate in me'. See Galatians 5:6 for the same participle.

2:1 He has spoken generally up to this point in the letter. His ministry to the Gentile churches included the Colossians (1:24*a*, 25*b*). Now he makes the allusion more pointed and unmistakable, as he intends to establish a personal bond between himself and the Colossian readers (Lohse). By the use of an introductory form he borrows from the letter-writing conventions of his day (**I want you to know**), he wishes to enforce an important matter (as in 1 C. 11:3). This is simply that his pastoral solicitude extends not only to the Gentile congregations he has personally founded and visited, but also to other groups whom he does not know at first hand (*cf.* Rom. 1:13). The Colossians fall into the latter category. It is equally for them that Paul expends his energies—by his care, his prayers (he strives, 2:1, as Epaphras does, in a ministry of intercession, 4:12) and by his letters. Hence the reason for the letter he is at present dictating and sending to them.

The Colossian church, however, is not the only congregation in the region. Nearby **Laodicea** is included, and this church will receive a separate communication (4:16) which will be circulated to the Colossians. They in turn are to pass on their letter to Laodicea. Little is known of that church, though one other letter addressed to them has survived in Revelation 3:14–22. Still other congregations are in Paul's mind, expressed in the phrase **all who have not seen my face.** The Greek adds 'in the flesh', but this simply underlines the statement that these churches, like the Colossians and Laodiceans, were personally unknown to Paul. Perhaps a church at Hierapolis (also in the Lycus valley, twelve miles distant from Colossae) is in mind in view of 4:13. Some copyists add this place name to the text of 2:1. But the phrase is evidently intended to take in all the Gentile churches not of direct Pauline foundation.

2. that their hearts may be encouraged as they are knit together in love, to have all the riches of assured understanding and the knowledge of God's mystery, of Christ.

Paul wishes for all these Christian groups a true unity in love and a firm adherence to truth.

There are several textual and translation problems to complicate the verse. **Knit together,** 'united', is one way in which the Greek verb *symbibazein* (see G. Delling, *TDNT* vii, p. 764) may be taken, and its correctness here is supported by 2:19 where the unity of the Church is pictured as the inter-connectedness of the tissues of a human body which is under the control of its head. **Love** is like that network of ligaments and tendons which binds all the various members into a unity (so 3:14). On the other hand, the verb can carry a didactic meaning (so Dibelius–Greeven and Spicq, cited in *TDNT* vii, p. 764, note 10) with the sense of the Vulgate *instructi in caritate*, and this meaning of 'being taught in love' is paralleled by the use of the verb in 1 Corinthians 2:16, Acts 9:22; 19:33. It also paves the way here for the transition into understanding and knowledge. On balance, however, the first-mentioned translation is preferable in the light of the later verses in the letter (so Lohse, Bruce).

There is an appeal to clear-sighted appreciation of theological truth in the second part of the verse. The object of this **assured understanding** is given as **knowledge of God's mystery, of Christ.** Textual witnesses are divided over the exact wording (see the evidence displayed in B. M. Metzger, *The Text of the New Testament* (Oxford, 2nd edn, 1968), pp. 236–8. The *RSV* translates the text which is the most difficult to account for except on the ground that it was the original and that later scribes attempted to clarify the sense by their additions. It is also the text which has the strongest internal support and it is attested by P^{46}, B and Hilary. The other variants are evidently attempts at improving this text. Beare [Commentary, *ad loc.*] regards the textual data as more intricate and pronounces the text as corrupt), but the sense is not greatly affected. Christ as the image of God (1:15) unlocks the secret of the divine nature and provides the key to the riddle of God. He is the repository of all 'insight', 'understanding', and 'knowledge'—all apparently much-used terms in the discussion raging at Colossae.

3. To say more about the way Christ reveals the Father, Paul goes on: **in whom are hid all the treasures of wisdom and knowledge.** 'Wisdom' and 'knowledge' are given in Romans 11:33 as the two constituents of the divine character which are seen in human redemption and God's control of history. There they are coupled (as in vv. 2, 3 with the word for 'riches'), and the whole train of ideas and words suggests a conscious indebtedness to the figure of wisdom in Proverbs 2:3ff. (*cf.* Sir. 1:25; see too Isa. 45:3 LXX). Paul is remarking 'that Christ has become to Christians all that the Wisdom of God was, according to the Wisdom literature, and more still' (Moule). He is using an appeal to Jewish sources partly because the false teaching at Colossae on its Jewish side was insisting that Jesus Christ was only one mediator and one source of revelation among many. His counter-insistence is to place an emphasis on 'all', declaring that Christ embodies in his inmost being ('hidden' in the sense of 'deposited', 'stored up') the totality of the divine attributes which are represented by those elements in the divine nature in its manward relation: 'wisdom' and 'knowledge'.

4. Paul's polemical intention in so naming Christ as the sole repository of what men may know of God's character is all but proved conclusively by the words which follow. **I say this in order that no one may delude you.** This way of translating is to be preferred to that which renders: 'What I mean is, nobody is to talk you into error' (Moule, Bruce) or which makes the antecedent to this the whole paragraph from verse 1 to verse 3 (Masson). The warning against 'being tricked' (a verb found only again in the New Testament at Jas 1:22: 'deceiving yourselves') is clearly one to be heeded in the presence of a determined attempt to do just that by errorists who would employ beguiling speech, i.e. the art of persuasion (Lohse). For the first time in his letter Paul puts his probing finger on the false notions which were being introduced into the Colossian assembly and identifies their presence.

5. For though I am absent in body. If Paul were present in Colossae, he would spare no pains to deal with the menacing situation. But his imprisonment renders this out of the question and his responsibility for this church is not a direct one. None the less, he has such a vivid sense of his kinship with these readers that he can speak of actually being among them in spirit. 1 Corinthians 5:3–5 shows that this is no empty expression but speaks of a presence charged with power (*cf.* E. Schweizer, *TDNT* vi, pp. 435f., on these verses. Paul's spirit [Gr. *pneuma*] is a sign of his authority, and exerts an influence even when he is not present physically). He views approvingly their steadfast intent to close ranks and stand firm, with no yielding to erroneous propaganda. The language he uses is drawn from military formation (**order,**

firmness). So 'the apostle is "with them" as a general standing before his troops and reviewing the battlelines' (Lohmeyer). And he has much to say by way of commendation and hope that they will not break ranks and lose their oneness (v. 2) in the face of an intruding enemy. This verse suggests that the heresy has not gained a lasting foothold at Colossae, and that Epaphras' report has been more of a danger which encroached on a section of the church than of a serious problem deeply entrenched in the community. But Paul will take no chances, and so launches into a full rebuttal.

PAUL CONFRONTS THE SITUATION
AT COLOSSAE 2:6–9

Paul's confidence in the healthy state of the Colossian church does not prevent him from addressing it in terms of advice (vv. 6, 7) and warning (v. 8). He could not take for granted the continuance in the faith which he feels sure they are displaying (v. 5). This is his typical pastoral counsel, to exhort his people to remain firm and to be unshaken when impending dangers threaten.

6. As therefore you received Christ Jesus the Lord is more than a reflection on the personal commitment to Christ which the readers have given, though it includes that. Paul's verb 'to receive' (Gr. *paralambanein*) belongs to the semi-technical vocabulary in early Christianity which took over from rabbinic Judaism the idea of transmitting and safeguarding a tradition (*paradosis*). See '*Ābôth* i.1 for the Jewish background. The clearest New Testament examples are 1 C. 11:2, 23f.; 15:1, 3; Gal. 1:9, 12; 1 Th. 2:13, 4:1; 2 Th. 3:6, using the key verbs 'hand over . . . receive'. See O. Cullmann, 'The Tradition', *The Early Church*, ed. A. J. B. Higgins (London, 1956), pp. 55–99. That tradition delivered to the Colossians in the initial evangelism of Epaphras (1:7) was essentially christological. It centred in the person and place of Jesus Christ, and it claimed the allegiance and commitment of those who heard the kerygma and yielded to its appeal. That response would be expressed in faith-declared-in-baptism, as the succeeding verses make clear (2:11f.).

We should certainly see an allusion to the early days of the Christian mission at Colossae in this verse, in view of (*i*) the reference to **just as you were taught** in verse 7; (*ii*) the contrasting danger which presented itself at Colossae in the form of a **human tradition** (v. 8) which Paul's appeal was meant to counteract; and (*iii*) the nature of the false teaching which was a christological aberration, from Paul's viewpoint. So Paul sets the primacy of Christ as Lord at the forefront of his recall, in conscious opposition to the error being inculcated at Colossae. As Masson remarks, 'If the heretical teaching really cast a slur on the universal primacy of Christ (1:15–20), it was extremely important for the apostle to remind his Colossian brethren of the lordship of Jesus Christ'. The appropriate response to that lordship is obedience to Paul's teaching.

so live in him. Paul summons his readers to make good their baptismal profession. Having confessed him as Lord (Rom. 10:9; 1 C. 12:3; *cf.* Ac. 8:37 D), they are called to live their lives in acknowledgement of his lordship, which excludes all lesser loyalties, especially to the astral spirits in the rival teaching (2:8). Paul's verb **live** is practical (lit. 'walk' in the sense of 'conduct your life', as in 1:10).

7. **rooted and built up in him and established in the faith.** These are three participles which belong together, with a pardonable mixture of metaphors. Paul begins with the language of horticulture (**rooted,** as a tree which sends down strong roots into the soil). Then he proceeds with an architectural metaphor (**built up:** Gr. *epoikodomoumenoi*, is a present tense to denote the continuous growth in contrast to the perfect participle of **rooted** which suggests a once-for-all firm rootage in Christ). The two elements of 'rooted–built up' are found side-by-side in 1 C. 3:9.

The third verb **established** is a legal term, suggesting a contract which is ratified and made binding. So Christians at Colossae are reminded of their initial pledges of faith by which their community life as believers was begun. **Faith** is more likely to mean their adherence to the apostolic gospel than personal trust, since Paul is recalling them to the need to remain steadfast in the face of the assault mounted by false teaching (1:23).

A fourth verb **abounding in thanksgiving** is more an accompaniment of the preceding summons than part of the apostolic exhortation. Perhaps it consciously goes back to 1:12 with its summons to gratitude to God for the saving events of the gospel. E. Lohse thinks that it is an invitation to join in the christological hymn of 1:15–20 by which the community acknowledges that it lives under the sole lordship of Jesus Christ, the Church's head. See 3:16f. for a similar call to hymnic confession.

8. This verse pinpoints for the first time in the letter the presence of the false teaching at Colossae, which Paul felt to be such a danger. **See to it,** i.e. be on your guard lest you be made a prey of. The verb (Gr. *sulagōgein*) is a rare term, meaning to kidnap, to capture and carry off as a captive or prize of war. Paul's choice of this term shows how seriously he regarded the malicious intent of the false teachers, who are not named. But the Colossians would be able to identify the person(s) concerned.

by philosophy. 'Philosophy' carried a broad range of meanings, from the Greek pursuit of knowledge and wisdom to the Jewish description of the sects within Judaism (Josephus, *Ant.* xviii.11). Apparently in this text it represented the claim which the errorists were making to master the secrets of the universe by their esoteric knowledge (Gr. *gnōsis*). Paul uses their word; and then proceeds immediately to pass a judgement on the claim as spurious. **Empty deceit** is obviously intended to expose the hollow shame of this theosophy.

Two reasons for Paul's negative attitude are given. The false teaching is (*i*) **according to human tradition,** which is perhaps a veiled glance at the secret transmission of formulae and passwords in the gnosticizing religion at Colossae. For Paul this is a clear sign of the man-made nature of the teaching as opposed to the apostolic message which claimed a divine authorization and was available to all men. *Cf.* 2:6 for the contrast. (*ii*) More seriously for Paul, the specious philosophy gave a place to **the elemental spirits of the universe** (i.e. demonic powers; see Introduction pp. 10–14) which rivalled that of Christ. This is the gravamen of Paul's indictment directed against a 'system' which took the place of Christ, either by demoting him to an inferior position within the *plērōma* or by insisting that his mediatorship alone was insufficient to bring men and women into touch with God. The following two verses are Paul's rebuttal of the aspersion cast on the Church's Lord.

9. For in him (and not in the cosmic powers) **the whole** (not in part) **fullness of deity dwells bodily** (not in a fragmentary way, which would make Christ the head of both universe and Church but not exclusively so). The different parts of this verse are open to discussion. Clearly **in him** stands in an emphatic position, as though Paul were intending to point to the contrast between Christ and the powers. In the Colossian 'heresy' the spirit forces of the universe were thought of as repositories of divinity and as acting as intermediaries between the high God and the world of men. Paul establishes the error of this idea by his insistence that 'all' the divine essence (Gr. *theotēs*, which is a strong term for deity, 'an abstract noun for God himself' [Arndt-Gingrich] as opposed to a similar term *theiotēs*, meaning the divine qualities or characteristics, as in Rom. 1:20) resides in the person of Jesus Christ.

It is **in him**—and not in angelic intermediaries—that the divine fullness dwells in its totality. Nor is the Christ simply another spiritual aeon or cosmic cipher. He embodies the fullness of God in his human person; the fullness dwells in him bodily, whether in the sense 'really, not symbolically' (*cf.* 2:17; see J. Jervell, *Imago Dei*, Göttingen, 1960, pp. 223f.), or 'really, not apparently'—as though Paul were rebutting a denial of Jesus' full humanity by insisting on his 'full humanity . . . not a humanity which is a mere cloak for deity' (E. Schweizer, *TDNT* vii, p. 1077) or 'corporeally, as the head of the universe and the Church, not in a way which would make him one repository of deity among several others'. The latter view seems preferable in the light of Paul's subsequent remark that the fullness of God is both found in Christ and in the Church, his body. For a good discussion on the place of Jesus' human nature in recent study, see C. F. D. Moule, 'The Manhood of Jesus in the New Testament', *Christ Faith and History*, ed. S. W. Sykes and J. P. Clayton, Cambridge, 1972, pp. 95–110. On the other hand, his real sharing of our humanity in a sense which does not make the incarnation a charade is indicated by one meaning attached to **bodily.** The fullness of the Godhead came to live in a truly human life which was lived out in our world as the perfect 'image of God' in a human person (1:15).

ANTIDOTE TO THE COLOSSIAN ERROR 2:10–15

10. What Christ's office is as the embodiment of 'all the fullness of God' is now stated in a personal application to the readers. **You have come to fullness of life in him.** Paul is obviously making capital out of the word for 'fullness': 'fullness of life' answers to 'fullness of deity'; and 'bodily' is the link-term uniting what Jesus Christ is in himself and what he has become to his people, his body the Church. In effect Paul is saying: Christ embodies the divine *plērōma*; and you as his body have a share in that fullness. Together he and the Church form one indissoluble entity, the whole Christ. Possibly, as Dibelius remarks, Paul is consciously using a slogan which the false teachers were adopting when they promised 'fullness of life' to their followers at Colossae.

who is the head of all rule and authority. The 'rule of Christ' is his office as Lord over the powers of evil (*cf.* Rom. 14:9; Phil. 2:10, 11). In apocalyptic thought the overthrow of evil forces was expected at the end of the present age. Here it is announced as having already happened (contrast 1 C. 15:24ff. for a still future hope in Paul), and this special emphasis may well have been occasioned by the need to assert Christ's present lordship over every hostile spirit-power. He is at once their creator (1:16), upholder (1:17), and the Lord who has subjugated them (2:15).

11–15. This paragraph elaborates the theme of 'fullness of life in him' and shows how the Pauline readers came to its conscious realization. Certain steps are clearly marked out, and to that extent the author's thought is clear. It is when we press the details that our exegetical troubles begin.

In simplest outline, Paul is directing attention to such memorable experiences of the Colossians' life as baptism (vv. 1, 12), new life in a spiritual awakening from death (v. 13), forgiveness and a new standing before God (v. 14) because Christ overcame all their enemies and accusers (v. 15).

The key-phrase in this entire section lies in verse 11: **by putting off the body of flesh.** This is Paul's way of recalling the Christian's initiation to his new life in Christ. The noun rendered 'putting off' (Gr. *apekdusis*) suggests a clean break with a past life, though the metaphor is one of disrobing and stripping off an unwelcome set of garments. 'Put off the old nature with its practices' (3:9) shows the practical side of this transformation, using the cognate verb and in reference to a Christian's new way of life. The background allusion to a baptismal action when the new convert divested himself of his clothes for baptism and re-clothed himself after the rite is very suggestive, especially in the light of Galatians 3:27. Moreover, Paul elsewhere makes the contrast between 'circumcision' (in the Old Testament) and its replacement in the New Testament by Christian faith-response (Rom. 4:9–12) certified in baptism, which is explicitly mentioned at verse 12 of this chapter.

11, 12. So far the thought is clear, and our interpretation requires that we take **the body of flesh** to mean the believer's unregenerate nature which would tyrannize over him and hold

him in bondage. On this view, 'body of flesh' is virtually the same
as 'body of this death' (Rom. 7:24) or 'body of sin' (Rom. 6:6).
From this tyranny deliverance is promised by a cutting free from
bondage, a release symbolized in the Christian counterpart of
circumcision, **a circumcision made without hands,** i.e. one
which is wholly the work of God (a phrase found with this sense in
Mk 14:58 par. and 2 C. 5:1). Paul is emphasizing that it is the
work of God, experienced in baptism. In this view the response
given in the rite of initiation marks a new beginning in a life of
obedience to the heavenly Lord (so Lohse). It is also possible that
Paul is contrasting 'true' circumcision not with an Old Testament
counterpart but with a ritual practised by the heretics at Colossae.
For the Old Testament and Judaic background see R. Meyer,
TDNT vi, pp. 72–84.

On another showing, however, a more subtle cross-movement of
the apostle's thought is possible. This view (championed by C. A.
Anderson Scott, *Christianity according to St Paul*, Cambridge, 1927,
pp. 36f.) is governed by two preliminary convictions: first, it
wishes to give full value to the Pauline phrase **in the circumcision
of Christ.** This is held to mean not a spiritual counterpart to
circumcision which belongs to the Christian dispensation, but the
circumcision which Christ himself underwent (see Moule *ad loc.*).
To the question when did this occur? the answer (a second point)
is discovered in 2:15. The *RSV* disguises the presence of the verb
from which 'putting off' in verse 11 derives. 'He disarmed (lit.
stripped off, Gr. *apekdusamenos*) the principalities and powers.' By
his death on the cross, Christ dealt a mortal blow to his spiritual
foes and passed from under their control by forcing them to submit to him after they had 'engineered' his death; and so he
'reconciled' them by drawing the sting of their hostility (1:20).

This reading of the text is dramatic and exciting. Paul is consciously appealing to what Christ did in his saving work. He
stripped off all alien tyranny represented by the spiritual forces of
the unseen world which tried to hold him captive (1 C. 2:6–8). In
that submission to them at death and victory over them at the
resurrection, Christ represented his people. In that sense when he
was victorious over his enemies, they were victorious over the
same set of alien spirit-powers. The sacramental means by which
his victory becomes theirs is baptism, in which faith is a vital in-
gredient. It is **through faith** and **in baptism** that the believer's
new life is begun, as Masson aptly remarks. And the risen Lord

imparts his own life and plenitude to his Church which is risen with him (3:1), and as such called to make a daily affirmation of freedom from the evil powers which work on frail human nature to pull it down (3:9). This second interpretation coheres with this apostle's thought throughout the letter, and should be preferred, however strange the drama seems to us as a cosmic, dualistic struggle.

13. More easily comprehended is the next part of Paul's description. **You, who were dead in trespasses and the uncircumcision of your flesh** matches a similar, if longer, expression in Ephesians 2:1. But the addition of the second part of the phrase means that the Colossians were Gentile and, before their incorporation into God's people, lay outside the scope of his covenant mercy (as in Eph. 2:11, 12). Such was their plight. Two areas of need are covered. Morally they were cut off from the life of God as alienated sinners; and religiously they stood afar off from God's presence as an outcast and disadvantaged people.

Now all this has changed, and a new order has been introduced with Christ's coming. God has brought life to those in spiritual death and forgiveness of those held down by evil powers. The present reality of the resurrection life which Lohse finds to be a sign of post-Pauline theology is probably accounted for by the polemical situation at Colossae and the need to stress the completeness of Paul's gospel to meet the Colossians' case here and now, without the supplement of alien theology which was offering a gnosticizing remedy for a full communion with the divine.

14. The meaning of forgiveness is illustrated by the use of vivid picture-language. **The bond** is that of an IOU signifying a debt to be paid. Examples of this 'certificate of debt' are given by A. Deissmann, *Light from the Ancient East*, London, 1927, pp. 334ff. It **stood against us.** What exactly does Paul have in mind? How does the next phrase **with its legal demands** fit in? And how is Christ's action in setting aside the bond by **nailing it to** his **cross** to be related to the general picture? If we work backwards from the reference to the action of removing the legal document, it would appear that it was not the law *per se* which Christ abolished. Paul never so speaks; the nearest he gets to this is Romans 10:4 or Galatians 2:19. See C. F. D. Moule, 'Obligation in the ethic of Paul', *Christian History and Interpretation, Studies Presented to John Knox*, ed. W. R. Farmer, C. F. D. Moule, R. R. Niebuhr, Cambridge, 1967, pp. 401–4. Rather it was that aspect of the law which was 'against us', i.e. when it condemned the man who failed to keep it. Of this aspect he speaks in Galatians 3:13 under the phrase 'the curse of the law'.

The content of the phrase **which** was **against us** is then to be read as the 'legal demands' (Gr. *dogmata*: so Percy, pp. 88–90); or, in the light of a cognate verb (Gr. *dogmatizesthe*) in 2:20, it refers to the heretics' false ritualistic prescriptions. It was by these strict requirements that the law became an instrument of condemnation. But the obedient Christ endured that curse on sinners' behalf (Gal. 3:13, 2 C. 5:21) and so **cancelled the bond.** This sense of the law's demands which bring condemnation is seen in 2:20 where judgement is being passed on the Colossians for their failure to measure up to the heretics' code of rules and regulations.

The way in which Paul can closely identify Christ's self-sacrifice with the body of flesh, representing human sinfulness, has suggested to some recent interpreters (especially O. A. Blanchette, 'Does the *Cheirographon* of Col. 2, 14 represent Christ Himself?' *CBQ* 23 (1961), pp. 306–12; A. J. Bandstra, *The Law and the Elements of the World, An Exegetical Study in Aspects of Paul's Teaching,* Kampen, 1964, pp. 158ff.) a new line in regard to our understanding of the bond (Gr. *cheirographon*) that was inimical to us. There is a difficulty with the traditional view, *viz.* that it is awkward to equate a certificate of indebtedness signed by men with a divine exhibition of condemnation in the bond which is nailed to the cross.

There is evidence, drawn from the Old Testament and Jewish literature, to show that the idea of a book of works kept by God and recording all men's sins was familiar. The actual term *cheirographon* is used of this book in an anonymous Jewish apocalyptic writing dated in first century B.C. Here the book is held by the accusing angel who notes down all the seer's sins. The seer asks that they may be wiped out. There is another book containing the seer's good deeds. The following words may be Paul's explanatory gloss on the noun *cheirographon*. The phrase 'which was against us' serves as an identification of the book of evil works.

If this notion of a book of indictment presented by a grand inquisitor at the heavenly court lies in the background of our text, it paves the way for the view that the bond was not a certificate of debt signed by men but one presented by malevolent spirits. Then the 'legal demands' may have nothing to do with the Mosaic law, but may stand for the ordinances (Gr. *dogmata*) which form the basis of the angelic indictment, *viz.* that man is fleshly and unspiritual and out of harmony with the divine, a typical gnostic indictment of mankind. This view suggests that Paul has taken over an existing statement of Christ's saving work (set in hymnic form) and redacted it to bring it into line with his teaching. The original 'hymn' of two strophes said no more than that it was 'against us'. Paul adds a redactional gloss in the words 'consisting of ordinances. That which was against us' as a prelude to the verb 'he removed'. He did this for a special reason. He wished to amplify the nature of the charge which the angelic indictment brought against men. In the light of 2:20 he sees the ascetic requirements (given in 2:23) as demonic and anti-Christian and a threat to the Church. He therefore proclaims that there is no reason for his readers to consent to a way of life which is a deliberate denial of his gospel and to a reversion to demonic tyranny which has been overcome by Christ's action in defeating the evil powers and cancelling their accusation against mankind.

The grounds for the above argument are partly textual and partly metrical, based on the assumption of a pre-Pauline hymn in 2:13–15 and Paul's redaction of it. For details, see my essay, 'Reconciliation and Forgiveness in the Letter to the Colossians' in *Reconciliation and Hope*, ed. R. Banks, Exeter, 1974.

Christ assumed a human body in his incarnation and took that body to the cross, also bearing our sins and becoming identified with man the sinner in his death (2 C. 5:21; Gal. 3:13; Rom. 8:3). This is Blanchette's argument to link *cheirographon* with Christ's body bearing our sins. The gnostic *Gospel of Truth*, xx.23ff. speaks of Jesus taking (? wearing) 'that Book' as his own and being nailed to a cross where he affixed the ordinance of the Father to the cross. A. J. Bandstra rightly supports the sense 'wearing' since the text goes on to say: 'Having divested himself of these perishable rags' (his flesh), he clothed himself with incorruptibility, which it is impossible for anyone to take away from him' (xx.34, R. McL. Wilson's translation in *New Testament Apocrypha*, vol. i, London, 1963, p. 524).

The association of 'wearing' and 'setting aside' recalls the previous verse (v. 11) where Christ divested himself of his body of flesh on the cross (2:15). Christians repeat this experience sacramentally when they accept the 'circumcision of Christ' and are united with him in his death and victory. The result is the same as that given in Romans 6:6: 'Knowing this, that our old nature was crucified (with Christ) that the body of sin may be done away'—a possibility whose antecedent must be that Christ became one with our sin, 'wore' it as a garment in his human body and so accepted responsibility for it on our behalf when the angelic accuser levelled a charge against mankind.

This he set aside, nailing it to the cross. Cancelling the certificate of indebtedness and nailing it to the cross go together, though it is not certain how the latter action referring to the historical crucifixion of Jesus bears upon the wiping out of the charge. The Greek verb *exaleiphein* means to rub out, wipe away and so obliterate from sight, as writing on wax or a slate was removed. Dibelius–Greeven suggest that the bond is like the *titulus* or sentence of condemnation which was posted over the criminal's head as he died on the gibbet (Jn 19:20). So the crucified Christ assumed our tale of guilt and made it his own responsibility in death. Against this, 'there seems to be no evidence for the alleged custom of cancelling a bond by piercing it with a nail' (Moule). See further A. Deissmann, *Light from the Ancient East*, pp. 332f.

The effective action seems more to lie in the removal of a list of sins by wiping it clean. For this Isaiah 43:25 (LXX) provides some anticipation: 'I am the one who wipes out (Gr. *exaleiphōn*) your iniquities and I will not remember them.' As a preparation for the Jewish service for New Year (*Rôš-hašānāh*) there is a litany extending over ten days during which the prayer '*Abînū Malkenū* is recited. This takes its name from the opening invocation: 'Our Father, our King!' and two consecutive lines run:

> Our Father, our King! blot out our transgressions, and make them pass away before thine eyes.
> Our Father, our King! erase in thine abundant mercies all the records of our guilt.

The nailing of this document, now wiped clear of all its accusations, is then a subsequent action suggesting 'an act of triumphant defiance in the face of those blackmailing powers' (Bruce) who were threatening the Colossians in the heretics' system.

15. He disarmed the principalities and powers. Paul continues with the message of Christ's triumph. The spirit-forces which accused you (he is saying) Christ has finally defeated, having divested himself of their clinging attack. He stripped away their rule and showed them up for what they were—usurpers and tyrants, domineering over human beings and making them the

plaything of fate and iron necessity in subservience to an astrological cult. His cross was the scene of the public exposure, and of
Christ's resounding triumph.

This line of interpretation gives full weight to this Greek
participle which is rendered 'he stripped off'. Lohmeyer cogently
argues that the imagery is not drawn from the battlefield where
an enemy is 'disarmed' (so *RSV*) but from a royal court in which
public officials are degraded by being stripped of their honour.
H. Schlier *TDNT* (ii, p. 31, n. 2) follows Lohmeyer in treating the
verb as a 'divestment of dignity rather than despoiling of weapons'.
The middle voice of the verb is better explained as a true deponent
in preference to the active and transitive sense used to denote the
personal interest of the one who acts (*cf.* Arndt-Gingrich, *sv*, and
A. Oepke, *TDNT* ii, p. 319).

It is still an open question whether the full force of the middle
voice should be given. The choice is between taking the verb to
mean, 'He stripped the evil powers of their dignity and authority'
(so Lohse); or, by giving the full meaning to the deponent, 'He
divested himself of the principalities and powers of evil'. The
latter is the sense taken by the Greek fathers and preferred by
Lightfoot: 'The powers of evil, which had clung like a Nessus robe
about His humanity, were torn off and cast aside for ever.' This
interpretation makes the participle govern **the principalities
and powers,** and yields the translation in *RV*. There is a third
view, adopted by the Latin fathers and in recent times by J. A. T.
Robinson, *The Body*, London, 1952, p. 41, which would make
Christ's action relate to the divesting of his flesh. Yet again it is
possible to combine these early Greek and Latin interpretations in
the manner taken by C. A. A. Scott, *Christianity according to St Paul*,
1927, pp. 34ff. This is the view which states that Christ (who is the
subject of the participle) stripped off from himself the evil forces
which attacked him and that he did so by stripping off his flesh,
since it was his flesh (i.e. his frail humanity) which the evil powers
assaulted. 'Flesh' in this context means 'the medium through
which He had become involved in the human experience of the
hostility of the evil Potentates and Powers, the spirit-forces which
had usurped authority over men' (Scott, p. 35). As Moule points
out (p. 103), the transition between these two views is one that
Paul may well have made in spite of the absence of any precise
term for 'flesh' in the text. Paul's description of Christ's reconciliation in 1:22 ('in the body of flesh by his death'), however,

makes clear his close association of Christ's death and the medium
of his bodily existence.

He **made a public example of them, triumphing over them
in him.** One further action also highlights the way in which
Christ's victory-in-death disgraced the would-be conquerors. He
not only made a public spectacle of them by showing up their real
character as usurpers and rebels against divine authority, but led
them in a triumphal procession as the defeated enemy. The
demonic powers (as in 1 C. 2:6–8) presumed to attack him as
weak and helpless (apparently regarding him as a mortal man,
identified with the human race over which they claimed their
rights—a gnostic idea). But he repelled that assault by turning
them into captives and conquered rebels whose bluff had been
called. He led them in public procession, remarks Paul as he blends
a historical illustration with the mythological concept, just as the
victorious Roman general paraded his captives of war in chains
through the streets of the city at the conclusion of a foreign
campaign (on the verb *thriambeuō*, see G. Delling, *TDNT* iii,
p. 160). I suggest that Paul's choice of this word is consciously
governed by his use of a rare verb in 2:8 (to carry off as a captive
of war) and it is his way of rebutting the insinuation that the
Colossians are the helpless victims of the false teachers with their
angelology: on the contrary, Paul says, the evil powers are subservient to the victorious Lord. So these demonic powers are his
'prize of war', held up to public spectacle as he mounted the cross.
From that cross (Paul's Gr. *en autō* is better understood as 'triumphing over them in it', the cross) he reigns and receives the homage
of his foes, who are now 'reconciled' and subjugated (1:20 is
illumined by this verse). On the subject of Paul's teaching on the
antagonistic motif and the *Christus Victor* theme, see R. Leivestad,
Christ the Conqueror, London, 1954.

DEFENCE OF CHRISTIAN LIBERTY 2:16–23

This lengthy and involved section falls into two parts containing
both a statement of what was being introduced as a series of
cultic practices at Colossae (2:16–23) and a call (begun at 2:20)
by the apostle which summons his readers to act upon the teaching
they have received from his representatives, notably Epaphras
(3:1–4). Our knowledge of the 'Colossian heresy' (as Lightfoot

termed it), at the most, fragmentary and indirect, is derived from this passage. But we are hindered by the cryptic nature of this part of the letter. Some verses are so tightly constructed (notably vv. 18, 21, 23) that access to their clear sense is not possible to the modern interpreter. One further complication is that, on occasion, Paul seems to be citing the actual wording of the heretical slogans (clearly in v. 21; and probably also in vv. 18, 23) before giving a judgement on their pernicious character. Ancient writers did not use quotation-marks or footnotes, so there is no certainty in this regard, and our knowledge of the actual language of the Colossian 'cultus' is at best inferential.

The whole passage is best described as 'defence of Christian liberty' (so Masson). This writer aptly remarks on the close connection between doctrine and practice. False notions about the person and work of Christ which are denounced in 2:8–15 have their inevitable corollary in strange aberrations on the practical level. Paul then proceeds to show the folly of any course of action based on wrong theological premises. He has pointed out in clear terms the real nature of the specious doctrine which is being taught at Colossae: it is nothing less than 'philosophy, empty deceit' (2:8), which stands in diametrical opposition to Christ. Indeed, the evil powers which are seen to be behind the false practices and regulations (2:20) were defeated and publicly disgraced by Christ. It is wrong for the Colossians to accept a way of life based on such wrong-headed notions.

In the course of his practical discussion, Paul will have an even more damaging criticism to level against these teachers who are 'bursting with the futile conceit of worldly minds' (v. 18, *NEB*). They do not hold fast to the Head (v. 19), that is, Christ. Thus wilfully departing from the Church's Lord and the universe's ruler, they are branded as self-condemned heretics whose teaching is to be utterly refused. And if their doctrine is thus in error, their ethical admonitions are clearly shown to be misguided as merely 'human precepts and doctrines' (v. 22) and as emanating from 'self-made religion' (v. 23). Paul gives a 'blow-by-blow rebuttal of their pretentious claims' (Lohse).

16–19. Therefore links the present section to the foregoing with its demonstration of Christ's victory over evil powers. With his victory standing to the credit of his people, they can ill afford to give attention to mistaken criticisms which the false teachers would pass on them. The points at issue are enumerated.

16. Let no one pass judgement on you in questions of food and drink. These are prescriptions belonging to an ascetic way of life. There were various reasons why abstinence from food and drink was practised in the ancient world. One was a belief in the transmigration of souls which led to the idea that consuming animal meat was a form of 'cannibalism' (see G. Bornkamm, *TDNT* iv, p. 67). Another view (more important in this context, in the light of v. 18) was an importance attached to fasting as a prelude to receiving a revelation from the gods (see the hellenistic texts given by J. Behm, *TDNT* iv, p. 926).

with regard to a festival or a new moon or a sabbath. The holy days, whether annual, monthly, or weekly, were also the subject of controversy at Colossae. Again the root principle needs to be noted. Paul is not condemning the use of sacred days and seasons. Nor does he have in view the Jewish observance of these days as an expression of Israel's obedience to God's law and a token of her election (a frequent OT idea, e.g. Hos. 2:11). What moves him here is the wrong motive involved when the observance of holy festivals is made part of the worship advocated at Colossae in recognition of the 'elements of the universe', the astral powers which direct the course of the stars and regulate the calendar. And so they must be placated (see E. Lohse, *TDNT* vii, p. 301; G. Bornkamm, 'Die Häresie', p. 148). It is bad religion leading to man's bondage to 'fate' that Paul attacks.

It is an open question whether the main influences on this Colossian theosophy were Jewish or pagan. The allusions to dietary restrictions and to sacred days and festivals seem, at first glance, to settle the issue in favour of a Judaizing tendency. J. B. Lightfoot in 1875 pointed to the example of the Essenes who practised a type of asceticism and separatism. Since then, the literature of an Essene-like sect at Qumran has given more understanding of their discipline and ethos, notably in the observance of a heterodox calendar with diverse feast-days from those of Palestinian Judaism. Moreover, certain verbal correspondences between the Dead Sea Scrolls and this epistle have been explored by W. D. Davies, 'Paul and the Dead Sea Scrolls: Flesh and Spirit', *The Scrolls and the New Testament*, ed. K. Stendahl, London, 1958, pp. 166–9; and P. Benoit, 'Qumran and the New Testament', *Paul and Qumran*, ed. J. Murphy-O'Connor, London, 1968, p. 17. The latter concludes: 'A return to the Mosaic Law by circumcision, rigid observance concerning diet and the calendar, speculations about the angelic powers: all this is part and parcel of the doctrines of Qumran.' This may be so but the singular absence of any debate over the Mosaic law at Colossae and even the absence of the word for law (*nomos*) should make us pause before accepting too close an identity, as E. Lohse reminds us in his essay, 'Christologie und Ethik im Kolosserbrief', *Apophoreta*, Göttingen, 1964, pp. 157f. This consideration militates against W. Foerster's thesis ('Die Irrlehrer des Kolosserbriefes', in *Studia Biblica et Semitica*, Wageningen, 1966, pp. 71–80) that the heresy was a sort of successor to the Qumran teaching. For a more balanced assessment of the evidence of the Scrolls see E. Yamauchi 'Sectarian Parallels: Qumran and Colosse', *Bibliotheca Sacra* 121,i, (1964), pp. 141–52.

17. These are only a shadow of what is to come. The reason for Paul's attack is now supplied. Religious observance expressed in subservience to the 'regulations' of verse 20 betrays a misunderstanding of God's purpose in bringing men into the perfect light of his revelation in Christ. Such observance means being content to live in the shadow-side of religion where fears lurk and inhibitions abound. The 'shadow' presages what is to come; and the time of the substance has arrived, thus antiquating all that pointed forward to it. That 'substance' is **Christ.** His new age delivers men from the bondage of fear and superstitious dread. He sets them free from false notions and insubstantial hopes, and gives them a taste of reality in religion as they come to know in him true communion with the living God. This reality is what Paul means in his earlier references to the 'hope of the gospel' (1:5, 23) which his readers are not to abandon. It is likely that Paul is here employing the contrast 'copy/original' which derives from Plato and was used in the Colossian philosophy. Perhaps the teachers were insisting that 'full reality' (*plērōma*) could be attained only by way of veneration paid to the 'copy', i.e. the angels, and obedience to their ascetic regimen. If so, Paul turns the tables on them by giving a christological twist to the contrast. **Substance** is in fact one rendering of the Greek term (*sōma*) for 'body'. This has suggested to some interpreters (Lohmeyer, Masson, Moule) but not all (E. Best, *One Body in Christ*, London, 1955, pp. 121f.) that Paul has the Church as Christ's body in view. In fellowship with Christ and his people 'all the great "realities" were found—pardon, sanctification, communion with God, etc.— of which ritual, whether Jewish or non-Jewish, was only a shadow' (Moule). This reference to a corporate expression of faith, found in Christ, seems required by the train of thought which follows. There Paul will continue the contrast between false religion and the true faith of the body, of which Christ is the head (v. 19).

18–19. These verses abound with difficulties both linguistic and conceptual. Mercifully the drift of Paul's thought is clear. **Let no one disqualify you.** It is couched as a warning lest his readers should allow themselves to be cheated out of their prize (see E. Stauffer, *TDNT* i, pp. 637–9, for Paul's use of *brabeion*, 'prize' which underlies *katabrabeuein* here) by heeding the false teachers who offered as a substitute for his gospel a system of religion which was the product of their own minds. Paul obviously has a low opinion of these sophists. He bluntly calls these men the victims of a worldly outlook because they refuse to submit their thinking to divine revelation, and boast in their native wisdom and pride (see Rom 1:21, 22; 1 C. 2:14f.; Phil. 3:19 for similar judgements on men who despise God's way of life and devise their own religious customs and ceremonials). But Paul's Greek is still more expressive. They are controlled by 'the mind of the flesh' (*cf.* Rom. 8:7) and are willing victims of an arrogance and self-conceit which gives them an unfounded sense of superiority over their fellow-Christians. Bornkamm ('Die Häresie', p. 144, n. 14) sees a Pauline sarcasm here, since Paul uses the verb 'puff up' in his debate with gnostics at Corinth: they are boasting of their acquaintance with divine 'fullness' (*plērōma*) and being full of knowledge (*gnōsis*), when all that they are 'full of' is their pride! **not holding fast to the Head.** They stand under the most tragic of all condemnations: they are willing to be detached from Christ, the head of the Church. So they put themselves out of touch with the source of all true life, just as a limb loses its life once it is severed from the human torso.

The human body provides the analogy for Paul's description in this verse. As an anatomical structure, it is supplied with and bonded together by joints and ligaments and so grows in strength and size as God purposes its growth (so Moule). The application is pointed. Human limbs are meant to be an integral part of the human frame. Once they become detached, they lose that vital contact with the source of life and nourishment. Paul is saying: the false teacher who ceases to depend on the head, ceases to belong to the body. He who cuts himself off from Christ cuts himself free from the Church (Masson). So closely are Christ and his body joined: and so important is it for his people to remain in living union with him who is their head. False teachers have proved themselves self-excluded from the Church by reason of their forsaking Christ as true God and man; let the Colossians not be enticed into the same trap (2:8).

For Paul, the danger facing the Colossians was a serious one, full of momentous consequences. The key-terms are found in the phrase: **insisting on self-abasement and worship of angels, taking his stand on visions, puffed up without reason by his sensuous mind.** Recent study of this verse, notably by F. O. Francis, 'Humility and Angelic Worship in Col. 2:18', *ST* 16 (1961), pp. 109–34, has identified certain conclusions, as follows:

(a) **insisting on** (Gr. *thelōn en*) indicates the desire on the part of the errorists to impose their views on the Colossian church. Francis renders 'bent on' to show the strength of this determination and its attractiveness. Other translators (G. Schrenk, *TDNT* iii, p. 45, n. 13; E. Percy, pp. 145ff.; Masson, *ad loc.*) give 'delighting in' from a Septuagintal model of the verb, e.g. 1 Samuel 18:22: Saul had delight in David. A. Fridrichsen, '*Thelōn*. Col. 2:18', *ZNTW* 21 (1922), p. 135–7, takes the participle as an adverb to qualify the verb 'disqualify', 'deliberately'. So Dibelius–Greeven: 'Let no one wilfully condemn you.'

(b) **self-abasement** is literally 'humility' (Gr. *tapeinophrosunē*). Often used in a good sense of a Christian virtue (as in 3:12), the word here must carry the sense of mortification or self-denial. Specifically it may well mean 'fasting' as in the Hebrew *ta'anîṯ* and as used by second- and third-century Christian authors (Hermas, Tertullian). Francis draws attention to an important strain of Jewish pietistic literature which offered the reward to ascetic practice of entering into the heavenly realm and catching a vision of the divine. But Lohse finds fault with this view since it restricts too narrowly the meaning of self-abasement. For him 'it describes the eagerness and docility ("readiness to serve") with which a person fulfils the cultic ordinances'.

(c) **worship of angels.** The difficulty here is to know how to interpret the phrase: is it 'worshipping of angels' or 'worship conducted or practised by angels' which is reprobated? Francis argues for the latter (*loc. cit.*, pp. 126–30) with great ingenuity and so relieves his interpretation of the difficulty (seen on the first view) that there is little evidence that within orthodox Judaism the Jews worshipped angels. See A. Lukyn Williams, 'The Cult of Angels at Colossae', *JTS*, os 10 (1909), pp. 413–38. *Cf.* E. Percy, pp. 149–55. There is, however, a fatal objection (voiced by Lohse) to the second interpretation, *viz.* this reading 'breaks down because of the statement in verse 23 where the worship is explained as a cult performed by men'. Nor is it valid to argue from the fact that the Jews did not worship angels, since the Colossian situation is thoroughly syncretistic and included pagan elements (J. Lähnemann, p. 138, n. 106). In some way veneration must have been paid to the angels as part of the cultic apparatus of this religion.

(*d*) **taking his stand on visions.** The first three words are clearly a paraphrase of the single Greek verb *embateuōn*. Its primary meaning is 'to enter', whether in a neutral sense ('set foot on') or an aggressive sense ('invade'). Sometimes the meaning is figurative, as in the English idiom: 'to go into detail' (see 2 Mac. 2:30).

Some commentators, both ancient (Chrysostom, Athanasius) and modern (H. Preisker, *TDNT* ii, p. 535f.) argue for this last-named sense. Preisker insists that Paul is refuting an insatiable thirst for knowledge which characterized the gnostic-Jewish philosophy at Colossae and elsewhere (2 Tim. 3:7; 2 Jn 9). The meaning is then: what he had seen in a vision, he tried to investigate (in the hope of gaining deeper insight into divine mysteries).

This view certainly would seem cogent, were it not for the further evidence of another meaning which makes the verb something of a technical expression in the mystery religions. It refers to the initiates entering the sanctuary to consult the oracle on completion of the rite (see S. Eitrem, '*Embateuō*. Note sur Col. 2, 18', *ST* 2 (1948), p. 93). Dibelius–Greeven call attention to the inscriptional data from the sanctuary of Apollo at Claros (second century A.D. ?). On this reconstruction, Paul is referring to a cultic ceremony—the initiate enters the oracle grotto at the completion of his mystical experience—and the claim of the Colossian teachers is that they too have penetrated the secrets of the universe and received a climactic vision. There is no need to argue that these words in our text are consciously borrowed from the mystery cultic practice. Clearly the two situations are not parallel, as critics of Dibelius have remarked (see S. Lyonnet, 'Col. 2, 18 et les mystères d'Apollon Clarien', *Biblica* 43 (1962), pp. 417–35), but there are two observations to be registered in favour of some interpretation akin to that of Dibelius–Greeven. First, the Claros inscription does contain the word used by Paul and in a semi-cultic context which Paul's writing seems to require. This point would give the interpretation the edge over Francis' view which maintains that the entry is into heaven as part of the general theory of the journey of the soul from earth to the heavenly regions; but the evidence he gives does not contain the exact verb *embateuein*. Secondly, Lohse states an important fact when he stresses that Paul in verse 18 is not arguing against the Colossian heresy explicitly but simply citing the heretical watchwords. There is no need (he proceeds) to insist that the text must be altered to produce a rendering which would be a polemic against the cult and its pretensions (Bruce, *ad loc*. has a full note on the conjectural emendations of this verse; they are all variations of Lightfoot's proposal to read the verb *kenembateuein*, 'to tread the air'). Our understanding of the situation at Colossae is assisted if we regard all the terms, 'servility' in regard to the spirit-forces, 'veneration of angels' and 'penetrating into visions he has seen' as slogans of the false teachers. They formed the cultic procedure by which devotees could gain a knowledge of the 'elemental spirits of the universe' (2:8) and could lay claim to some esoteric experience which unlocked the mysteries of life and destiny. The conclusion that a pride in special knowledge (Gr. *gnōsis*) lay at the root of the Colossian error seems certain in view of Paul's next phrase, which does pass judgement on the claim—unless we run together the two parts of Paul's sentence as suggested by N. Turner, *A Grammar of New Testament Greek*, Edinburgh, vol. iii, 1963, p. 246, and translate 'upon what he vainly imagined in the vision of his initiation'. Elsewhere Paul commented that an inordinate aspiration to knowledge of divine mysteries serves only to fill the claimant with conceit (1 C. 8:1; *cf.* 1 C. 4:18: on these texts, see W. Schmithals, *Gnosticism in Corinth*, Nashville, 1971, pp. 141ff.).

20-23. One final proof that verse 18 refers to the heretics' fear of the astral gods which could only be appeased (they believed) by a regimen of asceticism, abstinences and angel-veneration is given in verse 20. **If with Christ you died to the elemental spirits of the universe, why do you live as if you still belonged to the world? Why do you submit to regulations?** Paul recalls what happened when the Colossian Christians passed in their baptismal experience from paganism to fellowship with Christ. By their faith-union with him in his death and resurrection (2:12-15; Rom. 6:4f.) they passed from under the control of these cosmic powers and were 'transferred . . . to the kingdom of his beloved Son' (1:13). No longer held captive in the domain of darkness, they rejoiced to take their place in the heritage of God's people (1:12) and confessed a new allegiance and lordship (2:6). The vividness of Paul's writing brings out the dramatic sense of this transition from bondage to liberty in Christ. J. A. T. Robinson's translation (*The Body. A Study in Pauline Theology*, London, 1952, p. 43) succeeds in capturing the unusual construction: 'Ye died with Christ out from under the elements of the world', suggesting a death to an old order which liberates the sufferer from all the claims that order had on him (as in Paul's argument of Rom. 7:1–4).

The application is made in the form of a rhetorical question and a rebuke. If this decisive change in your loyalty happened to you in your baptism, and you henceforth determined to live under Christ's sole command, it is 'downright absurd' (Lohse) to go back to living as though Christ had never set you free. In particular, why do you listen to spurious teaching which would bring you into bondage to a legal code and impose on you a series of taboos and negative rules? The passive verb *dogmatizesthai* has the force: 'let oneself be dictated to'.

'Do not handle, Do not taste, Do not touch.' The prohibitions of verse 21 are given by Paul as part of what the propagandists were teaching. It is they, not he, who are laying down the regulations. In this list, the first and last verbs are almost synonyms and the line of distinction between them is hard to draw. It looks as though all three verbs are warnings against the consumption of food and drink, though possibly there was a disdain of marriage if the first verb (Gr. *haptesthai*) has a sexual connotation as in 1 C. 7:1; so Robert Leaney, *ExpT* 64 (1952–3), p. 92. Gnostic teachers (according to 1 Tim. 4:3) forbade marriage, but there is no explicit taboo on sex-relations in this epistle. The plain sense is that Paul is warning against a false scrupulosity in matters of food and drink (2:16) which is 'part of a piety paralysed by an uncertainty of what precautions to take to safeguard a purity which is always threatened' (Masson). The rule-of-thumb in this legalistic religion is then applied: avoid *all* possible sources of defilement, and practise by your abstemiousness a rigorous discipline for fear of losing your 'spirituality'. Jewish scruples and fear of ritual defilement are well illustrated in such parts of rabbinic teaching as '*Abôdāh Zārāh* ('Strange Worship') and the sixth division of

Tohôrŏth ('Cleannesses') in the Mishnah. But the taboos in this verse are pagan.

Paul's teaching, on the contrary, is a charter of freedom. His line of reasoning is meant to provide some rationale for his opposition to a false ascetic piety. We may set down some of the principles on which his counterclaim rests:

(*a*) **Why do you submit to regulations?** (v. 20) renders a Greek verb (*dogmatizesthe*) which recalls verse 14. There Paul has described the work of Christ on the cross as one which wipes out the charge brought against mankind by evil spirits. That condemnation is expressed in terms of the 'legal demands' (Gr. *dogmata*) which formed the charge-sheet of indictment. But Christ's death did more than wipe the slate clean and give men a fresh start. Not only are the accusations blotted out; the reign of the spirit-powers is brought to an end. This fact lies at the heart of Paul's question in verse 20: 'Why do you allow yourselves to be dictated to by regulations which have no authority?' In effect, why do the Colossians wish to re-impose a superstitious religion on themselves when Christ's cross has for ever set men free from this type of bondage?

(*b*) Matters of food and drink are of no consequence in the practice of Christian piety (Rom. 14:17)—when a test-issue is made of abstinence or enjoyment. The reason why items of food and drink cannot affect a Christian's relationship to God is given in verse 22, referring to things which **all perish as they are used, according to human precepts and doctrines.** This picks up the same thought as is used in the gospel teaching (Mk 7:6, 7 = Mt. 15:8, 9). Both passages go back to a common Old Testament source for authority: Isaiah 29:13 (LXX), which reads: 'But in vain they worship me, teaching the commandments and teachings of men.' The Pauline use of the text drives home a single point. The Colossians have no reason to pay heed to false ascetic rules, for what these teachers recommend are simply human ordinances, born out of man-made fears and frailties (*cf.* 2:5; Tit. 1:14 for a similar indictment). Food is quickly forgotten as it passes through the mouth into the digestive system and so 'perishes'.

(*c*) **These have indeed an appearance of wisdom.** Rules and regulations to order human bodily functions and appetites have a semblance of appeal. They appear to offer a life of self-discipline and mastery of the instincts. They give the impression of being for human good and of leading to self-conquest. And perhaps uppermost in Paul's mind is the value placed on self-denial (especially fasting) as a preparation required to receive a vision (v. 18). But while Paul elsewhere values the need for self-mastery (1 C. 9:24–7), in this context he speaks only in a critical voice of this kind of asceticism.

His chief complaint lies in the word translated **rigour of devotion** (Gr. *ethelothrēskia*), which is a composite term meaning either 'self-made religion' or 'would-be religion'. The latter rendering suggesting the thought 'pretended' or 'quasi' piety (proposed by B. Reicke, 'Zum sprachlichen Verständnis von Kol. 2:23', *ST* 6, (1952) p. 46) is not as acceptable as the former, which seems to be the necessary sense needed in Paul's argument. See K. L. Schmidt, *TDNT* iii, p. 159 for the construction of the word: *ethelo-* has the sense 'self-designed', 'self-appointed'. The gravamen of Paul's charge is that the errorists have imported on to the scene at Colossae a manner of worship which is essentially their own innovation. It is branded by Paul 'self-made', i.e. bogus, and so for that very reason invalid and not to be entertained by his readers. The Colossian sophists may express their pleasure (note the same Greek verb in v. 18 as in the prefix: *ethelo-*) in their religiosity and ascetic piety. It may give them inward satisfaction in keeping their body under iron discipline. But it is 'of no value in combating sensual indulgence' (Moule) and 'it entirely fails in its chief aim' (Lightfoot).

Or rather, perhaps it succeeded only too well by inducing a state of trance-like ecstasy which in turn led to a visionary experience. The term in verse 23 may well be 'a sarcastic borrowing from his opponents' language' (so W. L. Knox, *St. Paul and the Church of the Gentiles*, Cambridge, 1939, p. 171, n. 1) like a similar quotation from their terms in verse 18. Or more likely it is Paul's deliberate parodying of their claim in verse 18 by his coined term expressing his ridicule at what purports to be ultimate truth.

Paul grants that asceticism may produce visions, but his condemnation falls upon the motive and the result. The motive is a desire for spiritual experience which by-passes Christ and seeks gratification in a sensuous elation. The end-result is a sense of spiritual pride and this Paul terms a capitulation to **the indulgence of the flesh,** i.e. man's unrenewed nature.

This way of looking at 'self-made religion' would explain Paul's negative attitude to what seem to be wholesome practices

(fasting, self-denial, and keeping the appetites on tight rein).
'Paul is handicapped by the difficulty of admitting any value in
external practices without appearing to justify the claims of his
opponents' (Knox, *ibid.*).

**23. they are of no value in checking the indulgence of the
flesh.** The final words of the verse are problematic (see Moule,
pp. 108–10). One would expect a continuance of Paul's criticism
in pointing out the inherent weakness of a legalistic ritualism.
Therefore an ancient interpretation, shared by both Greek and
Latin Church fathers (see G. Delling, *TDNT* vi, p. 133), that
Paul's charge against asceticism is that it does not 'satisfy the
reasonable wants of the body', can hardly be correct. The apostle
is not timidly remarking that ritualism fails by 'not holding the
body in any honour'. On the contrary, his word is one for 'flesh',
not body; and the Greek word for the former, *sarx*, must carry
Paul's more usual sense of 'lower nature', 'sensual indulgence' (as
in v. 18). The obvious weakness in this type of religious endeavour
is that it provides no check for man's lower nature which, though
using his bodily instincts and appetites to hold him prey, is really
different from them. His 'flesh' (*sarx*) gains control of the entire
person and rules it as 'the mind that is set on the flesh', but no
amount of bodily restraint or self-denial will hold this principle in
check. Behind Paul's term may be the rabbinic doctrine of the
'evil impulse' (*yeṣer hā-rāᶜ*) which, according to Jewish anthropology, held men in bondage and goaded them into sin. See W. D.
Davies, *Paul and Rabbinic Judaism*, London, 2nd edn, 1955, pp.
17–35. It requires a higher 'law'—'the law of the Spirit of life in
Christ Jesus' (Rom. 8:2), the power of the Spirit (Gal. 5:16–25)
and a 'true' mortification (3:5) which presupposes a new nature
(3:10)—to give a man self-control. The 'severe treatment' meted
out to 'the body', i.e. conformity to the ascetic way of life in
following regulations and taboos as a prelude to gaining access to
God's truth, is useless, since it leaves untouched man's real problem,
viz. his motive. It is therefore only a false claim to 'wisdom' (as
in 2:8) and a mock humility (Gr. *tapeinophrosunē*) which serves
simply to bolster a man's ego.

In short, Paul's accusation is that this religious 'piety' was
liable to abuse. It set out ostensibly to promote the devotee's
highest spiritual interest, but did so in a way which served only
to make him a proud man. It exploited his love of secret knowledge; it professed to offer him the key to the riddle of God and

the universe; it invited him to explore the secrets of destiny by placating the 'elemental spirits' and venerating angelic hosts; it promised a reward to a regimen of discipline, fasting and self-mortification in the granting of visions of heavenly things, true 'realities' beyond the world of matter and sense-perception; it gave him a sense of self-mastery which set him apart from other men who toiled with their temptations and vices.

All of this, Paul flatly objects, is so much 'beguiling speech' (2:4). In so far as it succeeds in its declared and pretended aims, it fails to keep the 'flesh' in check. Rather it promotes a selfish and senseless spirit which claims a private experience open only to a select few.

LIFT UP YOUR HEARTS 3:1-4

The transition from the preceding section of the letter to Paul's summons in 3:1 and following is not easy to see. Probably his thought goes back to 2:20: 'If with Christ you died . . .'. He did not wish to remain with this negative statement of the Christian's separation from the domain of evil powers. So he feels impelled to assert the positive aspect. The believers are also raised with Christ and called to a new life with its emphasis on positive and affirmative considerations.

1. If then you have been raised looks back to the new life begun in a faith-response and certified in baptism (2:12). Paul confidently makes appeal to this as an attested experience common to all Christians (Rom. 6:3ff.). His use of a conditional clause betrays no uncertainty. 'If' means 'if, as is the case', 'since'.

seek (Gr. *zēteite*) means the orientation of a man's will (H. Greeven, *TDNT* ii, p. 893) which can be directed either to an unprofitable goal (Rom. 10:3; 1 C. 1:22) or to a worth-while end (Rom. 2:7). Here Paul directs his readers' attention to **things that are above,** perhaps in conscious opposition to 'the things which are earthly' (Phil. 3:19). More likely, he is still reacting against the gnostic claim to gain a secret knowledge of 'heavenly' realities by close investigation (2:18). The verb *zētein* can have the sense of 'investigate' (Greeven, p. 893). If this is so, Paul is countering the heretical bid by calling the church to concentrate, on true knowledge of spiritual secrets which are hidden in Christ, now exalted to the Father's presence (2:2, 3).

The session at God's right hand draws obviously from the most
common early Christian *testimonium* taken from the Old Testament: Psalm 110:1. See J. Danielou, 'La Session a la droite du
Pere', *The Gospels Reconsidered—Studia Evangelica*, Oxford (ed.
K. Aland *et al.* 1959) pp. 689–98. It is used in several contexts to
assert the undisputed lordship of Jesus Christ who, at his en-
thronement, received a dignity equal with God (W. Foerster,
TDNT ii, p. 1089). Here, in the Colossian situation, the exalta-
tion of Christ calls the Church to rise with him above the control
of the cosmic powers and bids Christians to share with him his
life of freedom in God. It further suggests that Christ is the true
way to God, and since believers are already risen with him, there
is no need to seek access to divine mysteries by a recourse to the
mumbo-jumbo of gnosticizing religion.

The exigencies of the situation at Colossae may very well account
for Paul's insistence upon the present realization of the Church's
life in Christ. Christians are already raised with him and share his
heavenly life. Some commentators (e.g. Lohse) and writers
(e.g. R. C. Tannehill, *Dying and Rising with Christ. A Study in
Pauline Theology*, Göttingen 1967, pp. 47–54) see in this teaching
a sign of a post-Pauline author, as in Eph. 2:5–7. But the latter
text is much more descriptive of the Church's elevation to share
in Christ's present triumph and lacks the concrete situation which
may justifiably be seen in Colossians. Besides, the future hope of a
deeper union between the Lord and his people is stressed in
Colossians 3:4; it is lacking in Ephesians.

2. Set your minds (Gr. *phroneite*) is a complementary verb, to
match the call of verse 1. The contrast with those referred to in
Philippians 3:19 is clear. The verb *phronein* means much more
than a mental exercise and has little to do with a person's emotional state (*cf. AV*, 'set your affection'). Its sphere is rather that
of motivation, as motive determines a line of action and an
individual's conduct. 'Let your thoughts dwell on that higher
realm' where Christ is enthroned as Lord (*NEB*) is a prelude to
a course of action which is determined by motives which are
inspired by Christ's lordship and not conformed to 'worldly ways'
(**things that are on earth**). The link with 2:20 is obvious. There
Paul had challenged the Colossians to abandon their commitment
to living as 'men of the world' since they had died with Christ to a
way of life which would mean bondage. Now he exhorts them to
allow Christ's freedom to inspire and control their lives.

3. For (Gr. *gar*) is an important connection. Their new freedom in allegiance to Christ follows directly from their baptismal renunciation: **you have died** (*NEB* gives 'you died', which is a better translation. Paul is looking back to a specific occasion).

your life is hid with Christ in God. The allusion to 'hidden' takes the reader back to 2:3. Possibly Paul's term recalls the Greek idiom in which death is likened to a man's being 'hidden in the earth' (*cf.* Moule, p. 112 and W. Barclay, *ad loc.*). Less likely is a popular view (stated by Dibelius–Greeven, p. 40) that the Christian's life in Christ is concealed in a mystical way at present; one day (in v. 4) it will be made public for all to see.

4. It is true that Paul does look forward to a future epiphany of the glory in Christ; and in this unveiling the Church will have a share. **Christ . . . our life** (the possessive **our** is not so well attested as 'your', but it has superior claim to be regarded as original. A later scribe would have no difficulty in altering 'our' to 'your' to bring the description into line with the second person plural throughout this paragraph) is Paul's summary of the source of the believer's new life of freedom. At the *parousia*, those who now are called to share his freedom will receive divine approbation in the fulfilment of God's purpose in accepting them as his own. **Glory,** in the light of 1 C. 15:12ff., 42f., suggests the resurrection of the body, both Christ's spiritual body and the future prospect of the Christian's new bodily existence (Phil. 3:20, 21; 2 C. 5:1ff.).

TRUE SELF-DENIAL 3:5–11

5. The claims of a false asceticism have been exposed and refuted at an earlier point in Paul's letter (2:20–3). Now he turns to advocate what is for him a positive line of self-control, which is both opposed to indulgence (vv. 5–8) and affirmative of a life-style which befits the Christian character (vv. 10, 11).

Put to death is the obverse side of the indicative statement 'you died' (2:20; 3:3). The fact of a decisive break with the old life describes the subjective experience of an individual's conversion expressed in baptism (Rom 6:3, 4, 6ff.) and looks back in this epistle to 2:12. Paul goes on to apply that teaching in a call to his readers: 'Let your old self, your pagan life, which died in baptism, remain dead.' But this is no quiescent acceptance of a past event; it involves a determined resolve to have done with former ways of behaviour. **What is earthly** refers back to 3:2 and prepares for the list of vices to be refused in verses 5 and 8. *RSV* omits the term 'members' (Gr. *melē*) as 'those parts of you' which belong to the earth. The allusion is to a person's bodily existence, as in Romans 6:11–13, 8:13. His physical nature, whether anatomical or belonging to his appetites, is not regarded by Paul as sinful, but it can often be the instrument of evil because man's fallen nature so chooses.

To spell out his meaning Paul lists certain evil practices which plague man's physical existence by becoming expressions of his loss of self-control. The vices are five in number, corresponding to the same number in verse 8 and again to a list of virtues in verse 12. Some interpreters see a special significance in the repeated use of the number five (*cf.* Bornkamm, 'Die Häeresie', p. 151, who argues that the number 'five' derives from an anthropological idea in which a man's deeds are his 'members'), though the parallels drawn from Iranian religion seem remote from this passage, even if it does draw upon some traditional formulation, as Lohse believes.

The first list covers the following ethical vices. **Immorality** stands first (as in Gal. 5:19) and is expressly forbidden. The Greek *porneia* carries several shades of meaning in the New Testament, ranging from extra-marital sex relationships (1 Th. 4:3) to marriages contracted with partners who are within illicit degrees of kinship (probably the sense of the word in Ac. 15:20 as well as Mt. 5:32, 19:1). But see B. Malina, 'Does *Porneia* mean Fornication?' *NovT* 14 (1972), pp. 10–17. **Impurity** (i.e. moral uncleanness) emphasizes the reason why the stringent ban of immorality was taken seriously (1 C. 6:9; Eph. 5:5). It means very much the same as its associated term, and it is equally reprobated (Gal. 5:19). *Passion* is evil passion which leads to sexual excess or even perversion. (W. Michaelis, *TDNT* v, p. 928.) See 1 Thessalonians 4:5; Romans 1:26. **Evil desire** is also mentioned in the catalogue of 'the works of the flesh' in Galatians 5:16 and its moral character is seen in the adjective 'evil' (Gr. *kakē*) which some manuscripts omit. But the base element in 'desire' is clear from allied texts (1 Th. 4:5; Gal. 5:24; Rom. 1:24, 6:12, 7:7f., 13:14). **Covetousness** stands out as the last member of the list. It breaks the sequence by turning attention from sexual vices to a sin of greed. The latter is the normal sense of the Greek *pleonexia* (lit. a desire 'to have more', the *amor habendi* which

Roman moralists described). This, then, is the sin of possessive-
ness, an insatiable desire to lay hands on material things (*cf.* Lk.
12:15). But a sexual overtone could be given to the term if
1 Thessalonians 4:6 which uses the cognate verb *pleonektein* ('to
wrong his brother') has an act of sexual irresponsibility in view.
But the verb (as in 1 C. 6:10) can equally mean to covet in the
accepted sense, i.e. to be greedy of gain.

covetousness leads a person away from God and encourages
him to trust his material possessions. See E. C. Hoskyns and
N. Davey, *The Riddle of the New Testament*, London, 1931, p. 28,
for the interesting connection between the Hebrew verb 'to trust'
and *māmônā*, an Aramaic term for wealth (Mt. 6:24, par. Lk.
16:13) which the rabbis personified as a demon and a rival of God.
So **covetousness** is no better than **idolatry,** the devotion given
to a false god.

6. New Testament lists of ethical vices often conclude with a
sobering reference to the divine judgement to be visited upon those
who indulge in these habits. (See 1 Th. 4:3–6; 1 C. 5:10f., 6:9;
Rom. 1:18–32.) So **on account of these** evil practices mentioned
in verse 5 **the wrath of God,** i.e. his judicial displeasure and
retribution, **is coming** at the final Day, although its processes in
history and in personal life are already at work (Rom. 1:18).

7. In these you once walked. If Paul is drawing upon traditional matter which was part of the ethical teaching of the early
Church, now he applies it to the Colossian situation. His readers
were converted pagans, formerly oppressed by the sins which
stained their pre-Christian lives, and 'dead' to the new life which
they began as believers (2:13). Now they have been forgiven and
renewed (2:13*b*) and given a new beginning to life with Christ
(2:10; 3:1–3). 'Walk' is a favourite Pauline metaphor, borrowed
from his Old Testament–Jewish tradition, for a way of life. Walk-
ing in old ways for these readers is replaced by the call 'walk (i.e.
live) in him' (2:6), and so lead a life which pleases the Lord (1:10).

8. The contrast 'then' (pre-Christian experience) and 'now'
(what believers have become) is a common one in Paul. See
P. Tachau, *'Einst' und 'Jetzt' im Neuen Testament*, Göttingen, 1972.
Here the contrast is made between the Colossians' old life and the
new order of life upon which they have entered as Christians who
have abandoned their former mode of behaviour. They have 'put
away' (Gr. *apothesthe*) the evil pursuits and pleasures of verse 5.
That list is now replaced by a new catalogue, comprising sins of

speech. This area of social intercourse by which men communicate
with their fellow-men is one indication that Paul's concept of the
'old nature' (v. 9) is as much corporate as it is personal. See
Moule, p. 119. Paul is describing the new life-style which belongs to those who have found their place in a new humanity,
renewed in Christ the 'last Adam'. And the quality of life in the
fellowship of Christian believers is to be seen in the abandoning
of coarse forms of speech and the anti-social character of a way
of living which they have decisively rejected when they put off
'the old nature with its practices'.

anger and **wrath** go together, with little to distinguish them (so
F. Büchsel, *TDNT* iii, p. 168). Both outbursts of human temper
are destructive of harmony in human relationships. **Malice** (Gr.
kakia) is a general term for moral evil and is used in passages
which depict the havoc to human society wrought by evil-
speaking (1 C. 5:8, 14:20; Rom. 1:29; Eph. 4:31). **Slander** is
literally 'blasphemy' (Gr. *blasphēmia*) which in this context refers
more to a defamation of human character than to a curse directed
to God. Any type of vilifying of man, whether by lies or gossip,
would fall into the category of this term. **Foul talk** is a word
found only here in the New Testament and suggests abusive
language whether as crude talk or as a recourse to expletives. The
range of 'sins of speech' is extensive in this verse, and Paul has
one final item to add to his unattractive cluster (see the next
verse). All these ways of destructive speech are to be resolutely set
aside as part of the old life.

9. The call **Do not lie** may seem to come as an anti-climax but
the social effects of untrustworthy promises and pledges are
enormous. Possibly this challenge belongs to tradition, which is
used to round off the list in verse 8. The same admonition occurs
in Ephesians 4:25. The exhortation seems to be restricted to an
application within the Christian community, and so its seriousness
is given a pointed reference. Lying leads to a breach of Christian
fellowship because it breeds suspicion and distrust and so destroys
the common life in the body of Christ (Rom. 12:4) by which we
are 'members one of another'.

The reason for an abandoning of evil ways is now provided.
**Seeing that you have put off the old nature with its prac-
tices** translates a phrase which begins with a Greek participle
apekdusamenoi ('having put off'). This is matched by a corresponding participle in verse 10, (Gr. *endusamenoi*, 'having put on').

All commentators agree that there is a baptismal motif in these verbs, taken from the activity of disrobing and re-clothing for the act of baptism when the new Christian entered the water. The reference in Galatians 3:27 clearly locates the experience as baptismal, though Paul is just as emphatic that every reader of his epistles should be able to appreciate the 'inner' significance of the outward act (*cf.* Rom. 13:12, 14; *cf.* Eph. 4:24).

The problem posed by these aorist participles, denoting a past event, is to know whether they continue the sequence of the admonitions or look back to baptism as supplying the occasion when the believer's renunciations of his old life were made. In the first view (stated by Lohse, p. 141) Paul is continuing the line of his appeal begun with the call, 'Don't lie', and stressing the obligation which his readers must face and act upon to give up the habits which belong to their old nature by stripping off all that pertains to their former life and replacing it with a new way of living. The participles carry an imperatival sense, in accord with common rabbinical and New Testament usage (see D. Daube, 'Participle and Imperative in 1 Peter' in E. G. Selwyn, *The First Epistle of St Peter*, London 1947, pp. 467–88).

The alternative view (shared by Abbott, Masson, C. Maurer in *TDNT* vi, p. 644, and argued for especially by J. Jervell, *Imago Dei*, Göttingen, 1960, p. 236) is to be preferred as being more in keeping with Paul's attested teaching. He is recalling the Colossians to their baptism and urging them to remember its dynamic effect in releasing them, as a consequence of their now confessed faith-union with Christ, from their old way of life. He proceeds to urge them, in this participial expression, to act upon that baptismal confession by being true to it, and to become in actual fact—by their renunciation and acceptance of their new life, given them as they were raised with Christ—what they were declared to be in their baptism. Earlier parts of this letter—to go no farther afield into the subject of Pauline ethics (see V. P. Furnish, *Theology and Ethics in Paul*, Nashville, 1968)—confirm this way of stating Paul's intention. He can hark back to the Colossians' decisive, life-changing entry into God's kingdom (1:3) when they shared in Christ's stripping off from himself the alien tyranny of demonic powers (2:11, 25). This event was their baptism (2:12, 13, 20) which inaugurated in union with Christ the Lord their Christian standing (3:1, 3).

This interpretation aids our appreciation of the puzzling term:

old nature (lit. 'old man' or 'old Adam') and **new nature** (correspondingly, 'new man', 'new Adam'). It seems clear that these are not terms of individuality but are corporate expressions denoting an old and a new order of existence. So Paul is calling upon his readers (as in Rom. 6:6–14) to have done with their old life-style and it habits, inclinations and goals, and to live as those who, at the beginning of their new life in Christ, entered a new world as members of a new humanity which is alive unto God. Nor should we forget that, while Paul may well be utilizing traditional forms of (catechetical) expression which were current coin in the early churches, there would be special relevance of this teaching to the men and women at Colossae who were puzzled over rival directions for the Christian way of life offered in the name of false teachers in their midst (2:16–23). Paul's answer and antidote is a simple declaration of the lordship of Christ and what it means to live under that rule. His readers (he reminds them) were those who professed allegiance to the Lord Christ in conversion and renewal (2:13). Let them now act out that profession in pursuing ethical ideals whose pattern is set by their life in the 'new Adam', the new segment of humanity which draws its life from Christ Jesus.

10. Paul's conscious use of the contrast 'old' and 'new' in reference to 'Adam' is carried over into his further descriptions. The **new nature . . . is being renewed in knowledge** (i.e. the ability to recognize God's will and command [1:9] and then do it) **after the image of its creator.** Genesis 1:26f. lies in the background of this text, with its allusion to God's design for man to know him in obedience, fellowship and love as his 'image'. Jewish interpreters of the Genesis text made the possession of the divine image in man an ethical incentive, so that man showed his unique relationship to God by obeying his voice and following his ways. There was also the hope that the splendour and glory, which mankind had lost in Adam's fall, would be restored (SB i, p. 11; *cf.* R. Scroggs, *The Last Adam: A Study in Pauline Anthropology*, Oxford, 1966). But rabbinical interest did not extend to the contrast between the old and new man. This is something new in Paul and there is no non-Christian parallel (Jervell, p. 240).

The **creator** is evidently God, but the image (in the light of 1:15) seems to indicate Paul's christological teaching. The 'new man' may then be taken to refer to Christ himself (so Lohmeyer) in view of Paul's teaching elsewhere (e.g. Rom. 13:14) that the Christian puts on Christ at baptism (Gal. 3:27). In this way

Christ becomes the prototype or ground-plan of the renewal, both in its inception and its continuance, of the new humanity which Paul saw emerging in the life of the Church.

11. Here (in the life of God's new people in the world 'in the realm of the new man', Dibelius–Greeven) **there cannot be** (there is no verb expressed in the Gr.) any justification for the divisions of the human race which were so pronounced in ancient society. The classification extends to divisions based on nationality (**Greek, Jew**), religious life (**circumcised, uncircumcised**) and social rank (**slave, free man**). The teaching of Galatians 3:28 is repeated and amplified, presumably according to the needs of the Colossian readers (though this is denied by Lohse who wants to see the verse as traditional. Jervell, p. 251, has maintained that the apostle 'took up the formula, but employed it for his special purposes').

The theological reason for Paul's teaching on equality in the Church is seen in 1 Corinthians 12:13. All members shared in a single baptism by which they are incorporated into a new humanity. So it is this 'new creation' (Gal. 6:15) which counts, not divisions based on accident of birth and social position or emphasizing religious badges which the coming of Christ has rendered invalid.

In the list **barbarian, Scythian** stand out. The former is a term for non-Greeks, who did not speak that language. But Paul's ministry was directed to them (Rom. 1:14) no less than to those proud of their Greek culture. And **Scythian** was a strange kind of barbarian (Lohse), down on the social and cultural scale, 'little better than wild beasts' (Josephus, *Contra Apionem* ii.269). The term was applied to tribes around the Black Sea, which yielded a wretched slave class. Hence Paul includes these, with a possible allusion to what he will later say in his treatment of masters and slaves (3:22–4:1). Magnificently, all these social stratifications and hostilities are removed in the assertion that **Christ is all** that men need to enter a new world, and he is **in all** irrespective of their former condition in the old world.

THE DISTINCTIVE CHARACTER OF THE CHRISTIAN LIFE 3:12–17

Paul's lofty teaching on the life-changing significance of a faith-union with Christ expressed in baptism (3:9, 10) may well have

sounded too idealistic and impossible for Paul's first readers. The
apostle therefore proceeds to make his appeal more specific and
practical as well as more clearly understood and pointed. He
moves from a list of affirmative virtues to be cultivated (v. 12)
through a statement of how the Christian will react to certain
human situations when his equilibrium is disturbed (v. 13) to a
reminder that his distinctive badge is one of love (v. 14). Christ's
peace will act as an arbiter when choices have to be made (v. 15).
The Church's worship will serve a dual purpose by aiding his
growth in Christian knowledge and fellowship with his brethren,
and also by giving him an outlet for praise (v. 16). Indeed, the
whole of life is to be brought under the aegis of his discipleship as
he performs his tasks in the spirit of devotion to Jesus Christ
(v. 17).

12. In a previous section Paul has accented the negative requirements of the gospel's moral call (3:5–9). 'Put to death',
'put away', 'put off'—these injunctions are couched in the serious
tone of self-discipline and ethical rigorism. Now it is time to turn
to depict the manner of living which belongs to **God's chosen
ones,** his elect. The transition is made with the use of a Pauline
then (Gr. *oun*, 'therefore') which clamps together his earlier
admonitions and his following statement of the consequences
which flow from what the baptized Christian has experienced.
The term *chosen ones* (Gr. *eklektoi*) belongs to Paul's favourite way
of expressing the truth that men do not become Christians simply
by choice and decision on their part (Rom. 8:33; 16:13. See for
these verses G. Schrenk, *TDNT* iv, p. 190). Underlying human
response is the free grace of God who takes the initiative and so
moves the human will that it finds its true freedom in willingly
surrendering to the divine call (1 Th. 1:4; 2 Th. 2:13, 14).

In the text of 3:12 the word **as** is not meant to distinguish
Christians from another group called 'the elect' (such as the
angels) but it is simply a way of emphasizing identity. Paul's
readers are to act as God's chosen people are meant to do.

In this powerful reminder of the Christian's standing before
God and the responsibilities it brings, Paul in fact is accomplishing
two objectives. As Lightfoot has shown, the three descriptive
terms—**chosen, holy, beloved**—are borrowed from the Old
Testament and transferred from Israel after the flesh to Israel
after the Spirit. Paul may have had his eye on some false teaching
at Colossae which claimed that an esoteric group of gnostics

alone had the key to the Old Testament. *Cf.* 2:11–13, 20–3. He had a deep sense of the continuity of God's purpose which ran through both Testaments and he saw the Church as the fulfilment of God's purpose declared in the Old Testament. As Israel had been chosen to be Yahweh's special people (Dt. 4:37; 7:7; Ps. 33:12), so Paul's teaching claimed that the new Israel of the Church was the successor to the divine purposes. The Church was the elect community—a title also found of the Qumran sect (1QpHab 10:13; 'God's elect'; 4QpPs 37.ii.5: 'the community of his elect').

His more obvious purpose was to remind the Colossians that their lives should measure up to their profession. Let them become in practice what they already were by divine calling and design.

Five moral qualities are listed. **Compassion** is literally 'a heart of pity', an expression formed from two separate words which are found side-by-side in Philippians 2:1, 'affection and sympathy'. H. Koester, *TDNT* vii, p. 556, regards this reference in Philippians as paving the way for the term in our epistle and postulates a literary dependence. But this need not be so, in view of an almost identical phrase 'heart of mercy' in the *Testaments of the Twelve Patriarchs* (Test. Zeb. vii.3) and Luke 1:78. The Greek word often rendered 'heart' is literally 'internal organs' (Gr. *splanchna*). In ancient thought the viscera were regarded as the seat of emotional life (of God, Isa. 63:15, as well as of man, Jer. 4:19; Phil. 1:8). The second word (Gr. *oiktirmos*) signifies the outward expression of deep feeling in compassionate yearning and action. See R. Bultmann, *TDNT* v, p. 159–61. So the composite term conveys the sense of a deeply felt compassion which goes out to those in need.

kindness and **lowliness** are a pair, matching the Christian's relation to others and to himself. Again, he will show a genial regard to other people and do his best to help any in need, though strictly *chrēstotēs* is 'a kindly disposition toward one's neighbour not necessarily taking a practical form' (Lightfoot, on Gal. 5:22). Other references in the Pauline corpus are 2 Corinthians 6:6; Ephesians 2:7, 4:32. The Pauline writings continually remark on the kindness of God shown to needy men and women (Rom. 2:4; 11:22; Eph. 2:7; Tit. 3:4) who in turn will want to reflect the same generous regard and interest in their dealings with other people.

lowliness is the same word as is normally translated 'humility';

earlier (2:18, 23) it had been used in a bad sense of false humility, meaning either 'fasting' or 'mortification' or else expressing a sense of inferiority which underlies the cult of angels in that thereby man is helplessly in their power (so W. Grundmann, *TDNT* viii, p. 22). Now Paul includes it in an obviously different way, to denote the Christian's appropriate attitude of self-regard, exactly as in Romans 12:3; Philippians 2:3f., in becoming neither haughty nor self-depreciating. True humility is, as Masson aptly says, 'the sovereign antidote to self-love which poisons relations between [Christian] brothers'.

meekness and **patience** are partners also (as in Qumran's teaching, 1QS iv.3: 'a spirit of humility, patience . . .') denoting the exercise of the Christian temper in its outward bearing towards others. So Lightfoot comments, and he proceeds to define the terms by their opposites. **Meekness** is best seen by contrasting it with 'rudeness', 'harshness'; while the opposite of **patience** is 'resentment', 'revenge', 'wrath'. More fully, we may say that **meekness** (Gr. *prautēs*) has two elements in it: (*i*) a consideration for others; (*ii*) a willingness to waive an undoubted right (as in 1 C. 9:12ff.). Considerateness is advocated in Paul's teaching elsewhere (see Gal. 6:1; 1 C. 11:33; 12:14, 15; Phil. 2:4) and is seen in his own character and behaviour (1 C. 4:6; Gal. 2:18). See L. H. Marshall, *The Challenge of New Testament Ethics*, London, 1946, p. 300; and F. Hauck and S. Schulz, *TDNT* vi, p. 650, who show that in contemporary hellenistic thought 'meekness' was regarded as a sign of weakness and had no virtuous character. It denoted rather a servile, cringing self-abasement.

patience is a picture-word suggesting 'long-temperedness'; it 'refers to the endurance of wrong and exasperating conduct on the part of others without flying into a rage or passionately desiring vengeance' (Marshall, p. 294). Only our cultivation of this last disposition will make possible the tolerance and the forgiving spirit, spoken of in verse 13.

Two comments on these Christian graces may be made. 'All five concepts show how a Christian should deal with his fellow man' (Lohse, p. 147), primarily within the Church's fellowship, as verse 13 shows. Then, in each instance, Paul's choice of terms seems dictated by the qualities which in the first place are appropriate to God's attitudes and actions. God in Christ is merciful, kind, humble, meek and long-suffering (Rom. 12:1; 2 C. 1:3; Rom. 2:4; Phil. 2:5ff.; 2 C. 10:1). Nothing could be clearer than

Paul's intention to hold up the divine character as a sublime model and to encourage his Colossian friends to catch the divine spirit. See the discussion in Jervell, *op. cit.*, pp. 251f.

13. The twin dispositions of **forbearing one another and ... forgiving each other** continue in the same vein. The occasion of the latter is given in the words **if one has a complaint against another.** It is hardly likely that Paul has in mind a concrete situation in the Colossian church. The reference is more general, though his choice of a rare Greek word rendered **complaint** (or 'reproach': Gr. *momphē*) is unusual. It is used only in Greek poetry (see Lohse). Perhaps, as Masson suggests, we should understand: 'if anyone has a grievance or grudge against another person'. Then, there is room for the exercise of these peace-making attitudes as Christians seek to curb their impatience with a difficult person and to show a charitable and forgiving spirit. The reason and justification for this conciliatory mood are of the highest: **the Lord has forgiven you.** The Lord is Christ himself (a variant reading in the text) who mediated God's forgiveness (2:13). It is characteristic of Paul to recall the self-sacrifice of Christ in his act of salvation in order to provide the motive-power for Christians to turn their bitterness into forgiving love. This is part of what has been called his 'conformity'–teaching, in which Christ's human life is not simply a model to be imitated by following in his earthly footsteps. On the contrary, Paul emphasizes the total impact of Christ's incarnation and especially his self-offering on the cross as providing a paradigm of a life-style to which the believer henceforth 'conforms' (Rom. 15:7f.; Eph. 5:2, 25, 29, *cf.* 4:32; Col. 3:13, are the texts given by N. A. Dahl in his essay, 'Formgeschichtliche Beobachtungen zur Christusverkündigung in der Gemeindepredigt' in *Neutestamentliche Studien für Rudolf Bultmann*, Berlin, ed. W. Eltester, 1957, pp. 3–9 [p. 7]).

14. The excellence of **love** as the Christian's distinctive dress is given special place as we may have anticipated from the writer of 1 Corinthians 13, Romans 13:8, 10, and Galatians 5:6. **Above all** may carry the thought of 'on top of all the other "articles of clothing" ' to be put on (v. 12) (so Moule). **Love** is the uniting force (Gr. *syndesmos*, lit. a bond or link which unites and gives coherence. This assumes a sense similar to the Platonic usage: see G. Fitzer, *TDNT* vii, pp. 857ff.) which holds all other virtues in place, gives them motive and meaning, and so produces the fullness of Christian living. **Love** gives cohesion to the perfect life by producing 'the perfect fellowship that ought to exist among Christian men. Love is the bond that unites them in a common service' (R. Newton Flew, *The Idea of Perfection in Christian Theology*, Oxford, 1934, p. 70). Another interpretation is possible (discussed by Lohse, pp. 148f.) in the light of the observation that Paul never regards love as a uniting force linking other virtues. The suggestion is to give a final or purpose meaning to the genitive *tēs teleiotētos* (**perfect harmony**). The thought then is that love acts as a bond that leads to or produces perfection. See for this rendering Moulton-Turner, p. 212, and G. Delling, *TDNT* viii, p. 79. Also compare H. Chadwick, 'All Things to All Men', *NTS* 1 (1954–5), p. 273.

Paul's thought is never narrowly individual and pietistic as though his chief design was to write a manual for the interior life of sainthood. His concern is ever with the Christians' corporate life, and the perfection he sets before his readers is attained only in the fellowship of believers whose attitudes and living together reflect something of the graces of verse 12 and the spirit of verse 13. The variant reading is verse 14 (Gr. *henotētos* in place of *teleiotētos*), though not as strongly attested textually, captures the apostle's thought. Love gives a cohesion to the Christian qualities of life and unifies them.

15. The need to have a Christian community living together in unison and tolerance is further stressed. What happens when strife and friction enter as disturbing elements? The umpire in any dispute is Christ's **peace**—both the peace he embodies and which he alone can give—which is the desired prize in all Christian relationships (Jn. 14:27). 'He is our peace' (Eph. 2:14) in the special sense of uniting Jews and Gentiles in the Church as both groups are reconciled to God. The call here is to allow no alien spirit to creep into church members' relations with their fellow-believers, which would destroy that 'peace'. Probably the Old Testament idea of 'wholeness', 'integrity', 'soundness' (implicit in the Hebrew term *šālôm* = peace) is in the background.

The harmony of the Church is God's will for his people. **To which indeed you were called in the one body.** To that goal they are called as the one body of Christ of which he is the appointed head (1:18, 24). As he rules in his house and settles every faction (**rule**, Gr. *brabeuein*, means 'arbitrate', 'give a verdict' in either a legal case or an athletic contest though the nearest parallel to this verse is the action of wisdom in Wis. 10:12: 'in his

arduous contest she gave him the victory'), so his peace is realized
in the Church's becoming in fact what it is intended to be by
God's design. It is nothing less than the coming into visible
reality of that new man of verse 10. A new society is born and
grows and is distinguished by a corporate life of 'wholeness'
affecting every dimension of the Church's existence in the world.
W. Foerster can therefore correctly designate the peace of Christ
as 'a kingdom in which the believer is protected' (*TDNT* ii,
p. 414) as long as he seeks the will of the King and is obedient to
the head of the body. **In your hearts** is Paul's way of issuing a
call which embraces the whole of life. 'Heart' in the biblical
literature 'is supremely the one centre in man to which God
turns, in which the religious life is rooted, which determines
moral conduct' (*TDNT* iii, p. 612). A man shows his response
by the measure of his acceptance of a life-style patterned on the
spiritual qualities of verse 12 and a forgiving disposition which
reaches out to any who bear him malice (v. 13).

And be thankful. As it stands, this call looks as if it is the conclusion of Paul's admonitions. But it is more than simply a summons
to an expression of thanksgiving. It is rather, as H. Schlier, *An die
Epheser*, Düsseldorf, 1957, p. 249, interprets it, an invitation to his
readers to be a thankful people who know what it means to be
called out of dark bondage into the light of a new relationship
with God (1:12f.) and into the rule of Christ in his body, the
Church. The call to be thankful is directly related to the new status
of Christians in the 'one body'.

16, 17. One assumption which is made in recent study of these
verses (along with the parallel verses in Eph. 5:19f.) would throw
light on the arrangement of the verses. This is that the call, 'be
thankful' (v. 15*b*), is not an appendix to what has gone before, but
a sort of rubric or heading indicating the next topic of catechetical
instruction. See J. M. Robinson, 'Die Hodajot–Formel in Gebet
und Hymnus des Frühchristentums' in *Apophoreta*, *Festschrift*
E. Haenchen, Göttingen, 1964, pp. 194–235, especially p. 225.
This part-verse is to be linked with 1 Thessalonians 5:16: 'Rejoice always' as a call to hymnic praise at the head of a list of
seven admonitions (1 Th. 5:16–22). What is notable is that the
free rein which is given at Thessalonica, with the warning inserted: 'Don't quench the Spirit', is restricted at Corinth in the
injunction that the spirits of the prophets should be subject to the
prophets (1 C. 14:32), and at Colossae a decisive shift is made

away from ecstatic and spontaneous hymnic speech in the direction of a more stereotyped and didactic form of church worship.
In Paul's latest description the emphasis falls more obviously on
the instruction given by the word of Christ (i.e. the missionary
message which centres in Christ, 1:5; 4:3); believers are encouraged to teach and admonish one another by the use of the
gift of wisdom (1 C. 12:8) and so to share in the apostolic task
(1:28). This looks as if it is deliberately aimed at the heretical
claim to 'wisdom', since **the word of Christ** speaks of Paul's
message which is the antidote to a false wisdom (2:23). While
singing is mentioned as a feature of corporate praise and thankfulness, a restrictive ban on freely created and ecstatic songs (sung in
glossolalia = by the use of a tongue?) may be seen in the way in
which such hymnody is subordinated to the ministry of teaching
and exhortation. And it is 'in the heart' and 'to God' that the
most meaningful hymns are offered—not by the use of a tongue
and expressed publicly in the full congregation which is assembled
for worship.

The oldest allusion to early Christian **hymns** is found in
1 Corinthians 14. There is evidence to show that the 'psalm'
(Gr. *psalmos*) in verse 26 was in the nature of an ecstatically-
inspired hymn of thanksgiving to God, as the worshipper was
caught up in an emotion of ecstasy and poured forth his praise
in blessing God. Nothing, however, is known of the content or
form of such spontaneous creations (see G. Delling, *TDNT* viii,
p. 500).

We may assume that **psalms** in our present verse carries the
same notion, though older writers (e.g. Lightfoot W. Lock,
'Hymn', Hastings' *Dictionary of the Bible* ii, Edinburgh, 1899,
pp. 440f.) thought that probably the Psalms of David would be
included under this caption. **Hymns** are sometimes taken to be
expressions of praise to God or Christ (so Lock) but the term is
general in the biblical literature and is used of any festive hymn
of praise (Isa. 42:10. LXX; 1 Mac. 13:51; Ac. 16:25; Heb.
2:12). See Schlier, *Epheser*, p. 247.

spiritual songs is a phrase which uses a general term for a
musical composition (Gr. *ōdē*) with its special meaning decided
by the adjective 'spiritual', i.e. inspired by the Holy Spirit. There
are characteristic references in the Book of Revelation to the songs
of the heavenly worshippers (Rev. 5:9; 14:3; 15:3).

It is very doubtful if these firm distinctions can be drawn, and no exact classification of New Testament hymns seems possible on the basis of the different words. See Delling, *loc. cit.*, p. 499, and *idem, Worship in the New Testament*, London, 1962, pp. 86f. The adjective **spiritual** may be taken to extend to all the terms, leading to the conclusion that it is the Spirit who stirs the worshipper and directs his thought and emotion in lyrical praise, whatever be the precise musical form. On such musical forms as were practised, see W. S. Smith, *Musical Aspects of the New Testament*, Amsterdam, 1962.

Another general conclusion is that the common motif running through the variety of liturgical expressions is thanksgiving to God (Col. 3:16, 17; Eph. 5:20; 1 C. 14:16; 1 Th. 5:18) whose mercy in Christ, his person and work, no doubt formed the chief theme of Christian canticles, to judge from Colossians 1:15–20 (*cf.* 1:12); Ephesians 5:14; Philippians 2:6–11; Hebrews 1:1–4; 1 Timothy 3:16; John 1:1–14 (to mention the outstanding specimens of New Testament hymns). See W. G. Doty, *Letters in Primitive Christianity*, Philadelphia, 1973, pp. 61f.

with thankfulness in your hearts to God. These expressions of praise are directed 'in your hearts'. This does not mean a silent worship in contrast to 'with your voices'. Paul is using the term 'heart' (as in v. 15) to cover the whole of man's being. 'Man should not only praise God with his lips. The entire man should be filled with songs of praise' (Lohse).

17. These hymns to God (v. 16) which centre on Christ's mission and accomplishment and exalted place lead on to the call to do everything **in the name of the Lord Jesus.** Singing gratefully (v. 16) matches **giving thanks to God through him.** He is seen as mediator and advocate; by his redeeming work and intercessory ministry he makes Christian worship possible and stands in the divine presence to gather up the Church's oblation of praise and present it to the Father (Heb. 7:25, 12:24; 13:15; 1 Pet. 2:5). The theme is one of praise to God through Christ rather than petition and supplication (so A. Oepke, *TDNT* ii, pp. 68f.).

Further, Paul's pastoral concern may have developed in a more positive direction by the time he came to write verse 17 of our passage. If the two passages (1 Th. 5:16–22 and our present section) are parallel, his earlier warning, 'Keep clear of every appearance of evil' (1 Th. 5:22), is couched in severely negative terms. Now he re-phrases this prohibition to offer a total stance towards life in positive tones: **Do everything in the name of the Lord Jesus, giving thanks. . . .** The name of the Lord Jesus is not a magical formula to be thoughtlessly appended to prayer. Nor is it anything to do with mystical fellowship. Nor is the meaning of **in the name** to be restricted to Christian liturgical praxis, as W. Bousset, *Kyrios Christos*, Nashville, ET 1970, p. 132, takes it in his remark, 'Paul is thinking essentially about what goes on in the worship life of the Christians', as though 'word' and 'deed' could be separated into the liturgical practices of 'preaching' and the Lord's Supper. No such special meaning of the phrase 'in the name of' seems intended. Rather Paul seems consciously to be drawing upon Jewish forms in this phrase. Rabbi Jose (*c.* A.D. 100) is credited with the saying, 'Let all thy deeds be done for the sake of heaven' (lit. 'in the name of heaven') (*P. 'Ābôth* ii.12). Rather 'the whole life of the Christian stands under the name of Jesus' (H. Bietenhard, *TDNT* v, p. 274). The new convert was baptized 'in the name of the Lord Jesus' in the Pauline churches (1 C. 6:11) and made his baptismal profession by invoking that name (Rom. 10:9, 10). The meaning of the 'name' in these contexts is seen in the way that the new Christian on his profession and admittance to the Church passed under the authority of Christ and became thenceforth his 'property'. In his new way of life he is simply making good his baptismal allegiance by placing the totality of his life under Christ's lordship.

Whether this change of emphasis is correct or not, there is no mistaking the ringing, life-affirming tenor of verse 17. The reference, then, should not be confined simply to acts of worship performed in a church service but embraces the whole of life. However, there is a sense in which every phase of life is an act of worship and all our activities, even the most mundane and routine, can be offered up as part of the 'living sacrifice' we are called upon to make (Rom. 12:1). See E. Käsemann, 'Worship and Everyday Life', in his *New Testament Questions of Today*, London, 1969, pp. 188–95.

FAMILY AND HOUSEHOLD DUTIES 3:18 4:1

'Without apparent transition Paul now addresses the members of the Christian family.' But we may query whether this remark of Masson's is correct. Is there in fact no logical connection between the two paragraphs? At first sight there seems to be none, and this apparent break in Paul's thought is appealed to by some scholars (e.g. Lohse) who maintain that he introduces here an independent section of admonitions drawn from contemporary ethical rubrics (so-called 'rules for the household'). True, there are several parallel sections in the New Testament (Eph. 5:22–6:9; 1 Tim. 2:8–15, 6:1–2; Tit. 2:1–10; 1 Pet. 2:13–3:7) which address practical counsels to husbands, wives, children, masters and slaves; and these draw upon maxims found in hellenistic popular philosophy, especially of Stoic origin (*cf.* Dibelius–Greeven, pp. 48–50). But we should recall how in his discussion of church worship (1 C. 14) Paul found it needful to include an injunction to spell out the general rubric: 'All things should be done decently and in order'. In particular, women members of the Corinthian congregation are counselled against speaking in public worship (14:33f.) and are summoned to be 'subordinate' (Gr. *hypotassesthōsan*). It is 'disgraceful' (1 C. 14:35) for their voices to be heard. Apparently Corinthian women, exploiting their freedom in society and their role in the church to pray aloud (1 C. 11:5–16), had gone to excess and were exercising and abusing a spiritual gift of tongues. Paul calls them to be subject to their husbands and to restrain their desire for knowledge by refusing to fathom deep mysteries (1 C. 14:34, *cf.* 14:2). Rather, let them consult their husbands in private. In a similar context, 1 Timothy 2:11 uses the same Greek term rendered 'submissiveness' (*hypotagē*) to caution women would-be teachers to keep silence in the church.

The inference is, then, that Paul's directory of public worship at Colossae is rounded off with a similar call. He has encouraged the Church to be attentive to the exercise of spiritual gifts, expressing thanks to God in song and profiting from a ministry of mutual exhortation and teaching. Now he will enter a cautionary reminder that order and decorum should mark out the conduct of women members. They should be subject (Gr. *hypotassesthe*) to their husbands in congregational assembly.

18. Wives, be subject to your husbands. The restriction is, however, of wider application; and we may remark that our understanding of a passage such as this is greatly enlarged by the discovery that Paul's thought moves in channels already cut out by both Jewish ethical teachers (e.g. Josephus, *Contra Apionem* ii.198–210, who gives a table of Jewish laws and prohibitions to do with marital relations, training of children, and love of parents)

and Greek popular philosophy. In particular, his language is
drawn directly from the teaching of the latter, with such characteristic phrases as **as is fitting** (this verse), 'what is pleasing'
(3:20), and 'justly and fairly' (4:1). But the important difference is
a twofold one. First, Paul grounds his teaching on a new basis of
obedience. Obedience to a person in his hierarchy of importance
is a reflection of a primary act of obedience to the heavenly Lord,
Christ. Then, his additional phrase **in the Lord** (3:18) indicates
that this is how a Christian should act and respond to others in a
'christianly' way which expresses a type of life suitable to those
who belong to Christ and are seeking to express his will in their
lives. That means, as Conzelmann remarks, that Paul's teaching
is one of principle and not timeless 'Christian' ethics, understood as legislation which is binding on all subsequent generations, irrespective of changing social conditions and developing
conscience.

In domestic relationships with their husbands and family,
Christian spouses are summoned to accept their place in the divine
ordering of family life (1 C. 11:3-9). A reason for being subject
to your husbands is supplied: it is **fitting,** i.e. socially acceptable
in that day. Attempts have been made to give a voluntaristic
sense to this call to obedience, but this can hardly be supported.
However, there is no harshness in the admonition as if Paul were
regarding women as inferior; he is appealing to an ordering of
society whose principle extends even to the Godhead (*cf.* 1 C.
11:3-9; 15:28). Paul is using here a Stoic maxim what insisted
that custom and usage determine in conduct which was 'the
right thing to do'. He christianizes it, however, with the phrase **in
the Lord.** It is part of the social order for her to take her appropriate place in society; indeed, Paul goes on, it is her Christian
duty (*NEB*).

19. Husbands love your wives. Husbands are reminded of
their responsibility: to love their wives. The splendid passage in
Ephesians 5:25ff. which takes its starting-point from this statement is not reproduced here; and in a sense what follows is a kind
of anti-climax. In neither passage are the wives commanded to
love their husbands (*cf.* Tit. 2:4), and the omission in the
Ephesians text is best explained in view of Paul's strict analogy
between Christ who loves the Church, and the Church which
obeys Christ. The warning **do not be harsh with them** is
a salutary reminder that Christian love is to be exercised in a

realistic fashion and should have a controlling influence on character and everyday living. In a strange quirk of human behaviour we can often injure thoughtlessly those we love the most; so Paul's caution is well taken: Husbands, do not be embittered (Arndt-Gingrich) against your wives by nursing resentment and harsh feelings (see W. Michaelis, *TDNT* vi, p. 125, who calls attention to Paul's prepositional phrase ['bitter *against* them'] which suggests that there was no cause on the wife's part to occasion that bitter feeling).

20. Paul's practical realism is again to the fore in his message to both children and fathers. **Children, obey your parents in everything** is a call modified by **for this pleases the Lord.** Children in the Christian household are called to act in a way which, above all, is acceptable and pleasing to the Lord. Actually Paul's Greek has 'in the Lord', and this seems to indicate that he is consciously qualifying a traditional maxim by this addition. And this is no exceptional case, for Paul uses the same word (Gr. *euarestos*, rendered elsewhere 'well pleasing') of the Christian's goal and motive in the entire range of his life (Rom. 12:1f., 14:18; Eph. 5:10; 2 C. 5:9). Indeed, this is his life's ambition (see commentary on Col. 1:10). The filial obedience of children is thus part and parcel of the total response which believers of all ages and positions make to the will of God which is 'noble, well pleasing and ideal' (Rom. 12:2).

21. Fathers, do not provoke your children. Fathers are bidden to do nothing which would alienate their children. Paul's word (Gr. *erethizein*) suggests a desire to irritate either by nagging at them or, more seriously still, by deriding their efforts and wounding their self-respect (Paul's verb keeps company with other hurtful associations in Epictetus, *Enchiridion* xx: 'when someone irritates (*erethizein*) you' refers back to 'the man who reviles or strikes you'). The net result will be that children become exasperated and 'give up' on their parents in despair of ever understanding their mentality. While it would be a liberty to suggest that Paul is speaking to a modern situation, his insights are pertinent and helpful. We should not overlook how revolutionary these counsels were in the ancient world. 'The sensitive understanding of children, with the realization that they might become discouraged and lose heart, is a striking feature of this new chapter in social history' (Moule).

22. The 'household code' embracing wives, husbands, children and fathers, has so far been expressed in short, lapidary statements, with a minimum of comment or justification for the commands given. Now Paul turns his attention to another familiar feature in contemporary society: the slaves. His teaching (like that in 1 Pet. 2:18–25) follows the line set in 1 Corinthians 7:21–4 (*cf.* Eph. 6:5–8) and is addressed to *Christian* slaves. Paul is not making a social comment on a prevailing custom. He is addressing himself to Christian readers. For a short discussion of the New Testament attitude to the social implications of slavery and freedom, see K. H. Rengstorf, *TDNT* ii, pp. 270–3.

The Church was born into a society in which human slavery was an accepted institution sanctioned by law and part of the fabric of Graeco-Roman civilization. The problem was not one of an acceptance of the institution *per se* or how to react to a demand for its abolition (which not even the epistle to Philemon hints at, though there may just be a veiled confidence that Philemon will in fact set free the Christian brother Onesimus, in Phm. 21), but the way slaves were to accept their status, and the treatment Christian slave-owners were to give to slaves in their control. The traditional teaching on which Paul draws in his earlier admonitions to wives, fathers and children, lacks this new dimension. So Paul must reformulate traditional moral teaching to meet the pressing need of how converted slaves were to act and how Christian masters were to treat their slaves.

No call is issued to overthrow the system of slavery and Paul's exhortations do not reflect any knowledge of slave uprisings in the past (e.g. in 73–71 B.C. Spartacus led gladiators and slaves in revolt). He gives no countenance to a means of ending slavery by violence. One reason for this refusal may well be that Paul's ethic rejects a retaliatory motif (Rom. 12:21, 1 C. 6:7). Then an advocacy of violent overthrow of slavery would have been suicidal as W. Bousset has perceptively noted: 'Christianity would have sunk beyond hope of recovery along with such revolutionary attempts; it might have brought on a new slave-rising and been crushed along with it. The time was not ripe for the solution of such difficult questions' (*Die Schriften des Neuen Testaments*, Göttingen, ii, 1929, p. 101). See further on Philemon, pp. 149ff.

With this in mind we shall not be surprised to hear the summons: **Slaves, obey in everything those who are your earthly masters.** It follows the line of the New Testament generally, which is a call to acquiescence and not to protest.

Instead, the sting is partly drawn from this inhuman practice by the slaves' attitude as Christians, as well as by the apostle's earlier statement (3:11) that in the Church all such social distinctions of 'slave' and 'free man' are cancelled out. Paul's characteristic stress falls in verse 24b: 'you are serving the Lord Christ.' This is a consciously attempted play on words: 'Slaves . . . you are slaves of your true Master, Christ.'

What it means to be a slave of Christ (the precise title given in Eph. 6:6) is spelled out with some pointed application. It entails serving the slave-owner with **singleness of heart,** i.e. in honesty, with no ulterior motives (Moule). This is best taken in conjunction with the preceding negative: **not with eyeservice, as men pleasers.** The ethic Paul insists on is therefore one of true motivation. The slave should be diligent in his tasks, even if no one is there to observe him and then to reward him for his hard work. The work should be done in a disinterested manner, with no desire to impress and so gain favour with the boss. Or else the Greek term, rendered **eyeservice** (*ophthalmodoulia*, a rare word found only here and at Eph. 6:6 and not at all before Paul's writings) may mean 'merely such service as can be seen', and so superficial (Moule).

But Paul is sufficiently pragmatic to know that some motivation is needed. 'Work for work's sake' is not his way of putting the case. **Fearing the Lord** is a gentle reminder that even when no human supervisor is checking on us, the great Taskmaster's eye sees all, especially the true motive and the hollowness of 'work outwardly correct but without the heart put in it' (Masson).

23. Whatever your task, work heartily, as serving the Lord and not men. The same call to do one's work faithfully and well is repeated, and an extra motive is given, with further motives added in later verses. The menial occupation of the slave is given a new dimension of dignity if it is seen as 'serving the Lord and not men'. This admonition picks up the earlier rubric of 3:17 that every activity is to be brought under the control of Christ's lordship. In this context the meaning is more limited. The purpose implicit in the words 'work heartily' (Gr. *ek psychēs*, lit. 'from the soul', i.e. with wholehearted endeavour, as in Mk. 12:30 par.) is to lift the slave's tasks above the realm of compulsive necessity (in any case he had no choice: either he must work or be punished for disobedience or idleness) and give it a new freedom. Some of the ennui and distaste would be taken out of his forced labour if he could offer even his servitude to the Lord as part of the cost of discipleship.

24. Paul's ethical instructions do not disdain the thought of reward. For the slaves earthly commendation is not to weigh (v. 22). What should be sought is the praise of his Master, the heavenly **Lord** from whom **you will receive the inheritance as your reward.** Perhaps Paul is attempting a second pun in his use of 'reward' (Gr. *antapodosis*); it is found only here in the New Testament. A similar term (Gr. *antapodoma*) is found in the Greek Old Testament and in Romans 11:9 in the sense of 'punishment', 'retribution', (see F. Büchsel, *TDNT* ii, p. 169) and this type of treatment is what the slave normally associates with the master's attitude to him. The Christian slave's heavenly *Kyrios* is different. He takes note of his servant's fidelity and will not allow it to pass without acknowledgement. He can be trusted to pay his 'reward' at the end of the day—not in rebuff or fault-finding, but in the granting of a share of his possession (as in 1:12), eternal life (Masson). This is a surprising thought since, under Roman law, the slave could never inherit anything. Paul would be familiar with the rabbinic teaching which praised God's fairness in rewarding his faithful ones: 'Faithful is thy taskmaster who shall pay thee the reward of thy labour. And know that the recompense of the reward of the righteous is for the time to come' (*'Ābôth*, ii.16). **you are serving the Lord Christ.** Is it an indicative (so Lightfoot and *RSV*) or imperative (so Moule, Lohse)? The latter is preferred, since the best texts do not supply a preceding 'for' (represented in *AV*) and the admonition picks up the train of thought of verse 23 (also imperative) and as well as preparing for verse 25 with a connective particle 'for' to give the reason for the summary in verse 24c.

25. For the wrongdoer will be paid back. The prospect of future reward needs to be complemented by the sober realization that evil slave-owners who treat their slaves as chattels and think only in terms of punishment and penalties will themselves be judged at Christ's tribunal. Only this interpretation, which sees a change of subject from the slaves to their owners, we believe gives a meaning to Paul's connecting 'For . . .' and adequately accounts for Paul's verb in the phrase the wrongdoer (Gr. *ho adikon*, lit. he who does unjustly, who violates the law). The question is, how could a slave with no legal standing 'act unjustly' against his master? A. Schlatter (cited by Masson) believes that the slave may have imagined that his wicked action had no importance in God's sight because he was a slave. But his view hardly explains Paul's verb. *NEB* suggests that it was by dishonesty, as Onesimus proved dishonest (the same language is used in Phm. 18: 'and if he has done you any wrong') in his master's affairs and apparently ran off with some of Philemon's money or property. But G. Schrenk (*TDNT* i, p. 160, n. 11) shows the difficulty with this view. Further, the continuation of Paul's instruction (4:1), that slave-owners are to give their slaves what is just and fair, suggests that the earlier use has in mind slave-masters who were defrauding their slaves, and it is they who are threatened with the sobering reminder that all injustice will be answerable at the divine court, and that God the supreme Judge has no favourites. **There is no partiality** with him. Partiality (Gr. *prosōpolēmpsia*, from a Heb. phrase 'to accept or lift up the face', to show favour) is an attitude to men in which God has no part, in the biblical account (Ac. 10:34, Rom. 2:11; Eph. 6:9; 1 Pet. 1:17). Inhuman masters will not be able to bribe their way out of a full exposure of their misdeeds. Moreover, this is the sense of the parallel counsel in Ephesians 6:9 (so Conzelmann).

4:1. The remedy is clear, **Masters, treat your slaves justly and fairly,** and is in the hands of the slave-owners themselves. While Paul does not advocate a wholesale abandonment of the system, he clearly points to an amelioration of the slaves' lot. The masters should treat their slaves in as human and humane a way as possible. This requirement would include fairness in treatment and an honest remuneration (perhaps implied in the verb rendered treat (Gr. *parechō*, lit. 'grant')), with the possibility that there should be no unduly harsh measures of repression or victimization of those in a helpless position.

Again, Paul lifts the slave-masters' gaze above the social structure. **Knowing that you also have a Master in heaven:** he reminds them that as earthly masters (Gr. *kyrioi*) they too have a heavenly Master (*kyrios*), the same Lord Christ whose slaves are in their control. 'If both [masters, slaves] realize that they owe obedience to the one Lord, so both have in hand the true standard for their conduct toward one another' (Lohse). And their common Master dispenses justice to all irrespective of social status and worldly influence. He does not turn a favourable glance in the direction of the rich and important people and will call these slave-owners to render account at the final day.

CALL TO PRAYER, AND OTHER ADMONITIONS 4:2-6

After addressing specifically the different members of the Christian household, Paul then turns to offer some general admonitions. There is a summons to prayer, which resumes the theme of 3:17, and his own special case is singled out for mention. Then, Paul glides into a general exhortation to the church members to let their conduct and their speech be in harmony with their profession.

2. Continue steadfastly in prayer. The verb 'to continue' (Gr. *proskarterein*) is one which belongs prominently to the New Testament vocabulary of the Church's devotional and 'liturgical' life (Ac. 1:14; 2:42, 46; 6:4; Rom. 12:12). It suggests a certain persistence and determination in prayer, with the resolution not to give up (Lk. 11:5-13) or grow weary (Lk. 18:1-8). The noun from the verb is rendered 'perseverance' in Ephesians 6:18. W. Grundmann (*TDNT* iii, p. 619) sees in these gospel texts a different attitude to prayer from that customary in Judaism, which had fixed hours and set patterns of prayer. This new practice, both spontaneous and personal, was a novel feature of early Christianity as a sign of its power and vitality (see A. B. Macdonald, *Christian Worship in the Primitive Church*, Edinburgh, 1934).

Two accompaniments of 'persevering prayer' are mentioned. These are the need to cultivate the wakeful spirit and the thankful heart. 'Watch and pray' was Jesus' advice to the disciples both in the Garden of Gethsemane (Mk 14:38) and in his eschatological admonitions (Lk. 21:34-6; Mk 13:32-7). The reminder **being watchful in it** (i.e. prayer) **with thanksgiving** may be taken in several ways. Is Paul simply remarking on the believers' general stance: be watchful to continue the practice of prayer at all times (so Lohse)? Or, is he reminding the Colossians of the need to overcome the tendency to drowsiness when the mind at prayer concentrates in a spiritual exercise? Or, can it be that his thought takes in an eschatological dimension (see the uses of the verb, *grēgorein* in relation to the *parousia*, given in A. Oepke, *TDNT* ii, p. 338) as he bids his readers be on the alert in expectation of the coming Lord (so Conzelmann)? If the third possibility is preferred, this gives a more pointed nuance to the encouragement to prayer. Paul is saying: Don't give up in your prayers for the coming of God's kingdom and pray in anticipation that the cry *Maranatha* (1 C. 16:22) will be heard. 'Our Lord, come' is to be your eager longing, and never let this hope (3:4) grow dim, when you are in danger of being enticed away from the hope (1:23) of the gospel which my colleagues brought to you (1:5). Rather, remain firm and thankful that this gospel is your inalienable possession. Thankfulness of spirit will then mark out the Christian's prayer, as he has in review the mercies and mighty acts of God in Christ, past, present and to come. **Thanksgiving** is a theme which recurs in this epistle (1:2; 2:7; 3:15, 17).

3, 4. pray for us also. The specific request is that this church will take to its heart the needs of the Pauline mission and accept some responsibility in intercession for Paul and his fellow-preachers (as in 1 Th. 5:25). Paul writes as a prisoner (4:18) under close surveillance and restricted in so far as an active ministry of public preaching is concerned. He is 'bound' in chains (as his Greek verb *dedemai* makes clear in the light of 4:18: 'remember my chains', Gr. *tōn desmōn*) and is not simply 'in prison'. The gist of his request is that, by the Colossians' prayer on his behalf, the door of active service, now closed by his confinement, may be opened once more, so that he may 'tell the secret of Christ' (*NEB*) in a plain, uninhibited way.

Some allusions here help us to form a picture of what life was like for him in his prison. Whether they speak decisively to the vexed problem of the place of his imprisonment is not clear. We discussed this matter in the Introduction.

One thing stands out. Paul was no social or political prisoner, paying the penalty for a crime. His imprisonment was **on account of** his message as a Christian preacher. That message is described here as earlier (1:26; 2:2) as **the mystery of Christ,** that is, a technical term for the message of God's saving purpose in Christ, which proclaims the 'joining of Jews and Gentiles in one body under the head Christ [as] a cosmic, eschatological event' (G. Bornkamm, *TDNT* iv, p. 820). That 'secret' (Eph. 3:3ff.) is now being disclosed by the apostolic preaching, but while Paul is the messenger primarily responsible for its manifestation, now he calls on the Gentile churches to accept their part in seeing that his ministry is not hindered. They are summoned to do this by praying that **God may open to us a door for the word.**

It is small wonder that Paul chafed under the strain of seeing the door of missionary opportunity closed. He uses this expression of a 'door' in 1 Corinthians 16:9 and 2 Corinthians 2:12 (cf. Rev. 3:8) to indicate the scope of his evangelistic and pastoral labours and a ready reception which was given to his preaching (the metaphor, taken to mean an opportunity presented for someone to exploit, is found in the Jewish rabbinic writings; see J. Jeremias, *TDNT* iii, p. 174). It is part of his life's work to use all available means to enter into strategic missionary territory (Rom. 15:17–29). His present captivity is a limiting factor, which he longs to see removed. Then, with his freedom regained, he can display (Gr. *phaneroun*: a unique term for Paul's preaching of the gospel) the wonder of God's mystery in Christ, which he knows to be his bounden obligation (as the 'eschatological apostle') to do (v. 4). For a possible historical setting, see the Introduction, pp. 27f.

Early Christian communities were conscious of a distinctive identity. Men and women 'belonged' to the Church, but not in an exclusivist sense as though they felt themselves obligated to withdraw from human society (cf. the Qumran community). Paul now addresses a short group of admonitions to the readers, showing how they should live 'in the world' of contemporary society.

5. Conduct yourselves wisely. The call is for wisdom in our dealings with those outside the Church. This means, as E. Lohse comments, to live such a self-scrutinized life that no cause for stumbling or misrepresentation will be placed in another person's way (1 C. 10:32). 'Wisdom' is contrasted with what is a false species (2:23) and means, in this context, an understanding of the divine will and a resolution to do it (as in 1:9f., 28; 2:3; 3:16). It is essentially practical and realistic.

making the most of the time. Every moment is a precious gift to be exploited and capitalized to the full. The verb in Paul's Greek phrase (as in Eph. 5:16) is drawn directly from the commercial language of the market place (Gr. *agora*). The Greek is *exagorazomenoi* where the prefix *ex* denotes an intensive activity, a snapping up of all the opportunities (Gr. *kairos*, a moment of truth and destiny) which are available at the present moment (see F. Büchsel, *TDNT* i, p. 128). Another possibility, supported by J. Armitage Robinson (*Commentary on Ephesians*, London, 1904, at Eph. 5:16), is to take the verb in its more customary New Testament sense: to 'rescue' the time from the evil condition in which the present has fallen. This may be a good suggestion for Ephesians 5:16 in view of the following reason: 'because the days are evil'. But the context in Colossians seems to require the sense of 'exploit', 'use to the full'. See further, R. M. Pope, *Studies in the Language of*

St Paul, London, 1936, ch. 5. The Christian's stewardship of time as God's priceless commodity is the teaching here, with a call to invest our energies in occupations which will be a positive and attractive witness to those outside the Church's fellowship. **Outsiders** refers to the non-Christian world, and carried a semi-technical meaning (cf. Mk 4:11; 1 C. 5:12f.; 1 Th. 4:12) derived from rabbinical Judaism where *ha-ḥiṣonîm*, 'those who are outside', refers either to heretics or to 'the people of the land'. See J. Behm, *TDNT* ii, p. 575.

6. The winsome life which draws other people is not insipid and dull. Conversation is the index here, especially when it comes to the Christian's advocacy of the good news in personal talking and dialogue. **Your speech** (Gr. *logos*) seems to be a deliberate recall of Paul's preaching of the 'word' in verse 3. Christians owe it to the message itself to present it in an attractive dress, since its clearest profile is one which has the grace of God much in evidence. Grace (Gr. *charis*) and **gracious** are two words so intimately related that it is difficult to separate them. The caution Paul expresses is a reminder that the manner of speaking is almost as important as the content, when it comes to the influence the believer exerts on his friends. So in 1 Peter 3:15 the way the Christians defend their faith is the subject of apostolic exhortation: 'do it in a gentle and respectful manner' (Bruce).

seasoned with salt is the literal sentence, expressing an idiom in current use (*cf. NEB*, 'never insipid'). Salt was used in seasoning food and in preserving it from corruption. Either way, Paul's use of this metaphor is suggestive. The use of salt as a preservative is in the background of such verses as Matthew 5:13; Mark 9:49, 50; Luke 14:34, and may be Paul's intention here. We may compare Ephesians 5:4 with its rebuke of all corruptive forms of speech. This is the positive side. Let your speaking act as a purifying, wholesome influence, rescuing the art of conversation from all that debases and perverts. Or, possibly Paul borrows from the rabbinic idiom which uses salt as a metaphor for instruction in wisdom. See W. Nauck, 'Salt as a metaphor in instructions for discipleship,' *ST* 6 (1952) pp. 165–78. 'The Torah is like salt' is a common comparison (SB 1, pp. 232–6; ii, pp. 21–3; iii, p. 631). The virtue of this view would be that it helps to explain Paul's following remark. Christian witnessing is to be gracious and to concentrate on God's offer in Christ of the wisdom of God (1 C. 1:24, 30; 2:6), so that those who hear our words may sense that we are

speaking to their need and matching their questionings with
God's provision in the message of his love and wisdom in Christ's
cross, as in 1 Peter 3:15.

PAUL'S PLANS AND GREETINGS 4:7-17

Paul now turns his attention to the Church's desire to know about
his own situation. In anticipation of the sending of the letter he
announces that this will be entrusted to Tychicus. Onesimus also
will be a bearer of news as he accompanies Tychicus on his
journey. Then follows a list of personal names as Paul looks around
him in his imprisonment and sends various greetings to Colossae
in the name of the men who are close at hand. The nearest
equivalent to this list is Romans 16, which also picks out a list of
names for personal greetings. Paul had a genius for friendship;
and the evidence of his many friends, colleagues and helpers is
seen in these two chapters. 'We cannot but infer from the tale of
his friendships that Paul the Christian Apostle had a magnetic
personality' (C. A. A. Scott, *Saint Paul, The Man and the Teacher*,
Cambridge, 1936, p. 19. E. Lohse, 'Die Mitarbeiter des Apostels
Paulus im Kolosserbrief' in *Verborum Veritas. Festschrift* Gustav
Stählin, Wuppertal, 1970, pp. 189-94, also draws attention to the
parallel list in Romans 16. But he uses Colossians 4:10-17 to
argue that the purpose served by these references is not to convey
simple greetings but to describe a situation after Paul's death
when the Pauline mission needed confirmation in the eyes of the
churches that it was true to the authentic apostolic gospel. These
men's names are the guarantee of the post-Pauline mission which
the churches should recognize. This conclusion drawn by Lohse
is, however, by no means obvious or compelling.)

7. The Colossians naturally would be deeply interested to
learn how the apostle was faring in prison. **Tychicus** will be his
messenger. He **will tell you all about my affairs.** But Paul does
not disclose in the letter the kind of life he is experiencing in
prison (*cf.* verses 8, 9).

According to Acts 20:4, Tychicus was a representative of the
churches of Asia who had accompanied Paul on his visit to
Jerusalem. His name is a common one in inscriptions which have
been found in Asia Minor. He was sent to Ephesus (according to
2 Tim. 4:12) in his native region, and there is another proposal

to send him or Artemus to Crete mentioned in Titus 3:12. In both instances he plays the part of Paul's envoy to the churches, as here in his visit to the Colossian church (*cf.* Eph. 6:21).

Three parts of a commendation follow. Tychicus is warmly described as **a beloved brother** (a normal Christian practice to emphasize the way Christians thought of themselves as part of God's family; *cf.* 1:2). **Faithful minister** picks up the Greek term *diakonos* to describe his personal service to Paul. From this word we get our title 'deacon', but at this stage of development the word denotes 'not the holder of a fixed office in the community, but anyone who discharges a specific ministry' (Lohse). In particular, Tychicus was Paul's right-hand man and aide-de-camp, and the epithet 'reliable' is Paul's commendation of him. Does **fellow-servant** (Gr. *syndoulos*) mean that Tychicus was actually in prison with Paul? Perhaps not, since the same description is given of Epaphras in 1:7, but the case of Aristarchus (v. 10) and Epaphras (in Phm. 23) raises the possibility.

8. I have sent him means that Tychicus will be the letter-carrier, and this is a special way in Greek (an 'epistolary aorist' tense is used) of attaching a covering note to a letter in which the bearer is mentioned. He will be able to supplement the contents of the epistle with verbal messages to reassure the readers that Paul is in good heart. So they will be encouraged. Also he will be responsible to drive home Paul's teaching to the community by 'admonishing' (another meaning of Paul's Greek verb, *parakaleō*) the Colossians (2:2).

9. Onesimus is returning to Colossae for a different purpose. He was presumably the runaway slave whose conversion and restoration to Philemon the slave-owner form the subject-matter of the epistle to Philemon. To be sure, there is no compelling reason why we should identify the Onesimus of our text with the man of this same name in Philemon 10 since this was a common name, especially of slaves (so Calvin who doubts the common identity). The name Onesimus means 'useful' and would often no doubt be a convenient way of identifying a nameless slave in the hope that he would justify his adoptive name by his hard work. But the customary inference that it is one and the same person is reasonable in view of the close verbal connections and name-links between the two epistles as well as the parallels with Ephesians 6:21f. The way Onesimus is commended suggests that his Christian profession is now assured by Paul and he is to be welcomed back to his native townsmen (he **is one of yourselves**) with every confidence and given a warm reception into the church fellowship.

10. The description **my fellow-prisoner** used of Aristarchus presents a knotty problem. If Paul's captivity at the time of writing is that at Rome, we may trace Aristarchus' presence there to his joining the party in Acts 27:2. Perhaps we are to imagine he was actually in prison with Paul—a conclusion argued for by Lohse on the score that no qualifying term (e.g. prisoner 'in the Lord', or 'of Christ', as Eph. 3:1; 4:1) is added. *NEB* gratuitously adds this extension in its phrase 'Christ's captive like myself'. See Moule for arguments in favour of this implied addition, giving to 'prisoner' a metaphorical sense. Paul's use may be simply dictated by his fondness for military terms ('prisoner' is really 'prisoner of war', so recalling 2 C. 2:14; 10:3–5) both here and in Philemon 23 where it is Epaphras who is Paul's fellow-prisoner (however, with an accompanying phrase 'in Christ Jesus') and in the following verse, Aristarchus is named without description (as in Rom. 16:7). See G. Kittel, *TDNT* i, pp. 196f. This name belongs to a man of Thessalonica (Ac. 20:4) whose Christian origins would then go back to Paul's mission in that area (Ac. 17:1–9). His visits to proconsular Asia are reported in Acts 19:29; 20:4 and he would be known to the Colossians to whom his salutations are sent. If the letter was written from Ephesus, Aristarchus' visits would be in the near future.

Greetings also came in the name of **Mark.** He is evidently not too widely known at this time; hence he is commended as **the cousin of Barnabas.** Barnabas, on the other hand, is well known. Paul's link with Mark went back to their first encounter on the missionary journey to Cyprus (Ac. 13:5) and beyond (Ac. 13:13). Over this defection at Perga and Mark's decision to turn back to Jerusalem (where he and his mother lived, Ac. 12:12, 25), Paul and Barnabas fell out (Ac. 15:36–41), and Mark found his future service in the company of his cousin. It is pleasing to note that Paul and Mark are again on friendly terms, while an even more moving display of reconciliation comes in 2 Timothy 4:11 where Mark is unhesitatingly commended as a faithful Christian worker. At this stage, Mark is perhaps only slowly winning back his reputation in the Pauline churches and needs the special plea of Paul: **receive him,** i.e. without censure or doubt, **if he comes to you.** The community has already **received instructions** about him, probably from another person, not Paul himself. Exactly what these instructions were is anybody's guess.

11. A third member of the trio is otherwise quite unknown to us. But he was a man of sufficient importance for Paul to identify him by his double name: **Jesus who is called Justus.** 'Jesus' was his Jewish name, and 'Justus' was probably added to distinguish him from other Jewish Christians who bore the name 'Jesus', itself a common name among the Jews (Ac. 13:6) until the time of the second century A.D. when it disappeared as a proper name on account of the conflict between the synagogue and the Church (see W. Foerster, *TDNT* iii, p. 286). It may be found at Philemon 23 if a conjecture regarding case endings is accepted: see the commentary there. The practice of a double nomenclature is well illustrated in the case of Paul himself (Ac. 13:9), and it is attested that many Jews took hellenistic names similar to their Semitic names (see Arndt-Gingrich, p. 381, and A. Deissmann, *Bible Studies*, Edinburgh, 1901, pp. 315f.).

These men are further identified as Jewish Christians, **men of the circumcision,** who are praised for their support of Paul's work **for the kingdom of God,** i.e. his concern to bring the gospel to Israel and to point to the hope of the Jewish people in their Messiah (Rom. 1:16; 9:1-5; 10:1). Paul never lost his interest in this side of the gospel's appeal, temporarily frustrated because of Israel's disbelief (Rom. 11:25), though his special vocation to the Gentile world alienated him from his fellow Jews. It is not surprising that the three men mentioned are so few in number that they can be named. Exactly what is meant by the designation **men of the circumcision** has been discussed. Perhaps they were Jewish Christians of a particular stamp who took a non-proselytizing attitude to the law and co-operated with Paul in evangelizing the Jews on the basis of that law. See for this view E. E. Ellis, ' "Those of the Circumcision" and the early Christian mission', *Studia Evangelica* 4 (1968), pp. 390-9, who describes the apostolic tribute to these Jewish Christian preachers as an acknowledgement of 'a venture in ecumenical Christianity' (p. 396) as 'Paul and certain Hebrews were pursuing their distinctive missions in a co-operative fashion'. At all events, their faithful presence was especially gratifying to Paul. They have been a **comfort** (Gr. *parēgoria*—a touching word, found on grave inscriptions and used of consolation in the face of death's reality; see Moulton-Milligan, *Vocabulary*, *sv*) to him.

12. Paul now calls upon **Epaphras** to send his greeting. He has been linked with the Colossian church, presumably from its inception, and was apparently sent there by Paul (1:7). He came to Paul with news of the church's good order (2:5) in the face of stern conflict with false teaching (2:8ff.). Epaphras was a native Colossian and, like Paul, a slave of Christ in his service. Only in Philippians 1:1 does the title **a servant of Christ Jesus** appear again, there in reference to Paul's colleague, Timothy.

During his absence from the city, Epaphras' ministry had been one of prayerful intercession. Nor was this ministry taken lightly. He had 'laboured' (*RSV* gives **remembering you earnestly,** which is decidedly weak for the Gr. *agōnizomenos*) in his supplication, says Paul, using a term at the heart of which is the word for conflict and struggle (*agōn*). We are perhaps meant to take this term in a specific way. It is possible that Epaphras had come to seek Paul with news of the Colossian church and, finding him imprisoned, had himself been arrested and so had become the apostle's 'fellow-prisoner' (Phm. 23). Support for this understanding of Epaphras' conflict may be seen in 1:29 where Paul endures the same struggle. Perhaps in both instances it is conflict with the authorities or Jewish opposition (1 Th. 2:2) which has landed both men in prison (so E. Stauffer, *TDNT* i, p. 138, for this view of a physical hardship). But most commentators (Dibelius–Greeven, Lohse) take the noun to mean strain and effort for the Church.

Whatever it was, Paul knew this trial in his own ministry (see 1:29 where 'striving' translates the same Greek participle *agōnizomenos*). Nor should we overlook, with the reminder of Moule, the description of Jesus' Gethsemane prayers, in Luke's version: 'And being in an agony (Gr. *agōn*) he prayed more earnestly' (Lk. 22:44, cf. Ac. 12:5; Rom. 15:30).

The theme of Epaphras' petition for his congregation is set in true pastoral style. It is that they should attain to a maturity and conviction which will be an assurance to him that they are standing firm in the apostolic gospel. The choice of words seems clearly to reflect the situation at Colossae which threatened the infant community there.

The key lies in the second verb **that you may stand . . . fully assured in all the will of God** (Gr. *peplērophorēmenoi*). We have met several related forms of this participle earlier in our epistle (1:9, 19; 2:9, 10) and we may recall the teaching on 'fullness'

(Gr. *plērōma*) which runs through both the heresy and Paul's antidote. Paul has shown that the divine essence resides totally and without remainder in Christ, and that in him believers have come to fullness of life. Paul's prayer is that these Colossians may be filled with the knowledge of God's will in all wisdom and perception taught by the Spirit. And it is a further endorsement of the same teaching that Epaphras prays that they may be 'fully convinced and certain' of the truth of Paul's gospel. This is one meaning of the Greek verb *plērophoreisthai*. So Dibelius–Greeven and Moule. But it may equally be taken as equivalent to the verb 'to be filled'. Then it is Paul's counterblast to the teaching of the philosophy, and his answer is that, as Epaphras' prayer is answered, so the Colossians will be 'filled with everything that is God's will' for them. See G. Delling, *TDNT* vi, p. 310. In this way they may attain to perfection (Gr. *teleioi*, a term evidently chosen to counteract the gnostic aspiration to 'perfection' by their regimen and cult) and fullness of life (2:10) which will confirm them in apostolic truth and not permit them to be drawn away to erroneous ideas. **Mature** is 'perfect' (Gr. *teleios*) with the idea, taken directly from the Old Testament (Dt. 18:13; 1 Kg. 8:61; 11:4, 10; 15:3, 14, etc.) and Qumran literature (1QS iii.9f.), of obedience to God's will in practical living and not a speculative notion of attaining to a mystical experience by secret knowledge (*gnōsis*) or endowment of 'spirit' (*pneuma*), as in gnostic thought. The pastor's prayer, like the apostle's teaching, is aimed at offering a counterview to the 'philosophy' (2:8) lurking at the threshold of the church door. For the close correspondence in language between Epaphras' pastoral concern and that of Paul's missionary *agon*, see V. C. Pfitzner, *Paul and the Agon Motif*, Leiden, 1967, pp. 125f.

13. Just exactly how Epaphras had worked hard for his people is not clear. Perhaps Paul is continuing the idea of his labours in prayer, which included in their scope all the churches of the Lycus valley. Or, possibly, it is that Epaphras had done his best to answer the claims of heresy before he left his 'parish' to seek the counsel of Paul as to how best to answer the heretical propaganda (so Lohmeyer). There is no suggestion that Epaphras had deserted his post and needed to have his actions justified by Paul in spite of his 'short-lived defection' (Masson, who surmises that Epaphras failed because of incompetence to meet the arguments of the heretics and deserted the church). Paul's testimonial is rather that he has done his best in a difficult situation and cannot

be blamed if the answer to the false teaching needed a more
thorough treatment than he was competent to supply. The most
we can say with confidence is that Paul here pays him a fine
tribute and confirms that he has always had a deep concern for
the churches in the Lycus valley. For **Laodicea** see on 2:1 and
4:15, 16. For **Hierapolis** see W. M. Ramsay, *Cities and Bishoprics
of Phrygia*, vol. 1, Oxford, 1895, pp. 84ff.

This tribute to Epaphras forms an important part of W.
Marxsen's thesis (in his *Introduction to the New Testament*, Oxford,
[ET 1968], pp. 177ff.) in regard to the origin and purpose of this
letter. He sees that one of the chief reasons for the letter is to
supply an apostolic authorization of Epaphras whose teaching is
claimed to represent the mind of Paul. He argues that Epaphras
is thought to stand in an apostolic succession, now that the apostle
Paul is no longer alive (p. 180). Hence, the letter derives from a
post-Pauline period and reflects a developed ecclesiastical situation,
characteristic of the 'early catholicism' of the sub-apostolic age.

To read this type of role for Epaphras out of these two verses is
really a *tour de force* and to argue that Epaphras is recognized by
Paul as a fellow-servant who works in the church 'in the place of'
the apostle (from 1:7) is to confuse the ministry of Epaphras the
'deacon' with that of Paul himself as apostle to the Gentiles.
There is no suggestion of apostolic succession anywhere in this
epistle, where even Paul's apostolic claims are never explicitly thrust
to the fore. Paul calls himself a 'deacon' (1:24) and looks upon
Epaphras as a fellow-servant of Christ, along with Tychicus (4:7).

14. Luke and **Demas** are two names which recur in 2 Timothy
4:10, 11, but with obvious differences. Here **Luke** is called **the
beloved physician.** This has given rise to some speculation
(voiced by Lohmeyer and G. H. P. Thompson) that he was Paul's
attending doctor, but this is without foundation, and Philemon
24 calls him simply one of 'my fellow workers'. The profession
Luke had was so unusual that Paul comments on it and this
became an accepted part of Church tradition. The anti-Marcionite
prologue to Luke (c. A.D. 170) calls him 'a physician by profession'
and places his origin in Antioch. Jerome says the same: 'Lucas
medicus Antiochensis'. It is more doubtful, however, if we should
conclude from this verse, which separates him from Jewish
Christians (in vv. 10, 11), that he was a Gentile Christian, as is
popularly thought, mainly on the basis of this verse. There is
considerable evidence to argue the case that he was a hellenistic

Jew. See E. E. Ellis, *The Gospel of Luke* (New Century Bible), 1966, pp. 52f., drawing upon the pioneering work of E. C. Selwyn, *St Luke the Prophet*, London, 1901, and in *Expositor* (7th series) 7, 1909, pp. 547ff. If this is possible, it becomes equally feasible that he is to be identified with the Lucius of Romans 16:21 (so Deissmann).

Demas is passed over with a bare mention, but a consequence of this man's failure under trial is given in 2 Timothy 4:10. The fellow worker of Philemon 24 had deserted Paul at the time of his great need and returned to Thessalonica (his home?).

15–17. This short section stands out for a variety of reasons. For one thing, Paul now switches from conveying greetings to the Colossians on behalf of other people to a mention of his own greetings. In particular, he salutes the church at Laodicea and picks out the household of **Nympha**. The Greek name underlying the masculine Nymphas is Nymphodorus and the abbreviated form is uncertain. There is a textual uncertainty in the phrase 'in her house' (read by B, the harklean Syriac, Origen, 'Ambrosiaster'). Some authorities (the Byzantine and Western authorities) read the masculine pronoun (Gr. *autou* in place of *autēs*). This would make the name a man's name, which many commentators accept. Modern translations (*RSV*, *NEB*, *Jerusalem Bible*) opt for a feminine Nympha and render **the church in her house.** Lightfoot admits that, on face value, this is correct, but 'a woman's name . . . hardly can be so' because 'a Doric form of the Greek name here seems in the highest degree improbable'. This denial has been countered by J. H. Moulton who sees the alpha-ending in Nympha to be a true feminine form (*ExpT* 5(1893–4), pp. 66f.; *A Grammar of New Testament Greek*, vol. 1, Edinburgh, 1908, p. 48). But the case for Nymphas as a man's name is strongly presented by Moule, p. 28, n. 1, and Masson, *ad loc.* Lightfoot suggests that the original reading was *autōn* (for which there is some manuscript evidence in the Egyptian text) and that the original text read 'Nymphas and his friends'. Subsequent copyists altered this, not perceiving the classical constructions, some in the direction of Nymphas and others of Nympha. Perhaps the two names represent those of a married couple whose house was a meeting-place for Christian worship, a proposal made by F. Mussner, *Der Brief an die Kolosser*, Düsseldorf, 1965, *ad loc.*

The use of the home for Christian assembly is well attested in the New Testament period. In addition to the house of Nympha in Laodicea we know that in nearby Colossae Philemon's house was similarly used as a meeting-place (Phm. 2). At Philippi there was Lydia's home to which Paul resorted (Ac. 16:15, 40) and at Corinth Gaius is spoken of as 'host . . . to the whole church' (Rom. 16:23). Aquila and Priscilla seem to have made their dwelling-places available for Christian purposes both in Ephesus and Rome (1 Cor. 16:19; Rom. 16:5).

About these 'house churches' we know little. Christians were driven to meet in private homes out of necessity. Not until about the middle of the third century did the Church begin to own property for the purposes of worship (so O. Cullmann, *Early Christian Worship*, London, 1953, p. 10).

15. Give my greetings to the brethren at Laodicea. It is an unsolved problem of Paul's letters to the churches why he should single out these members of the Laodicean church for greeting when, on the usual view, he was writing separately to that church (v. 16). Perhaps, with Dibelius–Greeven, we should say that he wished to cement relations between the two churches in this way.

16. We have little definite information about the structure and content of early Christian worship. In this area of study every scrap of data is precious; and it is this fact which gives special importance to our verse. We learn that Paul expected that his letter would be read out to the assembled church, presumably at worship (see L. G. Champion, *Benedictions and Doxologies in the Epistles of Paul*, Oxford, n.d.). He advised that it should then be passed on to the Laodicean congregation for similar treatment there. Also there would be an exchange of letters by which his 'letter to the Laodiceans' would find its place as a document to be read out to the Colossians. To this practice, which involves both the distribution and public reading of Paul's letters (further attested by 1 Th. 5:27 and Phm. 2), we may trace one factor in the rise of canonical authority which came to be attached to these pieces of pastoral correspondence (see Polycarp's *Letter to the Philippians* iii.2). The reference in 1 Thessalonians 5:27 is important since it shows that the practice of reading aloud the Pauline letters during worship was established early. Thus Marxsen's further argument (*op. cit.*, p. 185)—that the public reading of Paul's epistolary correspondence is a mark of sub-apostolic Christianity—in favour of a later post-Pauline dating of the epistle falls down.

Not all these letters to the churches have survived. A case in point is the document here called 'the letter from Laodicea'. Obviously it is a Pauline composition sent in the first place to the church at Laodicea. The meaning of the preposition 'from' (Gr. *ek*) in the sentence **see that you read also the letter from Laodicea** is 'the letter that is at Laodicea' (Blass-Debrunner-Funk, *A Greek Grammar of the New Testament*, Cambridge, 1961, section 437) and is to be sent on from there to Colossae. It cannot mean, as some Church fathers (Theodore of Mopsuestia, Theodoret) supposed, a letter from the Laodiceans to Paul. Paul wishes that it should be circulated among the churches, or at least that it should be communicated to the Colossian assembly. He evidently thought that its contents were worth preserving and were appropriate for the Colossians to read. But did the church either at Laodicea or Colossae think the same? Were they willing to allow this document to drop into oblivion and perish, and to permit this *not* to happen in the case of what appears a much more ephemeral document, the note to Philemon?

Reluctance to draw this inference that the letter has been lost has motivated some interesting proposals. One view (first stated by John Mill in 1707: see Bruce *ad loc.*) is that the letter so described is really our epistle to the Ephesians (as in the canon of Marcion, which gave the title 'To the Laodiceans' to Ephesians in its list). Another view sees in the epistle to Philemon the presence of this letter, but it is rather the case that Philemon lived at Colossae (see Col. 4:9 for Onesimus as a slave of Philemon at Colossae), not Laodicea. No extant Pauline composition seems adequately to fit the description, and we are left with the inevitable conclusion that the letter to the Laodiceans has not survived. Perhaps it perished accidentally, being destroyed during the earthquake in the Lycus valley in A.D. 60–1 (so P. N. Harrison, 'Onesimus and Philemon,' *ATR* 32 (1950), pp. 268–94). Perhaps the letter was meant for a splinter group of the Laodicean church which resided in Colossae (so W. Schmauch in Lohmeyer's commentary, *Anhang*), and was destroyed once the church at Laodicea was united. But can we go further, and submit that it did not survive because it was deliberately suppressed, perhaps because its contents were critical (like an earlier letter from Paul to the Corinthians, written 'out of much affliction . . . and with many tears', 2 C. 2:4?) or because the Laodicean church, at the time when Paul's letters began to be assembled into a corpus, had

come under the judgement of Revelation 3:14–22 and had lost
its Christian character? We cannot tell. A full discussion of all the
possibilities provoked by this verse, including a treatment of the
apocryphal epistle which goes under the name of the epistle to the
Laodiceans, is given by Lightfoot, pp. 272–98. More recently,
C. P. Anderson, 'Who Wrote "the Epistle from Laodicea"?'
JBL 85 (1966) pp. 436–40, has sought to solve the set of conun-
drums posed by the existence of a lettter which will be relevant to
the Colossians as much as to the Laodiceans but which is distinguished from the Colossian epistle; by the disappearance of
the second letter and its consignment to oblivion; and by the fact
that we are unable to discover a sufficient motive for Paul's
writing the second letter. He submits that there is only one
circumstance which can account for all these facts, *viz.* that it was
Epaphras who wrote the epistle to the Laodiceans in view of his
inability to accompany Tychicus on the return to the Lycus River
valley (Phm. 23). The main hesitation we have with this theory
is the need to explain why Paul does not say explicitly that it is
not his epistle in question, but Epaphras'.

17. Archippus was a member of Philemon's household
(Phm. 2), possibly his son. He is personally addressed at the close
of the letter with a strong admonition to make good the service to
which he has been appointed. **See that you fulfil the ministry
which you have received in the Lord.** As with Tychicus'
designation as a trustworthy 'deacon' (Gr. *diakonos*) in verse 7, so
here we should interpret Archippus' 'diaconate' (Gr. *diakonia*) not
as a regular ecclesiastical office but as a specific task committed to
his hands. He is encouraged by Paul's words to fulfil his responsibility in the 'discharge of certain obligations in the (Christian)
community' (H. W. Beyer, *TDNT* ii, p. 88). We have no means
of knowing for sure what this task was. Possibly it had to do with
the collection for the Jerusalem church. This is a likely suggestion
if the Colossian letter was written during Paul's Ephesian ministry.
Paul often dignifies this responsibility as a service (Gr. *diakonia*):
2 Corinthians 8:1–6; 9:1, 12f.; *cf.* Acts 11:29f.; 12:25.

John Knox, *Philemon among the Letters of Paul*, Nashville, 2nd
edn 1959, however, has made this verse something of a lynch-pin
for his theory that Archippus played a decisive role in the release
of Onesimus. On his view Archippus was the slave-owner and the
main body of the epistle is addressed to him. Paul's recommendation to Archippus in that letter is pithily summed up in the

Colossian verse: the 'ministry' he has received is a roundabout way of reminding him of his duty imposed as a Christian obligation (**in the Lord**) to allow Onesimus to return as a free man to Paul. It cannot be said that this reading of the text is convincing. See further comments on Knox's theory, pp. 151ff.

We may only guess that Paul's personal encouragement to Archippus had to do with the local situation at Colossae. If Paul was still apprehensive about the threat to the church from heretical teaching and had some reserve about Epaphras' ability to deal with the matter on his return, then this is an appeal to the man on the spot to bend his efforts and do what is needful (his 'ministry') to defend the gospel against this propagandizing movement. This is then a call for Archippus to accept as his bailiwick the pastoral responsibility formerly held by Epaphras.

FINAL WORDS 4:18

18. I, Paul, write this greeting with my own hand. Remember my fetters. Grace be with you. Paul's letters were normally written by the hand of a scribe (Rom. 16:22 names Tertius as one such amanuensis) at the dictation of the apostle. See C. F. D. Moule's discussion, *BJRL* 47 (1965), pp. 430f. At this point in his letter-writing he himself takes over to append a personal message and final greeting, as he apparently does at Galatians 6:11; 1 Corinthians 16:21. It may be that this was to be seen as a mark of affection and personal interest, especially if the church at Colossae felt in some way disgruntled because Paul had not been able to visit them in person. See the commentary on 1:24; 2:1.

But a more sinister reason for this apostolic autograph may be sought. We learn from 2 Thessalonians 2:2 that Paul had to reckon with letters forged in his name which were being sent out to his congregations. One way in which he answers these forgeries was to append his own signature to the genuine letter as a token of authenticity (2 Th. 3:17: 'this is the mark in every letter of mine; it is the way I write'). It becomes just possible that there was this need at Colossae—and especially when letters from Paul would be circulating among the congregations of the Lycus valley—to safeguard Christians against the risk of giving heed to spurious documents, purporting to represent Paul's mind. So he adds a personal word **with my own hand,** exactly as he had done in 2 Thessalonians 3:17.

The call to **remember my fetters** matches this situation. 'The reference to "bonds" is not chiefly a matter of pathos but of authority' (Moule), and Paul is not morosely inviting his readers to spare a tender thought for him in his distress. Rather, he is summoning them to respect his authority (as in Phm. 9) as a prisoner for the gospel's sake and on behalf of the Gentiles whose interests he has at stake in his apostolic sufferings (1:23–5). He lies in prison on account of his vocation and because he will not surrender his commission to be an apostle and teacher of the Gentiles. The appeal to his fetters is therefore a powerful incentive which he calls into play that the Colossians should give heed to his teaching and not yield to the heretical doctrine which encroaches upon them. 'Remembrance' (see O. Michel, *TDNT* iv, pp. 682f. for the sense 'recognize', 'acknowledge') does not mean in this context primarily an invitation to pray for the apostle; it is more an obligation to heed his apostolic instruction and to honour him by remaining firmly committed to it in the face of those who would lead them astray from his gospel (2:4, 8).

Grace be with you is his closing note. With extreme brevity and economy of words he expresses the confidence that God's grace will sustain and defend his church. Epaphras, their minister, joins him in the same heartfelt wish (4:12). God's keeping power will see to it that, if they are faithful and fixed (1:23), the church will continue to enjoy the benefits of that gospel he has brought them in the person of his delegates. But human fidelity and perseverance are not enough. As Photius remarked in his ninth-century commentary, quoted by Lohse, 'They need grace to be saved; for what could a man do apart from grace?'

INTRODUCTION
to
Philemon

INTRODUCTION TO PHILEMON

1. THE OCCASION AND PURPOSE OF THE LETTER

This is the shortest of the letters which go to make up the Pauline corpus, and consists of 335 words in the original Greek. It is the only example in the extant Pauline correspondence of what may be termed a personal note (cf. C. H. Dodd, Introduction in *Abingdon Bible Commentary*, Nashville, 1929, p. 1292), although both E. Lohmeyer (*Kommentar*, pp. 171ff.) and Théo Preiss ('Life in Christ and Social Ethics in the Epistle to Philemon', *Life in Christ*, London, 1954, pp. 33f.) have drawn attention to the way in which the letter opens, associating Timothy with Paul and associating with Philemon the whole church which assembles in his house. They take these details to mean that the document is an 'epistle' (i.e. a document intended for a public hearing. A. Deissmann's attempt to classify Paul's correspondence as private communications [see *Light from the Ancient East*, London, 1927, pp. 230–302, 409] is now generally conceded as having failed. For a critique of Deissmann, see W. G. Doty, 'The Classification of Epistolary Literature', *CBQ* 31 (1969), pp. 185ff.) in which Paul writes in full awareness of his apostolic authority. This is confirmed by verse 9 in which the translation, 'Paul, an ambassador' (Gr. *presbeutēs*) is to be preferred to 'Paul, an old man'. In short, this brief epistle is to be seen not so much as a private letter of Paul as an individual (*Privatmann*) but as an apostolic letter about a personal matter (so U. Wickert, 'Der Philemonbrief—Privatbrief oder Apostolisches Schreiben?', *ZNTW* 52 (1961), pp. 230–8) or as J. Knox, *Philemon among the Letters of Paul*, Nashville, 2nd edn 1959, p. 59, expresses it: 'a letter to a church, embodying (would we say, "inclosing"?) a letter to an individual'. But it still remains true that the individual in question (Philemon) is seen as a member of the corporate fellowship of Christians all of whom have an interest in his decision.

The occasion of the letter may be inferred from its contents even though some details are obscure. A slave named Onesimus had wronged his owner Philemon who was a Christian living at Colossae (vv. 1, 2; *cf.* Col. 4:9, 17 with the other person named in the praescript) and had run off. Onesimus had in some way come into contact with Paul, either as a fellow prisoner or because he had sought refuge in Paul's company. In the latter event, it has been proposed that he could have benefited from Athenian law by which a runaway slave could seek asylum in the home of a friend at the family altar (see E. R. Goodenough, 'Paul and Onesimus', *HTR* 22 (1929), pp. 181–3). This provision was widespread throughout the empire (see F. F. Bruce, 'St Paul in Rome: 2. The Epistle to Philemon', *BJRL* 48 (1965–6), p. 89), and it may throw some light on Onesimus' desire to seek Paul's protection, though it is difficult to explain verse 13 in view of the further requirement that a delinquent slave must be sold, if he refused to return to his former owner.

The nature of the slave's offence is not certain. It is usually assumed that he had stolen money and then absconded (v. 18). But as Roman law required that whoever gave hospitality to a runaway slave was liable to the slave's master for the value of each day's work lost, it may be that Paul's promise to stand guarantor (v. 19) is no more than the assurance to Philemon that he will make up the amount incurred by Onesimus' absence from work. For this background see the fragmentary papyrus (*The Oxyrhynchus Papyri*, vol. 14, ed. B. P. Grenfell and A. S. Hunt, London, 1920, pp. 70–2) dated A.D. 298. The entire note, as reconstructed and translated by the editors, is worth quoting in full:

> Aurelius Sarapammon, called Didymus . . . to Aurelius. . . . I appoint you by this my instruction as my representative to journey to the most illustrious Alexandria and search for my slave called . . . aged about 35 years, with whom you too are acquainted . . .; and when you find him you are to deliver him up, having the same powers as I should have myself, if present, to . . . imprison him, chastise him, and to make an accusation before the proper authorities against those who harboured him, and demand satisfaction.

It may be that the slave had come on an errand to Paul and had overstayed his time. At all events, the primary purpose of the letter is to act as a covering note to ensure that Philemon will receive back his delinquent slave, although some scholars (J. Knox and P. N. Harrison, 'Onesimus and Philemon' *ATR* 32, (1950) pp. 268–94) regard the injunction of Paul to Philemon as a request that he was asking for Onesimus to be returned and allowed permanently to remain as his aide. Preiss (*loc. cit.*, p. 40) argues that Paul's language is insistent that the slave should be welcomed into Philemon's family, but this conclusion is somewhat strained. Verse

21, however, does contain an undertone of hope that Philemon will agree to the manumission of the slave. The various methods by which a slave could gain his freedom were as familiar as the institution itself. It was common for the slave to deposit money in a temple and for the god and his priests to officiate in the transference as his freedom was purchased. The remaining walls of the temple of Apollo at Delphi are covered with the names of slaves whom the god has set free (*cf.* C. K. Barrett, *New Testament Background: Selected Documents*, London, 1950, pp. 52f., for one example). But for forgiveness to be shown to a criminal slave who had escaped was another matter. Paul's plea was a revolutionary thought in contrast with the contemporary treatment of runaway slaves whom the master could take steps to arrest and then brutally punish. *Cf.* the wording in Oxyrhynchus papyrus 1643 (quoted above): 'you shall imprison him and whip him. . . .' The master could even have the slave crucified. A surviving papyrus (cited in Moule, pp. 34–7) dated in the mid-second century B.C. gives the text of a warrant for the arrest of a slave on the run. Rewards are offered to any person who finds him and brings him back or who can give information as to his whereabouts (e.g. in the temple of a god whose protection he has sought [seeking manumission?]). An even higher reward is promised to an informant who says that the slave is lodging with a private person; then not only would the slave be returned but the person who harboured him could be prosecuted and held liable for the loss of the slave's work incurred by his absence from his master.

Paul's bold request for Onesimus is therefore carefully prepared for by his approach of gentle language (vv. 8, 9) with its tones of entreaty, and leads to an appeal to Philemon's willing co-operation and consent (v. 14) and the promise to accept any liability which he may have incurred (v. 19).

But the letter does not stay on the surface of a simple request for a slave's life on humane grounds. A good illustration of a plea for clemency on a humanitarian level is seen in the younger Pliny's letters to a certain Sabinianus (*Ep.* ix. 21, 24). He intercedes for a young freedman who has sought refuge in Pliny's home and is full of fear at the prospect of his master's wrath. Pliny grants the master's right to be angry but tries to steer Sabinianus in the direction of clemency (Lat. *mansuetudo*, a Stoic virtue) because of the deserter's repentance, amendment of life and request to be forgiven. Sabinianus is entreated to be benevolent and to forbear his anger, which has been justly aroused. The tenor of Pliny's letter is quite different from Paul's, and the contents are obviously not the same. Paul says nothing about Philemon's 'rights' to exact vengeance nor does he even contemplate that Onesimus will be punished. (This omission militates against the view which sees a covert allusion to Onesimus in Colossians 3:25: 'the man who wrongs will be paid back for the wrong he has done', as though this section of the 'household code' had the case of Onesimus and Philemon in mind [cf. J. Knox, 'Philemon and the Authenticity of Colossians', *JR* 18 (1938), pp. 154ff.]).

Running through Paul's appeal is the current of Christian compassion (v. 12) and the powerful reminder that Philemon is already in debt to Paul himself (v. 19b) as owing to Paul's preaching of the gospel his very salvation under God. The characteristic notes are therefore: 'for love's sake' (v. 9) . . . 'refresh my heart in Christ' (by acceding to this request, v. 20) and receive this truant slave 'as you would receive me' (v. 17). The request ends with a parting shot (v. 21) that Philemon will go beyond the limit of Paul's desire; and this appeal is reinforced by the prospect of the apostle's visit (v. 22—this is surely meant to be taken as a serious intention and not as F. J. Hort proposed as 'in a playful way' a 'mere jest' (see P. N. Harrison, 'Onesimus and Philemon', p. 281) a hope that would spur Philemon to a ready acceptance of what was asked of him. There is every reason to believe that he did respond; otherwise the letter would not have been preserved at Colossae.

2. THE PLACE OF ORIGIN AND DATE

Paul writes as a prisoner (vv. 1, 9, 10, 23) and a careful comparison of names with Colossians 4:7–17 will show that this letter was sent from the same place as the Colossian epistle. Onesimus is to accompany Tychicus who was entrusted with the Colossian letter (Col. 4:9). Moreover, Paul's situation as a prisoner may well have drawn Onesimus into his company; some scholars believe that Onesimus had been caught and placed in the same cell as the Christian missionary and so won for Christ. But this can only be speculative.

The question of the precise location of Paul's imprisonment is raised at this point. For if (as has just been mentioned) Paul and

Onesimus were in prison together and Paul wore fetters (Col.
4:3, 18) and suffered some restriction in his ministry (Col. 4:3, 4),
Paul's circumstances are best described as those of a man in 'free
custody' similar to the conditions of his detention at Rome according to Acts 28:30f. On other grounds, however, it has been
proposed (chiefly by G. S. Duncan, *St Paul's Ephesian Ministry*,
London, 1929, pp. 72ff., 157ff.) that Paul was a prisoner at or near
Ephesus when he wrote this note to Philemon. He builds on the
request Paul makes (v. 22) for a lodging, and argues that this
promised visit to the Lycus valley is congruous with Paul's plans
at the time of his Ephesian ministry (Ac. 19–20). As events turned
out, Paul did not, according to the record in Acts, visit the region
of Colossae after leaving Ephesus. This may well be explained (as
by H. Conzelmann, *History of Primitive Christianity*, Nashville, 1973,
p. 99f.) on the assumption that he was released from Ephesian
imprisonment by being expelled from the province. He had made
things so uncomfortable for himself in the metropolitan area that
he later deemed it unwise to go back to proconsular Asia, and
had to be content to call in at the port of Miletus, and to summon
Church leaders in Asia to meet him there (so Ac. 20:16, 17; *cf.*
v. 23). However this may be, it is hardly likely that Paul would
have expressed a desire to visit Colossae when he was a prisoner
at Rome.

At Rome his plans were to go on to Spain (Rom. 15:23f., 28).
C. H. Dodd, who argues for a Roman origin of the letter to
Philemon (in *BJRL* 18 (1934), reprinted in *New Testament Studies*,
Manchester, 1953, pp. 90–9), concedes that this is a 'real point in
favour of the Ephesian hypothesis' (*loc. cit.*, p. 95), but postulates a
change of plan. His chief support comes from the fact that Onesimus was more likely to have fled to Rome and have sought the
anonymity of the imperial city where he was brought into touch
with the apostle; and Bruce accepts these arguments especially on
the ground that a threatening situation at Colossae may well have
led Paul to revise his itinerary and to visit the Lycus valley. He
mentions, if tentatively, a further pointer in the direction of a
Roman provenance of this epistle by drawing attention to the
inclusion of Luke and Mark in Paul's list (v. 24). 'Luke was with
Paul at Rome; we have no evidence that he was with him at
Ephesus. Mark is traditionally associated with Rome, not with
Ephesus' (*loc. cit.*, p. 87f.). But we cannot base much weight on
what are admittedly arguments from silence. For this line of

evidence, regarded as indecisive and neutral, see D. T. Rowling-
son's essay, 'Paul's Ephesian Ministry: An Evaluation of the
Evidence', *ATR* 32 (1950), pp. 1–7.

The placing of this epistle in a suitable period of Paul's life adds
very little to our knowledge of either the letter or Paul's mind. The
close tie between the letters to Philemon and the Colossians is a
datum which all interpreters accept (save for some exceptions, e.g.
E. R. Goodenough, *loc. cit.*, p. 182, n. 7, who does not think that the
Onesimus of Philemon is the same as the man referred to in Col.
4:9 and E. Haenchen, *The Acts of the Apostles*, Oxford, 1971, p. 474,
n. 1, who questions whether the Mark of Philemon 24 is the John
Mark of Acts 15:37, as Colossians 4:10 assumes). It follows that
if the case for a dating of Colossians in the Ephesian period of
Paul's ministry is preferred (see earlier, pp. 26–32), this will virtually decide the issue in respect of Philemon.

3. THE HISTORICAL VALUES OF THE LETTER

As a historical document, the letter throws unusual light on the
Christian conscience in regard to the institution of slavery in the
ancient world, and so complements and corrects what we find in
the so-called 'rules of the household' (*Haustafeln*) on the other New
Testament epistles (see especially Col. 3:22–4:1; Eph. 6:5–9; *cf.*
1 C. 7:21–3; 1 Tim. 6:1f.; Tit. 2:9f.; 1 Pet. 2:18–21). From these
traditional teaching-patterns Paul draws the framework of his
instruction, but he injects a moralistic tone with his reminders
that the slaves are 'serving Christ', that the owner has a 'master
in heaven', God who deals impartially, and that both slave and
owner are bond-servants of Christ. From that last position it is
a short step to a relativizing of slavery which in turn reaches
the point at which it becomes indifferent (1 C. 7:20–4) and has
lost its sting (Gal. 3:28; Col. 3:11)—at least, in so far as slaves
and masters are members of the one household of Christian
faith.

The main and striking feature of this epistle is brought out by
Bruce (*loc. cit.*, p. 90), *viz.* 'What this epistle does is to bring us
into an atmosphere in which the institution could only wilt and
die'. Paul's statement of verse 16 is the Magna Carta of true
emancipation and human dignity even if it is true that 'the
word "emancipation" seems to be trembling on his lips, and yet

he does not once utter it' (Lightfoot, *Commentary*, p. 321). The question is sometimes raised that the New Testament never condemns slavery explicitly and so it is defective at a crucial point. But part of the answer to this implied criticism is that Paul does not advocate a social philosophy which countenances revolution and violence. In the exigencies of the social structures of the Roman empire of Paul's day, slavery could be overthrown only by violent means (see the quotation of W. Bousset, given on p. 121 on Col. 3:22); and the apostle will be no party to class hatred or violent methods (*cf*. Rom. 12:17–21). *Cf*. *Diognetus* vii. 4: 'Coercion is incompatible with God.'

Furthermore, Paul's whole approach to Philemon is voluntaristic, leaving him to settle the matter by an appeal to his conscience. Though Paul could order him to act, he prefers to allow Philemon to respond with a measure of spontaneity and self-determination (see Preiss, *loc. cit.*, pp. 40f.). What matters to Paul is to secure Philemon's willing consent, not in perfunctory compliance but because he sees his duty as Paul wishes him to see it. This has been called 'the technique of Christian co-operation' (L. S. Thornton, *The Common Life in the Body of Christ*, London, 1950, p. 39), based chiefly on the common share which both men have in the realities of the faith and their common life as members of the one body. It is this feature, represented in both Paul's attitude to Onesimus as a child and a brother (there is no condescending paternalism in Paul's references) and his relations with Philemon as a joint-sharer in the Christian faith and experience, which lifts Paul's appeal on to a different level from contemporary humanitarianism seen in Stoicism. Paul bases no conviction on a common humanity shared by slave and master; rather he writes to a fellow-Christian about a slave who is a fellow-Christian. He employs a Stoic term in verse 8, 'what is required' or 'fitting', but quickly modifies it to his own ends.

The note to Philemon, then, while it is ostensibly about the treatment to be given to a law-breaking slave by his master, is more properly thought of as a witness to 'life in Christ' (*cf*. Preiss's title). The 'teaching' it contains is more of how the Christian life is to be lived in a social context. It aims to construct a 'network of new situations and the circuit of new relations which constitute the life in Christ, the life of the Church' (Preiss), and to set the particular issue of Philemon's treatment of Onesimus in that network. The apostolic attitude to slavery as an institution is nowhere

defined and, at best, has to be extrapolated from his teaching on
the life of Christian believers.

Another value of this small epistle derives from the important
place it holds in the reconstruction of Paul's correspondence
adopted by E. J. Goodspeed, *An Introduction to the New Testament*,
Chicago, 1937, pp. 109–24; A. E. Barnett, *The Letters of Paul*,
Nashville, 1947, pp. 157–60; and popularized by J. Knox (especially in his *Philemon among the Letters of Paul*, Nashville, 2nd edn
1959). Knox offers two identifications which, if accepted, would
modify our understanding of this letter and enlarge our picture of
apostolic Christianity. They are (*i*) that the real slave-owner was
Archippus, not Philemon to whom Paul appeals and whose ser-
vices he seeks to enlist in an attempt to persuade the former to have
compassion on Onesimus; and (*ii*) that Onesimus was set free to
return as Paul's aide; and he became in due course the bishop of
Ephesus in the second century, an identification attested (says
Knox) by Ignatius, who in his letter to the Ephesians shows that
he had read this epistle to Philemon and actually adopts the same
play on words which Paul uses in verse 20. Ignatius writes: 'May I
always have profit from you (Gr. *onaimēn hymōn*), if I am worthy'
(*Eph.* ii.2). With this identification assumed, Knox proceeds to
maintain that the same Onesimus, now a church leader, was
responsible for the collection of the Pauline letters and their publication—including the one to Philemon in which he had such a
personal stake.

Critical opinion on these two hypotheses has not been too
favourable. Moule (*Commentary*, pp. 16f.) rightly objects that Philemon's name standing at the head of the list of persons addressed
(v. 1) seems 'fatal to the theory that Archippus is primarily the
one addressed'. Further criticisms have fastened on such matters
as (*i*) the use which Knox makes of Colossians 4:17 (see commentary). For his reconstruction this verse plays a significant part
in identifying Archippus' 'ministry' as that of obeying Paul's
recommendation and accepting Onesimus. But this is by no means
obvious, since the verb Paul uses, 'you fulfil the ministry', is an
active word (so Moule) and the service Archippus had 'received'
is more probably something which had been 'handed on' to him
by tradition. Moreover, the delicacy of Paul's appeal in the letter
to Philemon is lost if he gives a blunt order to the slave-owner in
Colossians 4:17. (*ii*) The inferential nature of the relationship
between Philemon and Archippus in which the latter needs to

have pressure applied by Philemon is a weakness in the theory, since there is nothing to indicate such a relationship. We must remain content with Dibelius–Greeven's verdict: 'Speculation about Archippus' position in Philemon's household is idle'. (*iii*) H. Greeven, 'Prüfung des Thesen von J. Knox zum Philemon-brief', *ThLZ* 79 (1954), cols, 373–8, concentrates on Knox's translation of verse 10, which is taken to mean that Paul is asking for Onesimus to be permitted to remain (*Philemon*, pp. 19f.); and on the identification which Knox makes of the 'letter from Laodi-cea' (Col. 4:16) with the note to 'Philemon'. In this 'letter from Laodicea' we are meant to see the letter sent first to Philemon who was an overseer of the churches in the Lycus valley and who lived at Laodicea, the main town in the region. Paul wrote to him first of all so that his influence could then be brought to bear on Archippus in Colossae. In this way, it is claimed, we can do full justice to Paul's prepositional phrase: 'the letter *from* (Gr. *ek*) Laodicea'. But no such meaning is required, as we have observed (see commentary, p. 138), and Greeven can produce several reasons why this letter to the Laodiceans has not survived.

Bruce (*loc. cit.*, pp. 90ff.), however, is sympathetic to Knox's second point but unpersuaded by his attempt to give Archippus a distinguished role. He does concede the possibility that the identification of the ex-slave with the Onesimus who is mentioned in the first six chapters of Ignatius' *Letter to the Ephesians* as 'a man of inexpressible love and your bishop' (i. 3) is correct. Certainly it is a coincidence that this name should turn up in this way. However, it may be that we are stretching the long arm of coincidence too far in making the identification. A more cautious view would be to accept Lightfoot's suggestion, and think that the later bishop of Ephesus took the name of Paul's friend (*Commentary*, pp. 308f.). Lightfoot mentions another Onesimus to whom Melito, bishop of Sardis half a century later still, dedicated his volume of Old Testament extracts (Eusebius, *HE* IV. xxvi. 13f.). So the practice of revering 'Onesimus' by taking his name—perhaps because of its symbolic meaning—is not unique.

Even with this moderating view it is required to believe that Onesimus was set free and became a prominent figure in the Colossian church. Only then would a later bishop wish to accept his name (if he does have Paul's convert in mind) as a mark of honour. As P. N. Harrison notes (*loc. cit.*, p. 293), after setting down the views of Knox and Lightfoot, 'In either case, St

Paul's letter to Philemon must in fact have produced its desired effect.'

We should not fail to note the value in this epistle of the window it opens into Paul's character. He is the true man who is also an apostle, as Chrysostom aptly comments, full of sympathy and concern for a person in distress and willing to do all in his power to help, even at some cost (v. 19). Each of the parties involved was called upon to do something difficult: on Paul's part, to deprive himself of Onesimus' service and company; for Onesimus, to return to his master-owner whom he had wronged; for Philemon, to forgive. 'And each of the three [is to do] what he was called upon to do as a Christian' (C. A. A. Scott, *Saint Paul the Man and the Teacher*, Cambridge, 1936, p. 59). Moreover, Paul so identifies himself with both the slave and his master that he can fulfil the office of mediator, and represent meaningfully both parties. Our knowledge of Paul would be so much poorer if this slender document had not been preserved.

4. AUTHENTICITY

No serious objection stands in the way of receiving this letter as genuine; and A. Q. Morton and J. McLeman (*Paul: the Man and the Myth*, London, 1966, p. 89) raise no discordant voice. The Tübingen school of F. C. Baur (*Paul*, London, 1875, vol. ii, p. 80) did oppose this letter and dismissed it as a Christian romance, to be followed in this attitude by the Dutch radical W. C. van Manen (in *Encycl. Biblica*, iii, 1902, col. 3695). But these are aberrations.

ANALYSIS OF PHILEMON

PAUL'S LETTER

to

Philemon

1. Paul introduces himself by the term **a prisoner for Christ Jesus.** This word (Gr. *desmios*) is best understood in the literal sense. Paul is undergoing a confinement from which he hopes soon to be released (v. 22). This is preferable to taking his imprisonment to be metaphorical (so Moule, as though it were equivalent to that in Col. 4:10) or figurative (see A. Deissmann, *Light from the Ancient East*, London, 1927, p. 307, citing Lk. 13:16: 'bound by a daemon' and so unable to exercise a ministry of public preaching) or religious (with parallels drawn from the mystery religions in which the devotee in the temple is 'detained' by the god: see G. Kittel, *TDNT* ii, p. 43). Philemon 9, 10 seem definitely to indicate a literal captivity. His 'bonds' are a mark of his apostolic authority (see on Col. 4:18). **Timothy** is by his side, as in Colossians 1:1.

Philemon: the name of the recipient of the letter. He is praised, in a sort of *captatio benevolentiae*, intended to put Paul on good terms with his reader in view of the nature of the letter's request, as **our beloved fellow-worker** (possibly these are two separate terms). **Beloved.** Right at the outset Philemon is reminded that he belongs to a community of mutual love (*cf.* Rom. 1:7; Ignatius *To the Romans* i. 1). Paul is paving the way for a later description of Onesimus as he should be treated in that community (v. 16: 'a beloved brother'). **Fellow-worker** is a frequent name given to Paul's colleagues in the 'work' of the gospel (1 Th. 3:2; 2 C. 8:23; Rom. 16:3, 9, 21; Phil. 2:25; 4:3; Col. 4:11). Just how Philemon had laboured with Paul in missionary service is not clear; perhaps Paul is speaking in general terms.

2. Apphia our sister is often taken to be Philemon's wife, since her name follows directly that of Philemon. Her name was a common one (*cf.* Lightfoot). The most interesting datum is a grave inscription (cited by Dibelius–Greeven, appendix 6) which runs: 'Hermas in memory of Apphia his wife, daughter of Tryphon, a Colossian by origin.' Apphia's place as head of the household would be a deciding factor in welcoming back the runaway slave. **Archippus** is **our fellow soldier** (for this term, *cf.* O. Bauernfeind, *TDNT* vii, pp. 710f.) a title also given to Epaphroditus (Phil. 2:25) apparently in the same period of Paul's life, *viz.* at a time when he was a prisoner for his faith. If Colossians 4:17 means that Archippus has taken over some of the pastoral responsibility previously borne by Epaphras (see commentary; this is Lohmeyer's opinion), then 'fellow soldier' may have a special meaning, possibly drawn from a technical sense of the word.

The letter is no mere private note, addressed to one individual. 'In the Body of Christ personal affairs are no longer private, (Théo Preiss, 'Life in Christ and Social Ethics', *Life in Christ* ET 1954, London, p. 34), and this reminder is seen in the way in which Philemon is associated with the whole church which assembles in his house. **In your house** refers back to Philemon ('your' is singular). For the existence of 'house churches', see Colossians 4:15; *cf.* F. V. Filson, 'The Significance of the Early House Churches', *JBL* 58 (1939), pp. 105–12.

3. Grace to you is a greeting sent to the assembled company ('you' is plural), and the expression ('grace . . . and peace' is typically Pauline; see commentary on Col. 1:2).

THANKSGIVING AND PAUL'S TRIBUTE Verses 4–7

Pauline thanksgivings are more than conventional expressions. P. Schubert (*Form and Function of the Pauline Thanksgivings*, Berlin, 1939, pp. 12, 167f.) has drawn attention to the precise structure of verses 4ff., and it is one of his clearest examples to illustrate the principle that Paul's introductory thanks lead to the 'epistolary situation' of the entire letter. No fewer than seven terms in these verses are repeated in the body of the letter: 'love' (vv. 5, 7, 9, 16); 'prayers' (v. 22); 'sharing', 'partnership' (v. 17); 'the good', 'goodness' (v. 14); 'heart(s)' (vv. 12, 20); 'refreshed' (v. 20); and 'brother' (v. 20). Some of these terms may be coincidental, but the cumulative effect of the build-up of ideas which later are distributed at key points throughout the epistle cannot be fortuitous. See further J. Knox, *Philemon*, p. 22, and W. G. Doty, *Letters in Primitive Christianity*, Philadelphia, 1973, pp. 31ff., for references to recent literature on the structure of Paul's writing.

4. I thank my God. This is a common feature of hellenistic letters. The sender praises the gods for the health and well-being of his addressees, and assures them of his prayers on their behalf (e.g. the example in A. Deissmann, *Light from the Ancient East*, London, 1927, p. 184). Paul gives a distinctively Christian content to the formula by the way in which he goes on to describe the reason for his thankfulness (v. 5).

5. because I hear of your love. There are several matters raised by this verse. Normally, in the Pauline corpus, the verb 'to hear' in the context of Paul's thanksgiving indicates that he does not know the persons or communities at first-hand (Col. 1:4; *cf.* 2:1; Eph. 1:15; *cf.* Rom. 1:8; see Dibelius–Greeven, p. 103), and this would suggest that the apostle was not personally acquainted with Philemon (see H. Greeven, *ThLZ* 79 (1954), col. 376). The argument against this is the inference, drawn from verse 19, that Paul was responsible for Philemon's conversion. But that verse may mean no more than that Philemon owed his hearing of the Christian message to members of Paul's mission sent out from Ephesus (*cf.* Ac. 19:10), including Epaphras. Just as the Colossians' faith (1:5) and love (1:8) were reported to Paul by this man, so it may be inferred that Philemon's example was mentioned as the case of a Colossian who had responded to Epaphras' ministry. If the knowledge Paul has of Philemon is indirect, it becomes important to establish good relations with him in view of the nature of the request to follow in the body of the letter. Demetrius, *On Style*, who writes extensively on the art of letter-writing in the ancient world, makes it clear that a letter should be an expression of 'friendly relationship' (Gr. *philophronēsis*) between sender and recipient. Verse 5 performs that function, as verse 1 prepares for it by its uses of titles of endearment.

love . . . faith which you have toward the Lord Jesus and all the saints. If the terms are read in natural sequence, it follows that 'faith' must be understood as 'faithfulness', 'loyalty', since both the Lord and Christian people are the objects (so F. F. Bruce, *BJRL* 48 (1965–6), p. 81). Notice the apparent attempt to simplify this sentence in Ephesians 1:15. As an alternative, the structure of Paul's sentence may be chiastic, i.e. the terms are arranged in a 'cross (*chi*-shaped)' pattern, so that 'love' goes with 'saints' and 'faith' is directed to (Gr. *pros*) the Lord Jesus. On chiasmus, see N. W. Lund, *Chiasmus in the New Testament*, Chapel Hill, North Carolina, 1942.

The merit of the second interpretation is that (*a*) it permits the usual Pauline sense of 'faith' (Gr. *pistis*), meaning 'trust', 'confidence', to be given, with the preposition *pros* as in 1 Thessalonians 1:8; (*b*) it explains the variation in the use of the preposition *eis* before 'all the saints', meaning 'love for'—again typically in Paul's style (Rom. 5:8; 2 C. 2:8; 2 Th. 1:3; Col. 1:4; cf. Eph. 1:15); and (c) it explains why 'love . . . for the saints' as a composite phrase comes both first (for emphasis) and last in the sentence, since compassion and generosity rest on and are a proof of Philemon's Christian standing as a believer in the Lord Jesus. **The saints** are Christian people, forming the church at Colossae, as in Colossians 1:2. See commentary on that verse.

6. This is 'the most obscure verse in this letter' (Moule). **And I pray** is added by the English translators to show that what follows is the beginning of Paul's petition. It looks back to the phrase (v. 4): 'in my prayers' (Dibelius–Greeven, p. 103; Schubert, p. 12). As Moule observes, the two key phrases are 'the knowledge of all the good' and 'in Christ'. The last term is not the formula *en Christō* but *eis Christon*, and is capable of several interpretations ranging from 'bringing us into closer union with Christ' (the preposition conveying the thought of movement: see *NEB*) to 'for the glory of Christ' (as in 2 C. 1:21; 11:3; Rom. 16:5). The former is Moule's view, shared too by Dibelius–Greeven; the latter is that adopted by Lohse.

the sharing of your faith may promote the knowledge of all the good that is ours. Sharing is the meaning of *koinōnia* (see A. R. George, *Communion with God in the New Testament*, London, 1953, p. 183) but this is ambiguous. Does it mean 'your generosity, your willingness to share your goods which springs from your faith' (Lightfoot)? Or, 'your participation in the [Christian] faith' (R. Bultmann, *TDNT* i, p. 708)? Or, in a mediating view, 'the fellowship in which you have come to share by your exercise of faith' (H. Seesemann, *Der Begriff KOINŌNIA im Neuen Testament*, Giessen, 1933, pp. 79–83)? At all events, the main idea is clear. Philemon's faith is to show itself active in loving service (Gal. 5:6), presumably to 'all the saints' mentioned in the previous verse and in anticipation of the plea which will come later (v. 10). This activity or vitality (F. Hauck, *TDNT* iii, p. 805) is stressed in Paul's Greek adjective (*energēs*). The upshot will be a recognition (Gr. *epignōsis*) of all the good which he has as a believer (Lohse) or, preferably with Moule, which he will perform in the release of Onesimus. Thus 'all the good' matches as it looks forward to 'your goodness' in verse 14. As he consents to act out his faith in this specific way, he will come into closer relationship with his Lord, or his action will be a deed which glorifies

Christ. Either way it is the right thing for him to do, and eminently praiseworthy.

The verse is evidently the key to the subsequent appeal. It expresses Paul's prayer (and so his confidence) that his friend of whose faith and love he is assured (v.·5) will respond to the call. So he will give proof of his Christian status by acting in a way that will show specifically (by the release of the slave) that 'faith is made operative by love' and that he will do this as one who is confronted by 'the final arbiter of ethical conduct', Christ (W. Kramer, *Christ, Lord, Son of God*, London, 1966, p. 140 (34*b*). Paul's reference *eis Christon* may possibly point to the final day of judgement (1 C. 4:5*b*). So U. Wickert, *ZNTW* 52 (1961), p. 231.

7. Since Paul's appeal is to Philemon's love in action, he cleverly pays tribute to what he knows Philemon has already done in love. One particular deed may be in view in the phrase **I have derived much joy and comfort from your love** (so Lohse), though if the two men had not met in person, it is hard to see what it might have been. It can hardly be a reference to Philemon's help to the community at Colossae, since Paul speaks in personal terms. Probably we should understand a general reputation which this Colossian nobleman has. He has undertaken some relief work in the church, and **the hearts of the saints,** i.e. the lives of Christians, **have been refreshed,** i.e. encouraged and comforted (as Paul has been, to hear of it) by this action. Paul's language is tender and evocative. **Hearts** (Gr. *splanchna*) 'concerns and expresses the total personality at the deepest level . . . [a] term which occurs only when Paul is speaking directly and personally' (H. Koester, *TDNT* vii, p. 555). But the entire verse is full of ideas which play a significant role in Paul's letter-writing purpose. He will shortly remark that Onesimus is 'his very heart' (Gr. *splanchna*, v. 12) and that Philemon's acceptance of his request will 'refresh' him (v. 20). This verse, then, is both effusive and strategic.

PAUL'S REQUEST Verses 8–20

8. Accordingly links up with the foregoing statement of Paul's confidence in Philemon's character as a Christian man. At verse 21 Paul will reiterate that confidence. So here he prefaces his request with a 'therefore' (Gr. *dio*).

He could order Philemon to do what was needful, but he for-
bears **to command you to do what is required,** *viz.* to welcome
Onesimus back with clemency (a Stoic virtue) and even more as a
Christian brother (v. 16). 'What is required' (Gr. *to anēkon*) is an
ethical norm set by popular hellenistic philosophy (*cf.* the Stoic
ideal of 'what is fitting', one's duty; see *TDNT* iii, pp. 437–40).
The principle, used in Colossians 3:18 with the qualification 'in
the Lord', is equally here applied in a Christian sense as a version
of *noblesse oblige* (Eph. 5:3). Philemon is made aware of his duty
as a Christian believer; but Paul will not enforce it, for the reason
given in verse 14: 'not to compel you but to let you act freely.'

9. So he bases his appeal on other grounds: **for love's sake**
(whether Paul's love for his child Onesimus or for Philemon, or
Philemon's love mentioned in vv. 5, 7 [so Dibelius-Greeven], or
love as a regulative norm in Christian relationships [so Wickert,
loc. cit., p. 236, n. 16] is not clear). Paul's attitude, then, is not
dictatorial. Rather **I prefer to appeal** (Gr. *parakaleō*: see *TDNT*
v, p. 795, n. 166, for the verb as used by Paul in ethical contexts
where the note of entreaty predominates). Yet he does have
authority as Paul is **an ambassador and now a prisoner also
for Christ Jesus.**

ambassador (Gr. *presbutēs*) is strictly speaking 'an old man' and
is so taken in *AV* and argued for by Lohse; but a slight transcrip-
tional change gives *presbeutēs* (see Preiss, *loc. cit.*, p. 37f., for the
way in which these two words were treated as interchangeable
in antiquity). The sense, moreover, requires Paul's invoking of his
authority as an ambassador (*cf.* Eph. 6:20).

A further token of his 'right' to appeal to Philemon is the silent
witness of his imprisonment experiences because of his fidelity to
his calling. See the commentary on Colossians 4:18 with a similar
call to 'respect his fetters' by obeying his teaching. It has been
suggested that this verse indicates by its use of an emphatic adverb
in the phrase **and now** that Paul's imprisonment had only just
begun at the time he wrote—a likely supposition on either the
Ephesian or Roman provenance of Colossians–Philemon. See
earlier p. 25.

10. I appeal to you for my child, Onesimus. Now Paul
explicitly mentions his purpose in writing. The usual interpretation
of these words is that he has in mind the need to bring the case of
Onesimus to Philemon's attention: 'I am appealing on his behalf.'
This is more in keeping with the sense of the Greek phrase (the

verb and the preposition *peri*, as in 1 C. 16:12; 2 C. 12:8; 2 Th.
2:1) rather than the sense which Knox, *Philemon*, p. 22ff., gives:
'I am asking for him.' The purport is Paul's intercession for the
slave, not his request to have Onesimus returned as a permanent
companion (Knox, p. 25; Bruce, *loc. cit.*, pp. 93, 96). No support
for the latter view can be derived from verse 15 ('that you might
have him back for ever') where the meaning of the verb can only
suggest a new relationship in Philemon's home. See H. Greeven's
critique of Knox, *ThLZ* 79 (1954), pp. 373–8.

Onesimus—a significant name, now mentioned in the letter for
the first time but later the subject of Paul's playful handling (v. 11,
and possibly in v. 10: see below). It is a common name for slaves
found in inscriptions, partly because a nameless slave would
receive this identity-name ('Onesimus' means 'useful') in the hope
that he would live up to his adopted name in the service of his
owner. (See Lightfoot, p. 338.)

This man is Paul's **child** (Gr. *teknon*: a frequent Pauline designation of his spiritual protégés such as Timothy in 1 C. 4:17 and
the pastoral epistles) **whose father I have become in my imprisonment.** Teachers and holy men, in both Judaism (*cf.*
F. Büchsel, *TDNT* i, pp. 665f.) and the pagan mystery cults
(*cf.* R. Reitzenstein, *Die hellenistischen Mysterienreligionen*, Stuttgart,
1956, pp. 40f.) took the title of 'father' in relation to their students
and devotees. Paul's use of the imagery is seen in 1 Corinthians
4:14–17 and Galatians 4:19. **In my imprisonment** naturally
suggests a meeting of the two men in Paul's place of confinement,
as a result of which Onesimus had been won to the faith in Christ.

Knox (*Philemon*, p. 24) accounts for the case-ending of the name
'Onesimus' (an accusative) on the ground that the slave received
the name 'Onesimus', meaning 'profitable' for the first time at his
conversion, but it is just as likely that he became true to his slave
name at this time. The case of the noun is explained by its
attraction to the relative clause.

11, 12. he was useless . . . now he is indeed useful continues
the pun. Phrygian slaves had the ill repute of being lazy and good-
for-nothing. In one way especially Onesimus had belied his name
(*viz.* according to v. 18 he had wronged his master); but now he is
a changed man, and Paul is confident that a transformed person
as a 'new man in Christ' will show the proof of his conversion as he
is welcomed back to Colossae. This is the traditional way in which
I am sending him back to you is understood (Gr. *anapempein*

has the meaning 'return', 'send back': see Arndt-Gingrich, *sv*).
Knox *(Philemon*, p. 25) wishes to give a technical, legal flavour to
the verb, and suggests that Paul's action is to 'remit' the case of
Onesimus to Philemon for Archippus' attention and decision.
Meanwhile, Onesimus' future—whether to remain at Colossae or
to be free to be Paul's aide—is a matter on which Paul seeks
Philemon's consent (v. 13). But this reconstruction, while suggestive, hardly does justice to Paul's next sentence: **sending my
very heart,** which reads as though a permanent separation between the two men is involved. Paul is willing to give away 'part of
myself' (Moule's happy rendering of the Gr. *splanchna*: see on
v. 7), and this looks like a willingness to know personal sacrifice
as Onesimus returns to Philemon permanently (so v. 15).

13. If Paul were thinking simply in terms of personal self-
interest, he would advise that Onesimus stay with him to **serve
me.** The verb **to keep him with me** has a quasi-technical sense,
since *katechein* means the voluntary yet dutiful obligation on the
part of a hellenistic cult devotee to remain in the temple, at the
god's behest. No such background is to be seen here, although
Paul does invest his thought with a religious aura, since his imprisonment is for the gospel. Philemon's acceding to his earlier
request would set the slave free for this purpose, so it would lead
to Onesimus' service **on your behalf.**

14. but I preferred, out of a sense of fair play and respect for
the law which demanded that the deserting slave must be returned
to his legal owner (*cf.* E. R. Goodenough, 'Paul and Onesimus',
HTR 22 (1929), pp. 181ff.). There is also the personal factor involv-
ing good relations between Paul and Philemon. So **your consent**
is needful, and Onesimus will be sent back to Colossae so that his
master can deal with him in a way which is fitting to the occasion
(v. 8). What that suitable action entails becomes a little clearer
in the next section. In any case, Paul appeals to Philemon's
awareness of all the bounty he shares as a Christian (v. 6), and
trusts that his pardon of Onesimus will be freely given. **Not ... by
compulsion but of your own free will** is a common phrase to
emphasize a contrast, frequent in the papyri (see Lohse, p. 202).
Paul's tact shines through this sentence, with his clear sensitivity
to the need to place no constraint upon Philemon, other than the
constraining obligation of love (v. 7). And love cannot be commanded or evoked by coercion.

15. In a letter which is so full of nuances and hidden meanings it may well be believed that Paul's expressions are carefully contrived. His giving a providential aspect to such a sordid business as a slave's misdemeanour and escape is a case in point. **Perhaps this is why he was parted** (i.e. by escaping) **from you for a while** is Paul's way of dramatizing the episode. And his passive verb **was parted from you** may contain a conviction of the divine overruling (*cf.* in Hebrew the use of the 'divine passive', especially in the apocalyptic literature, which is a mode of expression to denote the hidden action of God as the agent responsible for what is done). Onesimus ran off but his restoration (**you might have him back for ever**) marks a new relationship, of a lasting quality.

16. That new relationship is now described **No longer as a slave but more than a slave, as a beloved brother.** For the first time Paul calls Onesimus a slave, though he has prepared the way for the mention by expressing the hope that Onesimus might have 'served' (Gr. *diakonein*, not *douleuein* from which the noun *doulos*, slave, comes) him on Philemon's behalf (v. 13). In that way Paul has put a new face on slavery by regarding the human condition as unimportant in contrast with a person's desire to fulfil his Christian vocation. This is his teaching in 1 Corinthians 7:21–4; and repeated in the 'rules for the household', especially Colossians 3:22–4.

Onesimus' new standing as a Christian is all-important, since this brings him into a new society in which all men are brothers; he will still be a slave **in the flesh,** as a man, but he will gain new dignity as Philemon's equal **in the Lord,** as a fellow-Christian. Whether Onesimus' manumission and freedom are implied in this assertion is uncertain. Probably Paul says no more here than to give a call to receive Onesimus back without punishment; at verse 21 he will put in a veiled plea for his release from slavery, as part of Philemon's anticipated 'obedience' to the divine will. Manumission in the contemporary world was followed by an acceptance of the former slave as his master's equal.

17. Onesimus' new status is based, in part, on his already existing relationship to Paul himself. And Paul acknowledges Philemon as a partner, lit. a 'sharer' (Gr. *koinōnos*) in God's grace and work. On the sense of this 'partnership, suggesting a common religious experience, see V. Taylor, *Forgiveness and Reconciliation*, London, 1946, p. 110, n. 2. It follows, then, that Philemon's attitude is to be determined by how he regards Paul. **Receive him as you would receive me,** i.e. with full acceptance. Onesimus is coming

back to Colossae as Paul's *alter ego* and is exposing himself to
Philemon's clemency—or wrath, which was not uncommon (see
Friedrich's commentary, pp. 194f.). Therefore he needs Paul to be
his intercessor, both by letter and promised visit (v. 22).

18. If he has wronged (Gr. *ēdikēsen*, as in Col. 3:25, but in
a different context) **you at all, or owes** (Gr. *opheilei*) **you anything.** This is usually taken to imply that Onesimus had stolen
or embezzled his master's money or property. But this conclusion
is no more than an inference. It is a conditional sentence; and it
may mean simply that his overdue absence from Colossae (on
Philemon's business?) or as an escapee meant that he owed his
master the value of the work he would have done if he had been
at work.

charge that to my account. Paul will take responsibility for all
that Onesimus owes. The underlying assumption is that Paul
knows the law by which a person harbouring a runaway slave
was liable to the owner for the loss of work involved in the slave's
defection. See Preiss, *loc. cit.*, p. 35. Oxyrhynchus papyrus 1422
contains a notice that persons who gave shelter to escaped slaves
were to be held accountable in law and could be prosecuted by
the slaves' master.

19. I will repay: a promissory note, sometimes called 'a certificate of indebtedness' (Gr. *cheirographon*, Paul's word in Col.
2:14: see the commentary) which pledges Paul to make good the
compensation to Philemon. He then adds a continuance of the
legal metaphor, as he enters a contra-account (Lohse) and reminds Philemon that *he* is the one who has incurred a debt. He
owes to Paul much more than a sum of money, **even your own
self.** Paul recalls Philemon's conversion through his ministry,
either personal or indirect as Paul sent out his colleagues to the
Lycus valley region including Colossae.

**20. Yes, brother, I want some benefit from you in the
Lord** (i.e. as a Christian, behaving in a 'christianly' way, by ful-
filling his request). This verb rendered **I want some benefit** (Gr.
onaimēn; the verb is *oninēmi* in the optative mood, used to express
a wish) is often thought to continue the word-play on the name of
Onesimus (cf. Moule; Bruce renders: 'Let me have this *profit*
from you as a fellow-Christian'). But it is doubtful if this link can
be established since the verb is a common one in current usage
(cf. Arndt–Gingrich, *sv*). See Blass–Debrunner–Funk, section 488,
1*b* for an emphatic denial of a play on Onesimus' name here.

Knox calls attention to the frequent recurrence of the verb in
Ignatius' epistles (six occurrences), especially at *Ephesians* ii. 2
where the exact wording is found: 'May I always have profit
from you (Gr. *onaimēn hymin*), if I am worthy.' The inference is
that Ignatius too is punning the name of the bishop of Ephesus
in the early second century, and that we are justified in seeing in
the Ignatian text a veiled allusion to Onesimus as the church
leader in that community (*Philemon*, p. 106). *Cf.* Bruce, *loc. cit.*,
pp. 92f., who is sympathetic with this proposal. But if there is no
intended play on words in the Pauline verse, and we recall the
frequency of Ignatius' use of the verb *oninēmi*, the case for an
identification in Ignatius looks very shaky.

Refresh my heart (Gr. *splanchna*) **in Christ.** Philemon has a
well-deserved reputation for this type of help (v. 7); Paul asks him
not to fail in this instance.

FINAL REMARKS AND GREETING Verses 21–5

21. Confident of your obedience. The note of apostolic authority sounds clearly, in spite of earlier tones of entreaty (vv. 8, 9, 14).
What Paul is really asking for is this man's compliance with his
request (v. 10) and action on his behalf. The **obedience** is directed
to God (as in 2 C. 7:15; 10:6, in the light of 2 C. 13:10; Phil.
2:12), even though Paul is the personal agent who lays the divine
commands on his people. The Greek *hypakoē* must be translated
'obedience' rather than 'readiness' or 'willingness' (as Dibelius–
Greeven suggest). *Cf.* U. Wickert, *ZNTW* 52, (1961), p. 233 for
a defence of the meaning 'obedience'.

Paul's hopes are high. He is confident that Philemon will meet
his wishes, and **do even more than I say.** Exactly what is implied in the **more** is uncertain. Knox (*Philemon*, p. 30), Preiss (*loc.
cit.*, pp. 39f.), and P. N. Harrison (*ATR* 32 (1950), pp. 276ff.)
believe that Paul is asking not only for Onesimus' pardon but for
Philemon's permission to allow the freed slave to return to be at
Paul's side. Nothing suggests this, as we have remarked on verse
15. Alternatively, Paul's words may just possibly carry an undertone of hope that Onesimus will be not only forgiven his wrong but
set free.

22. A subtle incentive calculated to stir Philemon to action is
probably to be seen in the words **prepare a guest room for me.**

This notice is a clear hint that Paul hopes to come in person and
visit Philemon. His future 'presence' (see R. W. Funk, 'The
Apostolic *Parousia*: Form and Significance', in *Christian History
and Interpretation*, ed. W. R. Farmer, C. F. D. Moule and R. R.
Niebuhr, Cambridge, 1967, p. 249ff.) is promised as a reminder
that he will hopefully arrive in Colossae—and see what effect his
directive has had. This feature at the close of the epistle is called
a 'travelogue'; it is no courtesy remark, but a deliberately phrased
convention, known from epistolary forms in the Graeco-Roman
world. See W. G. Doty, *Letters in Primitive Christianity*, Philadelphia, 1973, pp. 12, 36f.

your prayers. The pronoun is plural. Paul intends that his
letter and its contents will be read out in the church and Philemon's decision will become public knowledge (*pace* Bruce, *loc. cit.*,
p. 95, who remarks that such actions would put Philemon 'on the
spot'. But perhaps Paul intended to apply such congregational
and moral pressure).

granted to you. The passive voice (Gr. *charizesthai*) suggests that
it is God who can alone secure Paul's release, though Paul relies
on the prayers of the community to entreat God for this favour.

23. **Epaphras** is the Colossian leader who shares Paul's confinement (Col. 4:12). **my fellow-prisoner** is more probably to
be taken literally in view of verse 1 than as a reference to association with Paul in his apostolic tasks. See Colossians 4:10 for a
similar designation of Aristarchus. Paul's fetters (vv. 1, 9f., 13;
Col. 4:18) are shared by these men. One extra person may be
mentioned if we accept the suggestion made by E. Amling ('Eine
Konjektur im Philemonbrief', *ZNTW* 10, (1909) p. 261f.), that
in the phrase **fellow-prisoner in Christ Jesus** the last two words
are to be separated, 'in Christ' and 'Jesus'. The latter then becomes the name of the man, 'Jesus called Justus' referred to in
Colossians 4:11. The evidence is that, in this letter, 'in Christ' is
Paul's usual style but we should note (*a*) a letter of 335 words is
really too short to form an opinion and (*b*) Paul does write 'for
Christ Jesus' in verses 1, 9. But see W. Foerster, *TDNT* iii, p. 286
n. 18.

24. Greetings are also voiced by **Mark** (see on Col. 4:10),
Aristarchus (see on Col. 4:10), **Demas** (see on Col. 4:14),
Luke (*cf.* Col. 4:14) who are all spoken of as Paul's **fellow-
workers.** The name Philemon (v. 1) is brought into the same
orbit with this title, and Paul emphasizes yet once more the social

nature of the Christian ministry with its mutual obligations. On the picture which emerges from a passage such as this, which is that of 'a missionary with a large number of associates', and what that association meant in apostolic ministry, see E. E. Ellis, 'Paul and his Co-Workers', *NTS* 17 (1970–1), pp. 437–52. These allusions to Paul's fellow-workers are important in showing how much Paul respected the principle of collegiality in the Christian mission. In Acts the names of men with Paul appear more as those of travelling companions than of colleagues.

25. The grace is extended to the whole community who will hear the letter read out in corporate assembly. **With your spirit** ('your' is plural) means 'you' (E Schweizer, *TDNT* vi, p. 435).

INDEX OF MODERN NAMES

INDEX OF SUBJECTS